Civil Liberties United
Diverse Voices from the San Francisco Bay Area

Other books in this series:

Standing Strong! Fillmore and Japantown
Voices from WriteNow! Fillmore and Write Now! Japantown

Endangered, Species, Enduring Values,
An Anthology of San Francisco Area Writers and Artists of Color

Civil Liberties United

Diverse Voices from the San Francisco Bay Area

Edited by Shizue Seigel

Pease Press • San Francisco

Pease Press
1717 Cabrillo Street, San Francisco, CA 94121
www.peasepress.com
First edition June 2019.
Printed in the United States of America.
Orders: www.peasepress/CivilLibertiesUnited

Book and cover design by Shizue Seigel. www.shizueseigel.com

Cover art: Top - Kate DeCiccio "Black Lives Matter; Black Moms," wheat-pasted wall in West Oakland. Edsel Rivera photo.

Bottom: Jess X Snow and Roger Pete, "To Immigrants With Love" for Galeria de la Raza 2017. Edsel Rivera photo.

Library of Congress Cataloging-in-Publication Data

Civil Liberties United
Diverse Voices from the San Francisco Bay Area
Edited by Shizue Seigel
Library of Congress Control Number: 2019941693

ISBN: 978-0-9904173-9-2

Supported by the Zellerbach Family Foundation

About *Civil Liberties United*

In this book, 100 writers and artists of color, and white allies, celebrate the diversity that truly makes America great. Martin Luther King's dream has grown stronger in response to reactionary and repressive forces unleashed by the 2016 election. Civil liberties must be fought for in every generation. They are important to everyone living in America, not just those who happen to be targeted at a particular time. Those who remain silent allow the loudest to speak for them. Those who look the other way may be targeted next.

The vitality of the San Francisco Bay Area arises from its cultural diversity. Fully 60% of its residents are people of color, according 2019 US Census estimates, yet writers and artists of color remain under published and underrepresented. Many great social movements have flourished in the Bay Area's rich mix of people. Today, we join hands and declare that America IS great because it is all of us, ever evolving. Growth arises from the tension between who we were and who we aspire to be.

In an increasingly screen-based and polarized society, we don't retreat into fantasy but draw strength from the rich, reality-based perspectives around us. We don't have to choose between either/or. We claim both/and—both our unique individualities *and* our collective communities, both our creativity *and* our activism. Many of the book's contributors do much more than make art. They are organizers, educators, healers and helpers, working towards equality, justice and sustainability. They draw from roots in Native America, Africa, Asia, Latin America, the Middle East, and Europe.

Like previous anthologies from Write Now! SF Bay, this book comprises the thoughts and feelings of a wide range of people dealing with real issues of the day. It's the kind of book I wish I'd found in schools and libraries when I was young. Our minds need more than the privileged pronouncements and commercialized blandishments that lead to cultural obliteration.

Democracy must never be taken for granted. Now more than ever, we need to reach within ourselves and reach out to others to keep us moving foward. In times of fear and greed, old ways are dissolving to make way for new solutions. Each of us must claim our role in helping heal society and the planet.

—Shizue Seigel, Editor

Acknowledgments

Civil Liberties United is a project of Write Now! SF Bay. It was made possible with the support from the Zellerbach Family Foundation, our fiscal sponsor Intersection for the Arts, and the San Francisco Public Library.

Thank you to all the writers and artists who participated in Write Now! ongoing monthly writing workshops on race, culture and identity; and to all the others who submitted. Special thanks to Joan Jasper, Naomi Jelks, and Shawna Sherman for hosting Write Now workshops and events at the SF Main Library; to the editorial committee, Charlie Amore, Roji Oyama and André Le Mont Wilson, who carefully read and reviewed every written work submitted; to proofreader Rosalie Cavallaro; and publisher Ben Pease. Thank you to Edsel Rivera whose extensive photo archive introduced me to many street artists, to Lorraine Bonner for her powerful sculptures; Leon Sun for his photos from the Families Belong Together March and Rally; and Joan Osato' for her rich portraits of artists and families who participated in *The Black Women Is God* and SOMArts Dia de los Muertos exhibition *Honoring the Ancestors*.

Many people and organizations have enlarged my sense of the San Francisco Bay Area's creative community during this project and the projects that led up to it. Among them are:

Kim Shuck, current poet laureate of San Francisco; Avotcja, poet, musician and DJ at KPFA and KPOO; Elmaz Abinader, Faith Adiele, and Voices of Our Nations (VONA); the Asian American Women Artists Association and Shari DeBoer, Melanie Elvena, Nancy Hom, Michelle Lee, Susie Tagami, and Cynthia Tom; the Asian Pacific Islander Cultural Center and Vinay Patel and the ubiquitous Melanie Elvena; Dennis J. Bernstein of *Flashpoints,* KPFA-FM; Dan Brady and Sacred Grounds open mic; Summer Brenner; Jenee Darden of KALW-FM; David Erdreich; Fillmore Heritage Center; J. K. Fowler and Nomadic Press; Lisa "Tiny" Gray-Garcia and Poor Magazine; Evan Karp and Christine No of Quiet Lightning; Kearny Street Workshop; Robert Kikuchi-Yngojo and Nancy Wang of Eth-Noh-Tec; Eileen Malone and the Soul-Making Keats Literary Competition; Kathleen McClung; Choppy Oshiro; Jameel Rasheed Patterson; Reverie Writers; Edsel Rivera; Tony Robles and the Manilatown Heritage Center; Josué Rojas of Acción Latina; Deborah Santana and *All the Women in My Family Sing*; Karen Seneferu and Melorra Green, curators of *The Black Woman Is God*; Malik Seneferu; Thomas Robert Simpson of the AfroSolo Theater Company; Denise Sullivan and *Your Golden Sun Still Shines*; Kenji Taguma of the *Nichi Bei Weekly*; Robynn Takayama and Wesley

Teruya of the San Francisco Arts Commission; Alexis Terrazas of *El Tecolote*; Rosalyn Tonai and the National Japanese American Historical Society; James Tracy of the Howard Zinn Book Fair; Kelechi Ubozoh and Cassandra Dallett of Moondrop Productions; James Warner of Lit Crawl; Amos White and Bay Area Generations; Al Williams and the San Francisco African American Historical & Cultural Society; the Writers Grotto; the Writing Salon; and the late Rene Yañez and Rio Yañez, curators of Dia de los Muertos at SOMArts.

And books like this cannot survive without independent booksellers like Adobe Books, Alley Cat Books, Bird & Beckett, Bookshop West Portal, Browser Books, Christopher's Books, City Lights Books, Dog-Eared Books, Eastwind Books of Berkeley, Forest Books, The Green Arcade, Green Apple Books, and Pegasus Books Downtown (Berkeley).

About Write Now! SF Bay

Write Now! SF Bay began in 2015 with a series of six creative writing workshops facilitated by Shizue Seigel in San Francisco's Western Addition. We began with separate workshops in the Fillmore and Japantown to explore multiple displacements caused by migration, incarceration, redevelopment and gentrification. Later, the groups consolidated to become the free monthly writing workshops that now continue to explore race, culture and identity around the Bay Area.

Over 200 emerging and established writers and artists have participated in Write Now! workshops, our three anthologies and many public readings at bookstores and other venues. The ongoing workshops enable writers of all levels, ages, and backgrounds share prose, poetry, or projects in progress (with hard copies for written feedback) in a supportive, multicultural environment. Participants have the space to find their own voice and style rather than being told how to write or what to write about. Seasoned and beginning writers meet as peers and learn from each other. They develop a confidence and sense of community through regular attendance and by participating in public readings at bookstores and other venues throughout the year.

Write Now! SF Bay has attracted a wide range of participants: from mature 12-year-olds to professors emeriti; former gang members to city fire commissioners; very recent immigrants to established performers. It's a rich and constantly evolving community. For more information, see www.WriteNowSF.com.

Table of Contents

iii. ALL American

i. Sanctuary

Osha Neumann and Jason DeAntonis, "Water Lady," Albany Bulb,
Albany, California. Photo by Shizue Seigel.

Boundries
Kim Shuck

It's dangerous to be a
Secret centuries of practicing
Translucency can render you
Fragile or
Inaudible, changing political fashion regarding
Inclusion can trigger
Chameleon impulses can redraw
Ancient boundaries darker than they
Ever were can even create new
Fences or we can make real choices
Can choose to see one another

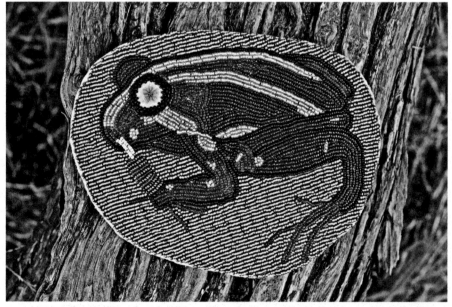

Kim Shuck, "Rattle Frog," bead work, 2013. Photo by Douglas A. Salin.

Bilingual
Kim Shuck

Skin a treaty
Stake it out flat for
Scraping and it will
Barely cover the distance between
Disappointment in a country that made you childish promises and
Our beloved dead arranged end to end from the
Mystic River to Achulet as the
Winter goes by it will go
White and stiff
An inconvenient reminder of things not finished but
Can be softened with random words in languages you don't
Speak like
Honor tattoos you
Can buy from local artists the hide can
Become a drum head for
Bonding with young people in a nearby park or
Shoe soles for walking a mile
Walking a mile a
Vacation in someone else's reality and you
Can tell that story for years to come
Years that you can keep track of on a
String of knots an
Invented anthropology while you whisper a
Word that you think means something about 'mystery' or 'sacred'
But really means
'Keepsake'

Kim Shuck is a complicated equation with an irrational answer. She has written three solo books and one chapbook. Her next book is being published by City Lights Press and will be called *Deer Trails*. In June 2017, Shuck was named the 7th poet laureate of San Francisco.

May Day
Tongo Eisen-Martin

under the house, but treated well by the 1970s

A class struggle
      sacred and soon

while we spend the new sea level at the store with morbid people who sell alcohol and alcohol for the man

                This morning is a zoo in love
                  A killing field's smile

Where they send applause in front of their troops,

                  "We got plenty of pain
                  to stay on this guitar
                  for one hundred years"

When a neighborhood is in pain, houses stutter at each other
In a theater of human and plaster

No one ever goes free, but the walls become more thoughtful and remember
our names

Men think they are passing around cigarettes
But really cigarettes are passing around men

                  houses stutter at each other
                  about the rich man's world
                  and the poor man's water
                  about the rich man's world
                  and the poor man's repetition

Ex-workers have hunched shoulders that fit between stairs and headaches /
An inverted purgatory / Of course their children feel at home everywhere

---

Tongo Eisen-Martin was born in San Francisco and earned his MA at Columbia University. He is the author of *someone's dead already* (Bootstrap Press, 2015), and *Heaven Is All Goodbyes* (City Lights, 2017), which received the American Book Award and other awards. Eisen-Martin is also an educator and organizer

Hands slur as they speak
      a man is lamppost high
      Is his lamppost's keeper

            the alarms are paved with gold

"futureless is this music and this music's proprietors"

            Children make better skylines out of wino's tales
          And it takes one (lamppost high… his lamppost's keeper)

        Incarcerated children next to the lightning
         Across the jar from purgatory

             Happy just to see something in motion,
             We welcome the north american drumroll

      A moth flies to the right of this definition of north america

      A moth flies to the right of twenty-five floors of brick astronomy

Europe rises to our 25th floor window
Carrying headaches and mirrors

We should close the window
But we haven't finished our cigarettes

"the alarm is paved with gold,"
the morbid person declares
while grinning and crying

          "you are going to get
         the gun under the counter wet,"
               we warn as we only grin

---

whose work centers on issues of mass incarceration, extrajudicial killings of Black people, and human rights. He has taught at detention centers around the country and at the Institute for Research in African-American Studies at Columbia University. He lives in San Francisco.

Without Teeth
Dee Allen.

Forty-two years ago,
His precious life
Was snatched from us.
The will of assassins:
Inert Black flesh.

A sudden rifle-blast
Ripped through the early April Memphis morning,
Then through him,
"The peacemaker."

A world based on total equality
Remained a dream
In stillbirth.
His life stolen
By parties unknown,
Given to the dark abyss.
His body, given to the cold ground.
His dream

Left unknown
Generations thereafter.

Forty-two years later,
The pin-drop
Is the only sound heard over an
Enveloping silence.
No one really mourns for him.
No acknowledgement of his untimely demise.
His life's work, done in vain.
Candles aren't lit
For the son of Atlanta's soil.
Activists have given the integrationist of yore
The collective brush-off.
A national holiday commemorating
His birth occurs every January and it's
Just another day off from
Slaving away for teachers & bosses.

Yes, he's been to the mountaintop without us.
Yes, he had a dream
And yet

No one knows what that dream was
Or for whom.

The sum of his achievements
On this earthly plane
Reduced to
Four or five
Simple words
Two phrases
Carrying little meaning to the average person
Now.

"I HAVE A DREAM."
"I'VE BEEN TO THE MOUNTAINTOP."

His other traits are clearly forgotten,
Lost in the dissonance
Of those same
Four or five words
Repeated like some holy mantra
In most minds of this generation:

Anti-war
Anti-imperialist
Pro-worker
Poverty's
Enemy
Third World
Insurrection's
Advocate
Mouthpiece
Against this Western Empire.

That man is never spoken of—
In Establishment circles.
That man was neutralised
Before his work could take fruition.
That Georgia preacher's son

Would have fought back, if tested hard enough.
Liberals,
Conservatives,
White Christians,
Corporations
Praising to the sky
"The peacemaker" today
Would've called him
"Troublemaker" yesterday.

So much easier to give accolades to a man of peace
Long after he's dead—

Accolades
Shouted out loud to
The great 20th Century Black Christian
Myth
Of a saint,
A non-violent man,
A once-living dream of racial tolerance,
A leader who ignored internecine wars elsewhere.

An Amerikkkan Black hero
Without teeth.

Safe in contrast
To other Black heroes of the past,
Starting with the shrewd inciters of
Slave revolts from Ghana to Ayiti* to
The Amistad, continuing through
Today's political prisoners
And the voices of the unheard
In city riots. But he's no less important to my people's
      history of survival.

In 1965,
While standing in the middle of
Scorched, riot-torn Watts,
That Georgia preacher's son
Who experienced a sharp, radical turn
In his outlook that reflected
His last three years

Is now
Softer & sanitised for everyone's protection.
A beloved Amerikkkan Black hero
Without teeth. No longer a threat.

No one
That is,
No one

Who dares to pick up a book
Can separate the man from the cherished
Public myth.
Forever behind the pulpit in Washington D.C.
Addressing anti-racist thousands
In a wide field of picket signs & banners.
Perpetual human paragon of civil rights
And only civil rights.

*What the Black natives of Haiti call their homeland.

Dee Allen. is an African-Italian performance poet based in Oakland, California. Active on the creative writing & Spoken Word tips since the early 1990s. Author of *Boneyard, Unwritten Law, Stormwater,* and *Skeletal Black*, all from POOR Press, and 18 anthology appearances including *Poets 11*: 2014, *Feather Floating On The Water, Rise, Your Golden Sun Still Shines, What Is Love, The City Is Already Speaking, The Land Lives Forever,* and *Extreme.*

Mel Waters, "Martin Luther King Jr. and Malcolm X," *Black History Month 2016* series, Mission District, San Francisco, 2016. Photo by Edsel Rivera.

Después del Discurso - Rafael Jesús González

a Martin Luther King Jr.

Una mujer me dijo que no fui cortés
con la oposición,
que fui duro
y que no animé
discusión.

Tal vez si fuera Cristo,
pudiera decir — Perdónalos
      que no saben lo que hacen. —
O la reina, y disculparme
por haber pisarle el pie a mi verdugo.

Pero solamente si supiera
que los verdugos
           fueran solamente míos.

¿Qué cortesía tengo el derecho a darles
a los que quiebran los huesos
    y las almas de mis hermanos,
        mis hermanas;
les niegan el pan, los libros
    a los hambrientos,
    a los niños;
        la medicina, el sanar
        a los enfermos;
techos a los desamparados;

que estropean los mares,
    que destruyen los bosques
        y los desiertos,
violan la tierra?

Afabilidad en los labios
de la furia justa
es pecado y blasfemia
    de la cual no seré culpable.

After the Lecture - Rafael Jesús González

for Martin Luther King Jr.

A woman said I was not polite
to the opposition,
that I was harsh
and did not encourage
discourse.

Perhaps if I were Christ,
I could say, "Forgive them
            for they know not what they do."
Or the queen, and apologize
for stubbing my executioner's toes.

But only if I knew
the executioners
                        were mine only.

What courtesy have I the right to give
to them who break the bones,
            the souls of my brothers,
                        my sisters;
deny bread, books
            to the hungry,
            the children;
                        medicine, healing
                        to the sick;
roofs to the homeless;

who spoil the oceans,
            lay waste the forests
                        and the deserts,
violate the land?

Affability on the lips
of outrage
is a sin and blasphemy
            I'll not be guilty of.

First published in La Bloga, Feb. 3, 2015. Rafael Jesús González bio on p. 232.

Life Light Remembered
Tureeda Mikell

"We are soldiers on the battlefield
With life light in our eyes," said Sis Sonja

1994, 23 years after volunteering
at the Black Panther Party free health clinic,
the *Tribune* calls,
Asking,
"How many guns did you have at the
Black Panther Clinic?"

How many guns?
Not - how many services were provided?
Not - how many programs were implemented?
Not - how many doctors or healthcare workers volunteered?
Not even why we'd care to put into practice such a program
with so many hospitals in our community.

No, didn't ask any of that!
Wanted to know how many guns we had.

Not what illnesses or diseases most
affected our communities or
how often we provided diabetes or sickle cell tests
or checked for high blood pressure, if at all.
Or... What may have been my program at that time,
I would have told her my interest in certain grains to regain genetic memory.

But she was more interested in
How many guns we had

Not who ran the clinic
or what hours or days
of the week we were open
Or... Who was our hero or she-ro
to set about such a task that sustains
    our health needs today.
No, the reporter didn't ask any of that.
She wanted to know,
How many guns we had?

Black men and women
Late teens, 20-somethings
Volunteered to become doctors, nurses, pharmacist, and therapist,
completed homework between
    seeing patients.
Black volunteer staff physicians
Tolbert Smalls and Eddy Newsome
tried to reverse curse of opioid addictions
purposefully placed in our neighborhoods
to weaken Black power base,
developed methadone program
to destroy heroin dependence.

We took vital signs,
Did sickle cell and diabetic tests
Provided prenatal care
Kept patient records
Organized charts, med rooms, pharmacy
Gave better care than Kaiser dared
Held life light in our eyes,
Books our bullets,
Educationally armed
Right to fight through walls that
Imprisoned us as violent, drug infested
Gun carrying, sex crazed jigga boos.

Kwame Ture warned…
"We must be politically prepared for what is coming. We have no choice.
The revolution is coming whether we want it or not! It is coming whether we
want it or not!!!"

How many guns did we have?
"We were soldiers on the battlefield
With life light in our eyes."

We are soldiers on the battlefield with life light in our eyes!!

Tureeda aka Toreadah, Story Medicine Woman, educator, has been called
an Activist for Holism, Word Magician. She is an award-winning poet and
director of Tree of Life Health Literacy Project, publishing 70 at-risk student
anthologies. She was an Eth-Noh-Tec NU Wa Delegate to China, a writer for
Rhodessa Jones of the Medea Project, and is a Bay Writing Project Fellow.

Lorraine Bonner, "Start 'Em Early," clay,
2014, 17.5 x 8 x 8 in.

Lorraine Bonner Artist Statement

I'm not going to talk about rights. The struggle for rights exists only within a framework of hierarchy and supremacism, in which the powerful have rights and others must constantly fight to win them, over and over and over again.

Freedom for ourselves and our children requires us to recognize and abandon this often invisible but universal system of malignant individualism, and to create, or rather rediscover, entirely different ways of organizing human life.

Instead of rights, I would like to talk about the African concept of Ubuntu, which means "I am because we are." Instead of a struggle for power, I call for an ecological network of "we," in which I am a node between the collaborative project which is my body and the collaborative project which is our culture and community; within the tapestry of all our relations: the animals and plants, the insects, birds and fish, even the bacteria and fungi; the pulse of earth and sky and water; the inhalations and exhalations of bright stars and dark endless cosmos, ancestors whose consciousness pervades the universe.

I am, we are, because all of this is. Art, music, dance, poetry live within the sacred rhythm and harmony of Ubuntu, beating in the heart of each of us, connecting us, making us whole.

I am not the only one saying this.

Lorraine Bonner. I was born into trauma, and to survive I sacrificed my heart and strengthened my mind. My mind carried me through education and work, and then, halfway through my life, clay slipped into my hands and began to reawaken my heart. My biography begins anew each day.

Lorraine Bonner's sculptures appear throughout the book.

sheer luck
Shizue Seigel

Swerving suavely through life
gyroscope spinning true,
inner momentum never disrupted
sliding along on greased wheels,
quarters jingling in your pockets
winning every coin loss,
you can afford to be flip
blank eyes, milky innocence,
a careless toss of smooth flowing hair.
Some people are golden.
Just lucky I guess.

There was a time when I worried
my young son would end up dead, drunk or in jail.
He had rocks in his brain,
broken glass in his heart.
The alphabet did flips across the page,
and girls who didn't think
Asian Americans date-worthy
confided in him endlessly
about their jut-jawed crushes.

The day the cops caught my son
crouched behind a bush
smoking pot with his pudgy white friend
pockets loaded with pen knives and a sharpened screwdriver
they could have been sent to Juvie
on a conveyor belt to prison.
But smoking while Asian and
carrying weapons while wussy
were not punishable offenses.
They were the wrong class and color
for involuntary servitude
So the cops laughed and
brought them home to their mommas.
Just lucky I guess.

Like the time the Highway Patrol smiled
when I said I was speeding towards my ex in-laws's latkes
because the engine on my new-to-me Mazda
was so quiet I couldn't tell I'd edged over 80.
Didn't even give me a ticket.
Just lucky I guess.

Not like my black sister-friend
stopped for a broken tail light in her dream machine
a new-to-her BMW convertible, cherry red
with a slightly frayed top.
The cop didn't like her attitude, threw her upside the car,
tossed her in jail, impounded the vehicle.

To ransom it, I loaned her $400 she didn't have.
She couldn't hold down a job for long.
She asked too many questions.
Her gaze was too direct. Her body too ripe.
The last words she heard before she died
were a joke about her black butt
from a well-meaning white male
who called himself a friend.
He was proud that he got her to laugh.
And laugh and laugh. What else could she do?
Just lucky I guess.

What you see is who you are.

Shizue Seigel is a Japanese American writer and visual artist. Her 20 years of creative activism are inspired by her family's World War II incarceration and her experiences in skid row, Indian ashrams, corporate cubicles, marginalized communities and public housing.

An Update - Richard Sanderell

When they came after Native People—attempting annihilation, murdering them stealing their lands, resources, cultures…you weren't Native, so you said nothing.

When they made Africans slaves—separating families, later acculturating their culture, music, killing them in the streets, prisons as new plantations… you were not African, so you said nothing.

When they forced Chinese to build USA's railways—made them cut their queues, forcing them into Chinatowns…you weren't Chinese, so you said nothing.

When the coal miners unionized—they were slaughtered, maimed for fighting to survive from those who stole the capital…you weren't a union man, so you said nothing.

When they rounded up the Japanese—put them into internment camps because USA didn't trust their loyalties, their own citizens…you weren't Japanese, so you said nothing.

When they rounded up, beat to death anyone who acts queer—or was dying of AIDS, who didn't have sex missionary style between a man and a woman…you do it missionary style, so you said nothing.

When they scapegoat farm workers or anyone with beautiful shades of brown as illegals—allowing exploitation of the worst kind from living in squalor, odious working conditions and pay so low no USAN citizen will work…you aren't a farm worker, so you say nothing.

When they burn Jewish synagogues—destroy their cemeteries, defile their very humanity, when buying something they got Jewed…you're not a Jew, so you say nothing.

When they come for Muslims—including citizens caught up in this kind madness of our enemies, and may be sent to camps…you're not Muslim; will you say something? Anything?

You may find the day comes when they come for you and there won't be anyone left standing!

Despite all, solidarity survives, she no longer suckles. Keep her strong, healthy, she's growing. You see what happens when she's murdered! Repeating your mistakes over and over is a proven way to madness.

Richard Sanderell is a Vietnam veteran against all of USA's wars. As an activist, he has supported Native Struggle since Alcatraz in 1969, vets' struggles and the issues of those we declare war against! In recent years, he's become a poet, jazz-poet. His work has been published in *District 11, 2017*; *Overthrowing Capitalism, Vol. 2*; *Bay Area Generations #41*; and *The City Is Already Speaking*.

Josué Rojas, "Amor for Alex: Perfect Lotus," acrylic on canvas, 2016, part of the *Gentromancer!* exhibition.

Josué Rojas is a painter and community leader, who became executive director at Acción Latina in early 2017. As an artist, educator and Mission native, Rojas has more than 20 years of experience in fine arts, community arts, arts leadership, and bilingual and ethnic media in the San Francisco Bay Area. His work and vision have been characterized by a commitment to San Francisco's cherished values of community arts and media, civic engagement, social justice and empowerment for migrant communities and marginalized communities at large.

Bullhorn
Tony Robles

I am a human being. I am a man, yet I feel like a pathogen. I walk in the city, the city that gave birth to me—and my mother and father—the city whose shadows cast over me—hiding my face, attempting to swallow me. I have a strange relationship with my city—upon whose streets I took my first steps. It slowly became disdainful, as if the fact that I was born in it were a source of shame—something to be extricated. It sees me as a pathogen, something to be exorcised from its streets, its public spaces—something that should be hosed and put down the drain. But I still walk the streets, a 5-foot 9-inch 185-pound pathogen. Why the hell should I leave? I'm from here.

So here I am—a full grown pathogen working as a housing-rights advocate carrying a bullhorn to the courthouse. A friend of mine is being evicted from her home of more than 30 years. Not quite a pathogen but they are treating her like one. A near pathogen who never missed paying rent in 30 years suddenly evicted because the new landlord wants to jack up the rent.

Why am I carrying a bullhorn? Well, we had a rally for my friend—the one being evicted—and I brought the bullhorn to break through the deafening silence of my town. The politicians must have jumbo marshmallows stuffed in their ears. The more the people cry out for housing justice, the less they are heard. It seems that anything that benefits the people is discounted, maligned or plain ignored. But back to the bullhorn: I carry it like a cop carries a gun. For much of my life my voice has been stuck in my throat in a knot trying to articulate thoughts and feelings in fits and starts. But with this bullhorn I have found my voice: "What do we want...Justice! When do we want it...NOW!"

On this day, the bullhorn decided to go AWOL. The thing didn't work. I bought new batteries and still the thing refused to work—refused to create a bigger voice and ensuing waves of revolution, undulating in the way a roll of toilet paper would do in a violent windstorm. So I had to speak with my own voice—no amplification—just solo. After stumbling, stuttering and lisping my way through the injustice of evictions—chanting and more chanting— I entered the courthouse.

As a pathogen, I am acutely aware of law enforcement, who are pathogen free—or so it seems. I enter a line where I wait to pass through a checkpoint. The checkpoint is manned (and, on occasion, womaned) by San Francisco Sheriff's deputies of various ranks.

The deputies have a variety of implements on their belts—mace, guns and other accoutrements that appear to weigh them down. It appears as if their pants could slide down exposing God knows what. Many of the deputies hook their thumbs on their belts and thrust their hips—as if urinating, insuring that none of their parts, should they dangle or come loose, fall to the floor. I take off my belt and deposit my belongings into a plastic basket. I walk towards the metal detector.

"What's that?" a deputy asks, looking at the bullhorn. He is a muscular guy who looks like he beats more than eggs.

"What the f*ck you think it is, a coffee pot?"

The deputy glares at me. "Oh, a smart ass?"

"Hey, I didn't say anything."

He snatched the bullhorn and put it on the conveyor belt. The other deputies gather around a video monitor like chimps watching a commercial for Chiquita bananas. "What is it?" asked one deputy.

"It looks like a coffee pot," said another deputy

"Kinda looks like a giant snow cone," said another deputy

"It actually looks like a vibrator," said yet another deputy

The bullhorn made it through in one piece and so did I. I gathered my belongings and headed towards the elevator. "You can't use the bullhorn inside the courtroom or anywhere inside the building," said a deputy.

"No sh*t," a voice replied.

"What?"

"Yes sir!" I said, entering the elevator.

The elevator took its sweet-assed time. I had to get to the 6th floor. It took forever to get to the 2nd floor.

"You're a real sh*t," a voice said.

I looked at the bullhorn in my hand.

"Did you say that?" I asked.

"Well, it sure wasn't your d*ck…and that ain't sayin' much."

"Hey, watch your f*ckin' mouth."

"What are you gonna do, start chanting?"

"This is serious business, ok, an eviction case. I don't need you f*cking me up…understand?"

Suddenly I heard the sound of a violin.

"Cry me a river," said the bullhorn

"You got a name?" I asked.

"Yeah," the bullhorn replied. "It's bullhorn…m*therf*cker."

We finally get to the 6th floor. I walk through the halls looking for room 620. A sheriff's deputy walks towards me.

"Be quiet, don't say nothin," I say to the bullhorn under my breath.

I almost pass the deputy when a voice calls out: "Hey handjob, you know where 620 is?"

I look at the deputy. My heart begins its speed bag routine.

"What did you just say?"

"Uh, nothin."

"No, I think you said something. Come with me."

I follow him to the elevator. We head back to the first floor.

"Who let this a**hole in here?" said the deputy.

I looked at the deputies. Their glances fall on me as if I were a garbage bin—not compost or recycle—just regular trash.

"What's with the bullhorn? You can't use that in here," a black deputy said.

"It doesn't work, it's broken," I replied, holding it up like a trumpet.

"Don't give me that Miles Davis sh*t," said the black deputy, not feeling the melody. He yanked the bullhorn away. I stood there, frightened that the little man or ghost or spirit that inhabited the bullhorn might say something else. The deputy looked inside the bullhorn, sticking his nose in first, then the rest of his face.

"You one big, stupid lookin' m*therf*cker," a voice said. I stood cringing.

"It was you!" A Chinese deputy said, pointing at me.

"Yeah," said a white deputy with a deep tan. "He's one of those guys who throws his voice—a ventrickulist."

"You mean ventriloquist?" I said.

The deputies glared at me.

"Look," I said. "I don't know where the voice is coming from. You said I throw my voice. Hell, I can't even throw a tennis ball, much less a pair of dice." The bullhorn was shoved back into my hands.

"You give us anymore sh*t and we'll shove that bullhorn so far up your ass that you'll be an alto—and I ain't talkin' about a sax," said a deputy who appeared to be the main shot-caller. As I walked towards the elevator, he deposited a very firm, very swift—hard and well-intentioned—kick into my ass. I looked back and was blinded by his smile.

I walked with bullhorn in hand whispering, "Shut your d*mn mouth and stay quiet." I navigated my way upwards and got off on the 6th floor. I make my way to Judge Kitteridge's courtroom. Two Asian deputies sit near the wall. A gaggle of court staff await the judge, their pores soaked in the perfume of power and authority. A deputy breaks silence: All rise…the honorable judge blah blah blah presiding.

The judge enters. He doesn't take a seat. His brilliant head of gray hair gives off a glow of florescent nights locked away in law libraries and walk-in closets.

"Be seated please."

The judge called the cases on the docket. He explained the procedures/protocols he requires from counsel and made clear the things that annoy him. My eyes fell on my friend, who after 30 years of residence in her building, is being evicted—through no fault of her own—but because the landlord wants to sell the building. She's the last remaining tenant in her rent-controlled building. She wants to stay in her home. The judge heard the attorneys in other cases. The judge stood, hips thrust out, arms crossed—like the deputies who seemed to all have been anointed with John Wayne's marrow.

One fellow, a young guy, was in court representing himself. The judge asked him why he hadn't paid his outstanding rent and why he'd waited so long to address the problem. The young man said that his mother had normally taken care of those things but had died and that he had become depressed. The judge looked at the young man.

"What's your educational background?" the judge asked.

The young man stood silent.

"Cut the f*cking bullsh*t, judge!" a voice called out.

The deputies looked at me.

"Yeah judge, I remember you," the voice said. "Well isn't this funny. You—a poor man's judge Roy Bean running the eviction court. People are being tossed out. They can't pay the rent and they have to see you, a giant intellect that barely passed the bar! Here come the runt…here come the runt! Yeah…tell it to the runt."

"Detain that man!" the judge said, pointing at me, his well-tanned face turning red.

The two deputies came around the table towards me.

"Up your ass, judge! Up your ass!" the voice kept repeating.

The deputies looked at me and realized my lips weren't moving. They looked at the bullhorn, perplexed. A deputy picked it up and held it like a trumpet. "What the hell?" he said.

The voice was clear as it vibrated from the bullhorn across the courtroom, making the walls move. Its words: "What do we want…JUSTICE! When do we want it…NOW!"

Tony Robles was born and raised in San Francisco of Filipino/African American heritage. His four books include *Cool Don't Live Here No More: A Letter to San Francisco* and *Fingerprints of a Hunger Strike* (Ithuriel's Spear). Nephew of the late activist poet and scholar Al Robles, and Russell Robles, co-founder of SOMArts Cultural Center, Tony is board president of the Manilatown Heritage Foundation and works for housing and senior rights.

Mel Waters, "W. E. B. Dubois," *Black History Month 2016* series, Mission District. Photo by Edsel Rivera.

Street Art

Mel Waters grew up in the San Francisco Bay Area, where his influences included hip-hop culture and his Filipino-American and African-American heritage. Mentored by seasoned graffiti and tattoo artists, he soon established a presence as a prolific street artist. Images from his 2016 series of Black History Month street portraits appear throughout this book. www.melwatersart.com.

Edsel Rivera, photographer, grew up in the Bronx of Puerto Rican heritage. Just short of completing an MA at NYU's Institute of Fine Arts in 1975, he moved to California. His love of San Francisco streets grew through his work as a taxi driver and letter carrier. Photographing street art is a passion; he's posted 7,000+ images on Facebook (Edsel Pretzel) and Instagram (Eggshell001).

I Know We Can!!!
Avotcja

We have been here before
We've sang in the face of the Klan
And danced with feet all bloody
On the decks of Slave Ships
On the "Longest Walk"
On Freedom Marches, in Jail cells
And Concentration Camps
Oooops Ghettos
That we we're supposed to call our home
We know this place
The Concrete Jungles, the Reservations
A curse of & by the uncivilized
Who have forgotten
The healing beauty of Grass & Trees
And the gift of clean Water to drink
And have lost their ability to love
We are familiar with
The senseless mayhem of perpetual War
The addictive lust for power
The intoxication of blood lust
And those who prefer
The inhumane sacrifice of their Souls
As they try to steal ours
Yes
We have been here before
We know the Hanging Tree, the rope
The rape of our bodies, our Cultures
The theft of our Songs & our Children
We have swam through the slime of misogyny
We've been here… we know
Racism, greed & stupidity have no conscious
And it is only a matter of time
Before the insatiable self-destruct
Before they devour each other
We've been through it all before
And we can get through it all again
We just have to be careful
Very careful…
The madness of this Narcotic is contagious

We must not get drunk on the stench of this poison
We have too much work to do
We must turn this suicidal Drug
Into fertilizer & let our tears
Fall down on deserts, glaciers & jungles
And run down the faces of
Good hearted people everywhere
I cry & I cry & I cry &
My tears come down like a Waterfall
An unending Waterfall for all the victims of
"Civilization"
We have been here before & together we can heal!
I know we can!!!

Avotcja has been published in English & Spanish in the USA, Mexico & Europe. She's an award winning Poet & multi-instrumentalist. She's a popular Bay Area DJ & Radio Personality & leader of the group "Avotcja & Modúpue" (The Bay Area Blues Society's Jazz Group Of The Year in 2005 & 2010). Avotcja teaches Creative Writing & Drama & is a proud member of DAMO (Disability Advocates Of Minorities Org.), PEN Oakland, California Poets In The Schools, Local 1000 American Federation of Musicians & an ASCAP recording artist. Her latest Book is *With Every Step I Take* (Taurean Horn Press 2013 available @ Small Press Distribution and/or Amazon).

ii. Locked Out, Locked In

Shizue Seigel, "Left Behind," *The National Interest* series, photocollage, 2008.

Questions commonly asked
by Norte Americano Border Patrol agents these days
Josiah Luis Alderete

State your nationality as currently perceived by these United States.
Can you spell where you are from using only American letters?
Can you regurgitate your original birth certificate with the raised seal?
State your mother's mother's mother's mother's maiden name
before the colonizer's baptised her.
Do you know the current location of any of the remains of your ancestors that
    we beheaded—specifically the heads?
Have you ever left flowers or explosives anywhere along the border where a
    brown man or woman was lynched?
How many family members do you have in your pocket right now?
Do you have anything in your blood that you would like to declare?
Are you able to provide us with any of your family members—specifically
    children—as collateral that you will return in case we need you to come
    down here again?
Can you lay your trauma on the table and keep it separate from any terror
That your family may have packed for you?
Were any of your bags packed by any ghosts that are not related to you?
Are you a monolinguist or a bilinguist?
Have you ever used a second language in an act of violence?
Have you ever used your second language to help others cross the border illegally?
Does speaking English hurt when you swallow?
Do you consider Spanish a colonized tongue even on Sundays?
Provide evidence of at least two locations in North America
where you have resided where the majority of the swear words spoken
    were in English?
Would you consider shortening or even changing your history
so that it's easier for Americans to pronounce it?
Have you ever driven across a border with the bones of a Conquistador in your
    trunk?
Are you able to provide us with a photo of one of your ancestors
In the process of committing a "foreign" act?
Do you dream in English more than three times a week?
Do you have any other unused languages stashed under your tongue?

Does your mispronunciation of English words follow immediate and sincere
shame?

Have you ever worked as a stereotype before?

Are there any bones out there not related to you that will speak up on your
behalf?

Can you provide receipts for any time that that you have been called
"wetback" "illegal" "beaner" "spic"?

Do you feel these statements were insults or acts of patriotism?

Would you press charges if someone shot you in English?

Do you read in between the lines of the National Anthem?

Can you imitate someone reciting the Lord's Prayer?

Do you set your clock back for daylight colonized saving time?

Do you cry at some point on the 4th of July while a Tijuana dubbed in English
Oliver Stone movie is playing?

How long did it take you to walk from here?

Do you remember the way back?

Could you take other people back with you?

Have you ever provided this service for money?

Did you smoke any milagros during your time in Mexico?

Would you like to talk to someone that you cannot relate to at all about this?

Did you need an interpreter for anything that I just said?

Would you consider your survival here an act of aggression against North
America's borders?

Or put another way:

Is the fact that you and your culture

not dead yet

despite everything that we have done to you so far something that should
concern us?

Wait here while we evaluate your answers and keep your hands where we can
see them.

Josiah Luis Alderete will tell you he is "a full-blooded Pocho Indio who refries
his beans and poesia in Spanglish." He was a founding member of the Molotov
Mouths Outspoken Word Troupe—a collective of politically engaged Bay Area
writers active in the early 2000s. Since then he's performed his work all over the
region and was featured in the poetry anthology *The City Is Already Speaking*.

Chip Thomas, "7089," wheat paste, Oakland, 2016. Photo by Edsel Rivera.

James "Chip" Thomas, MD, was born in Raleigh, North Carolina, son of an African American doctor. He has lived and worked on the Navajo Nation Reservation for over 25 years as an Indian Health Services physician. He is also a photographer, artist, and activist aka Jetsonorama. His large, wheat-pasted black-and-white images focusing on cultural visibility and social justice have appeared in the Southwest, in Oakland and elsewhere.

U Have the Right
James Cagney

You have the right to be right. You have the right To Claim, To Rename, To Redefine.

You have the right To Judge / To Frisk / To Choke. You have the right to remain standing; to remain whole, without being questioned. You have the right to ignore others' rights. To speak for all victims and tell a room of widowed mothers to shut up.

You have the right to Not See Color and firebomb diversity out of your field of vision. You have the right To Invade, To Displace, To Demoralize. You have the right to feel easily threatened. You have the right to the right side of history and to enjoy the good weather of a touring oppressor.

You have the right to trivialize the memorials of our dead while your missing daughters are canonized   their schools closed and festooned with roses.

You have the right to be inconvenienced by protests, by funerals, by the lives you didn't approve. Yfou have the right to ride to hounds   To turn lynching into a fraternal hazing workout   To turn lynching into a pop-up shop or video game app and award souvenirs.

You have the right to not see the problem / To browse safari thru our communities. To love wild animals while dismissing grown men as savages / as monkeys.   You have the right to prefer a comfortable lie over the truth.

You have the right to claim genocide as culture; To fellate weapons & sponsor the indignity of war; to see war as a product, to copyright its blood.

You have the right to justify torture and take selfies with the dead.
You have the right to be both the victim and the knife in the dark; To be the dark itself & the light glinting off the blade; to be ubiquitous and unseen.

You have the right to Ethnically Cleanse Until Culturally Clean & Repeat. You have a right to misunderstand history Just Enough then edit the facts that make you uncomfortable.

You have the right To Condescend, To Humiliate, To Desecrate; To redefine words used against you and dismiss our testimony; To control our prescriptions while telling us we're crazy.

You have the right to riot in the name of football; torch buses and Dumpsters not in your backyard—whether you win or lose; anarchy as good fun! Boys being boys! and all...

You have the right not to be questioned; to never be held accountable. To in fact do the accounting! To claim what hasn't been offered.

You have the right To Shoot & Not to Be Shot. You have the right to demand God act on your order with the Power of Now. You have the right to complain when our prayers get too loud.

If you ask me to swear on a Bible, I have the right to ask if you've read it.

Anything in your history can but will never be used against you.

Knowing and understanding that if you cannot remember which of your grandparents were members of the Klan, then your history will be expunged.

You have the right to hope your enemies don't read history. You have the right to have no enemies. You have the right to close your door on their grievances.

You have the right not to be sorry. You have the right to be armed and assumed innocent. You have the right to protect your best interests. You have the right of way. You have the right to be right.

James Cagney is a poet from Oakland, California. He has performed in venues and museums throughout the San Francisco Bay Area and beyond. His first book, *Black Steel Magnolias In The Hour of Chaos Theory*, is out now by Nomadic Press.

Between a Rock and an Immigrant - James Cagney
for Jakelin Caal / after Allen Ginsberg

America—goddamn.

This is what it's like being between Plymouth's
        Rock Wall and an immigrant

America, Liberty and Justice sure do make cute baby-goat names

America, your wig is powdered with coke but the lice don't seem to mind

America, I'm leaning in
I'm waiting for the conversation to turn to genocide so I can say
        ME TOO

America, wake up // You're missing the point

You invented terrorism but only use dark skin models in its ad campaigns

You award assassins with Black Friday arms deals

America, when I say you, I mean We
        the People, I guess.

I planned to make extra cash trademarking
                waterboarding
        but it's patented already.

Are there tortures you don't profit from?
Which bank do you entrust your Thoughts and Prayers?

America, can you say her name?
        As in a novena, not a marketing slogan.

America, nine people were murdered in a church
but the shooter on your flatbed truck is still hungry
11 people were murdered in a synagogue
But they brought it on themselves praying unarmed

20 children were shot at Sandy Hook
but your taste is for a loaded gun
over a living child

If you say you love children,
Emmett Till has four little girls he'd like to ask you about

Here I go—bringing up old shit, again.

America, you pass blood hand to hand,
                generation to generation

Has it ever occurred that YOU might be the savage,
                the terrorist,
the outside threat you're most afraid of?

Ask the Dakota Sioux their version of our history

Ask the buffalo about the endless pains

Ask the poisoned dead about the true
            meaning of Thanksgiving

Don't act like you don't know what I'm talking about.

You dropped the compassion units
from all your mindfulness classes

America, what do we tell our children
about this home of dead braves?

What do we tell our children, period.

America, you had a great idea, once.

You're a dry drunk
You throw a bomb then hide your hand
You're the main suspect and loudest victim, both.

Stop, Children… What's the sound of a maglite
hitting a migrants skull?
This is not setup for a bar joke.

This is me wondering why people are still crossing deserts
to escape slavery and oppression only to meet a walled promised land

In 1987, President Ronald Reagan demanded
Soviet leader Gorbachev: *Tear Down This Wall*
dividing East and West Berlin

After all these years, it never occurred to me
that we kept those bricks in storage

America, you're a big foster home where
the poor comes in for its abuse.

It's possible that the people who've passed the
Naturalization test know more of American history
than you do

And they still want to live here.

America, kneeling was once viewed as a sign of respect
or surrender / a sign of honor / or a pledge

When a black man kneels, the gesture becomes threatening

America, *there I go,* / *There I go* / *There I go...*

America, can you just   *say her name*?

Any name. Insert a name here like voting someone
off your island:_____

America, this year, my therapist
recommended I get a facelift.
I misheard her say Race-lift.

America, every time a siren rings
a black man gets his wings
and his mother kneels at an open casket
to sing the National Anthem.

What would it look like
Who would we be if we had
No one left to hate, or ban
Can you imagine this with your eyes open?

Texas Hold Em - Henri Jacob

With all this green you should have been a gardener
Red, white, & blue loop in my retina
To them I am cattle
Something to poke, prod, & brand
> *Here is the number that will follow you for life*
> *Smile for the camera*

Reduced to an asterisk
Another tally in a statistic that will be mass published & used as data to further
back the claims that we are uneducated, violent,
& feast on the flesh
of their Anglo-American beauties

Four walls encompass me
Deprived of all sensations
I stare into blackness
& watch my trial as it projects onto the concrete

Every thought echoes indefinably
Every thirty minutes an explosion is set off as
The guards tap the door to keep track of property

The clock ate itself centuries ago
I attempt to count to an hour
But this only leads to further hallucinations
The walls   c r a w l
        as if composed of arachnids
        The sink continues to move up & down like an unattainable pendulum
        Water is truth but the faucet is always out of reach
Each one of their laughs sounds like a death threat
The guards can't be seen
I identify them based on tone and verbiage
creating nicknames for them
My mind threatens to cut the power
        & abandon me for another host
        suicide sneaks into my subconscious
        But what I am to hang myself with?
                They took everything I own
                I am a digit

my claim to fame is

no

name in this

Criminal concentration camp
Genocide & gentrification make a great couple
Says one cockroach to the other
I evolve from boy to man
Crib replaced by cot

If you dare to call it that
In reality it is a cold carcass
whose base is a collection of rusted nails

Jail leads to professional unemployment.
I prepare my final poem to be written on the walls:
*Stripped to nothing but my pigment, they attempt to break me down layer by
layer and peel back my personality until it is nonexistent, revealing remnants of
my ancestors which they place into a Ziploc.*

Henri Jacob is a student of the Nicaraguan revolutionary poets & jazz poets.
Multiracial, of mostly Nicaraguan and Native American heritage, his work
grew limbs and learned to walk on 24th & Mission. "As a poet, it is our duty to
be a voice for the voiceless. We must breathe more poetry." Henri has published
a book of poems entitled *Poesia Libre* and a chapbook entitled *Poetic Tremors*.
He will be attending Naropa University this fall.

Artist unknown, "Dear Immigrants." Photo by Edsel Rivera.

Gell Ngnoy Yee: **Call Me Auntie**
Flo Oy Wong

On Angel Island near the open road,
A distance from Ai Fow, San Francisco,
The ocean billows.
I think of you, my *Gim Sahn** husband.
Our daughters and I have traveled
A long way to be with you.
We are latched behind barbed wire,
Soldiers with guns here.
Second daughter. . .shivers.
She asks. . .what she has done wrong.
What do I tell her?
I worry. . .
Will we answer the questions correctly?
In *Fah Kee Gwok,*** America, I am your sister,
Not your wife.
"Shhh!"
I warn our daughters,
"Maw Gong, Maw Gong,
Don't tell, don't tell.
Secret.
Maw hom ngnoy doo Mama.
Do not call me Mother.
Gell ngnoy yee,
Call me Auntie."

In November 1933, my mother, a "paper sister," was detained at the Angel Island Immigration Station along with my three older sisters. They stayed for six days for interrogation purposes before leaving to join our father in Oakland, California.

**Gim Sahn*, Gold Mountain, in Cantonese *thlee yip* (fourth dialect), is another Chinese name for the United States of America.

***Fah Kee Gwok* in Cantonese *thlee yip* (fourth dialect) means Land of the Flowery Flag, one of several Chinese names for the United States of America.

First published in *Dreaming of Glistening Pomelos.*

Flo Oy Wong, "Cutting the Birthday Cake," 1986.

Flo Oy Wong—artist, poet, educator—is a co-founder of the Asian American Women Artists Association (AAWAA). She began her art career at the age of forty. As an artist she received three National Endowment for the Arts awards. She started her poetry career at the age of seventy-five. Her parents were immigrants from China who were impacted by the 1882 Chinese Exclusion Act. She stands with immigrants.

Shizue Seigel, *"Jiichan,"* photocollage, 2007, 11 x 17 in.

Jiichan Ichiro: *Mottainai* - Shizue Seigel

Mottainai. Waste not want not.
Find a use for every bone and rag.
Jiichan. Grandpa. Make a life out of leavings.
You did not have the tongue to tell me;
I lacked the ears to hear.
Now I puzzle out the story
from scraps you left behind.

Jiichan. You only had to sigh
to let me know that I was loved.
On mornings when our breath hung in the air
and frost crunched underfoot,
we were two exiles without common language,
savoring in silence the coil of worm tracks in the mud
the call of birds we could not name,
bubbles trapped under ice.

Jiichan, your story spilled out petal by petal,
gnarled heartwood, gentled by time.
So much heartbreak. *Shimpai so da ne....*
You found your purpose where you could.
You learned to make do from the day you were born.
Shoganai, ka na! It can't be helped.

Your mother died to give you life.
She dropped in full flower like a headless camellia.
Your father emigrated to America to blot out his loss.
He left you in Japan in loving care of your baachan,
Your grandma raised you to a hopeful fifteen
'til you could join your father in California.

You found a stranger flanked by a jealous she-fox
of a stepmother with two demanding daughters.
You were the *chonan*, the eldest son,
with all of the duty and none of the privilege—
the family workhorse, your stepsisters' servant,
and your father and step-mom's old-age pension.
Oyakoko shinasai. Do your filial duty.
You tried, you tried! — for twenty years
until the day you broke free, rolled up some clothes in a blanket
and joined the *buranketto-jin*, the fieldhands who followed the harvest
south to north with only a bedroll slung across their backs.

Jiichan. You tumbled down the Central Valley
and back up the coast following the crops
—a rootless slip seeking a fresh bond, a strong graft,
a place to anchor your skills in the soil.
You came to ground as hired hand and then as the widow's foreman
managing 140 acres and thirty workers
planting peas and pole beans high up on the hill.

You would never fill the shoes of the widow's ghost.
But you could find comfort in the swash of the sea,
foraging for sea snails and singing songs
your grandmother taught you   on the distant shore of the same ocean.

The *iroha* that every schoolchild learns
uses each character of the alphabet just once
in a thousand-year-old poem that
etched impermanence into innocent hearts:

Iro ha nihoheto / Chirinuru wo...
Floral hues and fragrance / scatter inevitably
Who in the world / is unchanging?
Karmic mountains / crossed daily,
avoiding shallow dreams / and intoxications

Jiichan! As the world exploded into war
peasants became pawns in the board games of bureaucrats.
After an enemy sub shelled the Central Coast,
the FBI took you in dead of the night
with no time to pack your clothes.
Your crime? Living while Japanese
within five miles of the coast.
You weren't even head of household
just a hired hand who joined the Japanese Association
in place of your boss because she could not join.
Japanese rules allowed only to men,
not a Japanese widow who wanted her American-born
children of Japanese blood
to study the Japanese language after American school.
They were children caught between worlds—
ABCs with "I cannot tell a lie" George Washington
and his famous wooden teeth,
or *i ro ha* with honored emperor
tenno heika, stiff with gold braid.
Float like gentle petals with the wind—*I ro ha.*
Or stand pat with the red, white and blue.
When worlds collide, innocents are crushed.

Every able-bodied Issei who did anything whatsoever alien
in leadership, business, language, religion, martial arts
was tracked by Navy intelligence and the FBI.
They combed business directories, church bulletins,
and community newspapers, looking for names.
Better to be safe than embarrassed;
what bureaucrat wants trouble for a clerical slip?
An 80-year-old vet of the Russo-Japanese war? Lock him up!
A four-eyed mouse of a language teacher? Lock him up!
The treasurer of the Buddhist church?
Lock him up! Lock them *all* up.

Since 1939, lists of "potentially dangerous" grew.
Four hundred men, eight hundred at most—the Navy and FBI advised.
Take mostly men. Leave women and children alone.
Until the president had different priorities, other ideas…
mushrooming, mushrooming…
Two thousand…six thousand…
120 thousand imprisoned in American concentration camps

129 thousand dead in Hiroshima
80 thousand more in Nagasaki
How much vengeance makes America great?

Jiichan. Such a minor casualty of war
shunted to Department of Justice enemy alien camps
with Japanese immigrants, German bund members
and stranded Italian sailors—
blasted away to the badlands reserved for Indians
—Fort Missoula, Montana. Santa Fe, New Mexico. Bismarck, North Dakota.
The Germans had a name for fence sickness: *"Gitterkrankheit."*
Gitterkrankheit! That jailbird feeling—
innocence imprisoned for so long
that the guilt can never be shaken.

To mark off your days as a guest of the government
you re-made your life from scrimps and scraps
pieced from $12 a month pay and mail-order catalogs.
What you didn't spend on tobacco and rolling papers,
you spent on underwear, socks and shirts—the things you couldn't pack
when they loaded you in the back of a 2 a.m. truck.

"Kyampu de, porisuman demo, yori ni dorobo narimashita yo,"
you said, with eyes aglint with mischief.
"In camp, I was supposed to be a policeman, but in the night,
I became a *dorobo*, a thief." You stole lumber from the scrap pile
to build suitcases like store bought,
with dovetailed corners and steel-armored edges,
mail-order hasps and padded leather handles.

They stored gifts made by friends with time on their hands,
treasures of enforced ingenuity that you kept for a lifetime—
improvised brooches with safety-pin backs,
manzanita vases spelling out loyalty in dark and light wood
belts of black-walnut shell, sliced and polished,
threaded like conchos on Army-green bootlace.
A box of shoe-makers' scraps—oxblood red and ochre yellow leather
kept for half a century, in case of need
to patch a hole, improvise a hinge,
buffer an edge against bumps.
Ganbatte. There was something in you that never gave up.
It bent without breaking, like bamboo.

Actions speak louder than words.
Jiichan means love, though you never sat me on your lap,
never hugged or kissed or said that you were proud.
The warmth of callused hand on my shoulder never changed,
though I never learned to read the ripeness of the corn
by feeling through the husk.
o shimasho, ka na? Let's do it like this.
Wakarimasen, Jiichan. I don't understand.
Why didn't I pay attention?

After camp, your widow boss married you out of gratitude.
Duty. Obligation. Survival.
You would never measure up in her eyes
but you'd learned to take your own measure.

Struggling back to your feet in your 50s
two aging people stooping over strawberries
in a sharecroppers' camp
working together, *isshoni, isshokenmei,*
though you were both tired now.
You pooled your savings to buy a scrap of land
to grow bell peppers, corn and tomatoes.

But *Jiichan*, you chose not to waste
a single opportunity for joy,
refused to flatten life into daily gray,
refused to linger over the tea of bitterness.

How richly you deserved your rewards (you knew and I knew).
At the end of a long day, as you poured tea
over the last grains of rice in your bowl,
and sipped jug wine out of a teacup,
I stood behind your chair and
pounded your aching shoulders with child's fists.
Steel shatters but stone dances
a trayful of miniature mountains.

The leather scraps were still in the garage when you died.
Mottainai! Waste nothing.
Hone every experience to its essential lesson.

Manon Bogerd Wada, "Keepsaker," installation.

"Keepsaker" is a phantom ship intended for protection of passage and references a collective constellation of journey and migration. This work was installed at Fort Adams in Newport, Rhode Island, and responds to current "zero-tolerance" immigration policies that are interlinked within the consciousness of the site as a boundary and former coastal defense at the gateway of Narragansett Bay.

Manon Bogerd Wada was born in New York City and has been based in San Francisco for the past 20 years. She completed her BFA in Community Arts at California College of the Arts and is currently completing her MFA in Sculpture at Rhode Island School of Design. Through her art, Manon intends to give voice to marginalized narratives as an act of resistance.

Juice
Lauren Ito

Words weep
Connecting pen to paper
To calloused palms of cane
To cries for home out a boxcar window
To barbed wire dragging Jap blood from streets

Rid them from growing our food, everything they touch turns to ash
Rid them from teaching our kids, they're planting maggots in their brains
Rid them from the Laundromat on the corner, they've picked coins from my
pants pocket
Rid them from the corner store, I've had eye on that lot for a decade
Rid them from the house next door, neighborly doesn't look like

> Slit eyes
> > Buck teeth
> > > Rabid scowl
> > > > Jet black hair
> > > > > Pincers for fingers

Dr. Seuss told me so.

When cracking their heads like pomegranates
Pulp spatters on pavement
We go giddy
Slurp the tartness flooding streets
Hand our sons and daughters silly straws
So they too, can taste it
Engorge our bellies until we're drunk off it
Eyes rolled back, chins dripping, arms undulating with glee
We'll dance to a star spangled night only made for this America

In red juice, knee deep.

Opposite page: Shizue Seigel, "We Hold These Truths," mixed media. Dressed
in 1920s finery, American-born children of Japanese immigrants stand in
front of a Pioneer Days float bedecked with American flags and Japanese
irises. During World War II, they were driven from their homes and
incarcerated. Post-war hostility remained too high from them to return.

Gosei - Fifth Generation Japanese American
Lauren Ito

Chasing
Tattered tails of kimono silk
The crisp bow of an obi
A language that fell from our mouths as bombs fell like rain over Hiroshima

Whiteness
Did we quench your thirst?
Our ashes glaze your teacups
Mons steep in a dashi brewed from flakes of crackling skin

Excavating
A kanji-inscribed inheritance
My grandfather's sighs wheeze of Internment Camp dust
Slivers of polished sea glass rolling from shore to shore in a sea of tears.

Lauren Ito is a Gosei (fifth generation Japanese American) poet, photographer, designer, and community craftswoman from an island outside Seattle who now calls San Francisco home. Her writing draws from the diasporic experiences of Japanese Americans, exploring themes of inheritance, identity, and redefining home. Her work has been featured by the *Seattle Times*, Bay Area Generations, National Japanese American Historical Society, Japanese American Citizens League, Gears Turning, and Mission Arts Performance Project.

No, I'm Not the Maid, and Other Micro-Aggressions
Susana Praver-Pérez

Like water off a duck's back, they say.
      But it isn't really.
A seed of contempt is planted
      as they gesture
            with dismissive fingers,
      speak with their backs,
      say "Puerto Rican"
            with a curled lip.

I read between the lines and attitude
      slides off the page,
      rattles like a tremor
            shifting landscapes.

A whirling hiss of disdain
      rises like a tornado,
      knocks me
            off my feet
      before I even realize
      it's time to run for shelter.

Susana Praver-Pérez is an Oakland-based poet and co-founder of La Tertulia Boricua, a monthly Puerto Rican cultural salon that has been bringing creative community together since 2011.

Although Susana is passionate about writing, she's not ready to give up her day job at La Clínica de la Raza in Oakland, California. As a physician assistant she has been providing much needed medical services to underserved communities since 1980.

Miskito Sumo Rama Creole & Garifuna
John Oliver

Oh why they treat us bad
Oh why they doing us so
Can't they see we are humans?
Not because we are indigenous
Now it had been long time ago
Since we been oppressed
    So now it's time brothers & sisters
    To get out of distress

Look at my little Atlantic Coast
With so many people
Don't even know where they are coming from
Much less where they are going
Now these are rivers of poverty
That run through our veins
And if we keep waiting on better
We are going to wait the rest of our lives.

Miskito Sumo and Rama
Creole and Garifuna
This is no political problem
It's just indigenous rights.
The greatest weapon that can be used
To eliminate us on the coast
Is our self-separation
So that's why we must organize
And fight to stand up strong for our fight
So please let us all unite as one.

John Oliver lives in Granada, Nicaragua. This street prophet composes his poems amongst the cobblestones, selling and performing his work for tourists and locals.

Standing For Water

Tehmina Khan

1979 and we are there all over again.
The seventh grader inside me
goes from ambiguous brown girl,
who has to explain that Indian means
being from India, to *Eye rain ian.*

To be Muslim is no longer just
avoiding pork at birthday parties,
it now makes me *Eye rain ian.*
Someone from *Eye ran.*
And they say *Eye ran* but don't know what it is or where
or where India is for that matter,
and can anyone really find Santa Clara on a map?

Our neighborhood is white, black,
Mexican, and Filipino, and yet we
all try to erase ourselves when together,
silence the rhythms of our speech,
water down the flavors of our food,
hide our pain behind airbrushed masks,
and speak up only inside
the private sanctuary of our homes.

Eye ran, public enemy number one,
makes neighbors fly flags and yellow ribbons
in the faces of those who *do not belong.*
Soviet Union, USSR, not enemy but adversary,
worthy of being pronounced correctly,
an empire—strong but wrong,
and ugly, not beautiful like America.

The nightly news counts the days
that American hostages are held
by revolutionary students in Iran,
students who overthrew the tyrannical shah,
who years later will say maybe
it was a bad idea, taking hostages,
drunk on the power they held over the superpower.

Imam Khomeini is wise,
whisper grown up voices at
Indian Muslim dinner parties.
But he looks so mean, I think.
Islamic Republic—At last, a just society.
Mercy, Compassion…from God.
America cannot tell them what to do!

I get used to hiding in shadows
while flags of the citizenship imposed
by my birthplace are raised up high,
smothering the words that connect us to home.
You will be assimilated, resistance is futile.

I leave Santa Clara for Berkeley,
where we build shantytowns to protest apartheid,
march against United States' proxy wars
in Central America, organize for a free Palestine,
and feel the political become personal.
Caffeinated and armed with words,
we raise our voices, silencing fear.

When I help elderly immigrants prepare for
citizenship interviews, I tell them America is not beautiful,
and its power is ugly, but here you are, so be here,
and live here, and speak your stories and your language,
keep your grandchildren close, and tell them
who you are…who they are.

And 2017 is 1979, is Japanese Internment,
is the Chinese Exclusion Act, is Jim Crow Segregation,
is every treaty broken with First Nations.
But 2017 is also Sanctuary,
five centuries of resistance,
and all of us standing up for Standing Rock.
And we stand in the shadows
of a settler colony that wants us assimilated or gone.
But we walk in our own light,
as we weave our voices together into

a multicolored tapestry.
And speak a symphony of languages,
mathematical equations,
stories, prayers
to each other,
to the Divine
for water…for the water inside all of us.

Tehmina Khan has taught science to preschoolers, citizenship to octogenarians, and multilingual poetry to elementary school students. She now teaches English and creative writing at City College of San Francisco. Her work has been published in *Poets 11, Written Here, OccuPoetry*, and *Forum*. Tehmina's parents immigrated from Hyderabad, India, in 1963, moving from one university town to another until they settled in Santa Clara, California. Tehmina grew up in Santa Clara, studied at UC Berkeley, American University in Cairo, and San Francisco State. She now makes her home in San Francisco with her husband and son amid an ever-changing web of family and community around the Bay and beyond.

Next page: Anahita Miller is a mother, wife, and a medical professional. She is an Iranian American who has lived in four different countries and three different continents. She thrived and progressed while surviving childhood depression, revolution, war, immigration, and years of living in an ex-communist country. She is a writer who has many stories to share—stories about her eventful past and her winning battles.

Shizue Seigel, "Not Forgotten," watercolor. First published in *World Savvy: Population and Progress Collaborator's Guide*, 2013.

The Fear Box
Anahita Miller

"Kann ich bitte das Salz haben? Can I have the salt please," said the older German lady. I was headed towards the breakfast buffet, so I grabbed the saltshaker and placed it on her table with a smile.

"Can I please have some bread?" she added, again in German. My knowledge of German language was minimal, so I wasn't sure if I understood her correctly.

"I am sorry, but am not sure exactly what you mean? Did you ask for bread?" I looked over at my father, who was sitting at our table waiting for me to get my breakfast before he started eating his own.

"Oh my GOTT! You are not working here?" The woman's eyes widened and she immediately blushed.

"No. I am one of the guests at this hotel as well."

She apologized over and over again while I assured her that it was OK. We ended up chatting. She said that I looked exactly like the people who worked at the hotel, so she assumed that I was on staff. "I didn't mean to be racist," she said in thickly accented English. In America, people are scared of that word. I had to admit this German honesty was refreshing. She turned out to be a pleasure to talk to.

Later that night, kept awake by jet lag, I thought about what happened. I'd been annoyed, but not offended. And I didn't link her assumption with being racist. But the incident caused me to wonder. Was this a case of categorizing or of stereotyping?

My parents taught me to fear certain things and trust the others based on how they looked. In Iran, we'd had a holiday villa on the shore of the Caspian Sea. When my father and I walked through the area's lush natural foliage, he'd warn, "Be careful! The leaves with jagged edges, pointed tips, and a fuzzy surface are stinging nettles. They can hurt you. Wild mint looks similar, but without the fuzzy hairs that cause pain when you brush against them."

My own instinct and intuition tended to categorize things and people subconsciously. Is this division between what to trust and what to fear a natural part of our evolutionary survival, or is all this stereotyping somehow racist?

I closed my eyes and dug deeper into my past. I remembered that I was scared of all Afghani men back in Iran. They had escaped their country and come to ours as refugees. Most worked in construction as laborers. I hadn't been scared of them until one morning on my way to middle school. As I walked through a deserted alley, an Afghani man jumped at me, pulled down my compulsory scarf, ran his rough hands through my hair, and kissed my face and lips. Then, before I knew it, he ran away. At thirteen, I was shocked and frightened. After that, the idea became rock solid in my head: ALL Afghani men were dangerous. Period.

For many years afterwards, just seeing a man with Afghani features tensed my shoulders and raised my heartbeat.

It took many years and meeting wonderful new Afghani people whom I ended up caring for, respecting and trusting, for that category to open up and let Afghani men out of my fear box. Until then, I considered them all dangerous.

Why do we do that? Are we to blame for fearing something or someone after we have been exposed to bad experiences from similar things or people? Or was it a natural function of us humans to categorize and classify, so we can keep ourselves safe?

"All the Asian people look alike." I heard that over and over when I first got to America. To be very honest with you, they did look alike to me—at least Asian people from the same region. So did all the black people and all the white people. The only people who didn't look alike to me were the Iranians!

Then I overheard someone saying, "All the Middle Easterners look alike." I couldn't stop laughing. So it was the truth! When we are not familiar with certain features, all people having those features look alike to us. We are automatically categorizing and seeing everyone as the same. But are we all racists? Are we bad for thinking, perceiving or feeling that way?

The question circled in my head all night. Logically, I now understood that what I used to feel towards Afghani men was probably racist. But I couldn't help myself when they were all in my fear box.

I dug deeper in my mind. I had, and admittedly still have, the same feeling towards very religious people. In Iran, I was forced to learn Arabic (though my native language is Farsi), forced to memorize the Quran and forced to perform prayers. I was forced to cover head to toe and forced to fast during Ramadan even though I fainted over and over at school from lack of food. I witnessed torture, stoning, lashing, hanging and spent countless hours in jail because I let my hair show. I saw a ten-year-old girl forced to become a second wife to a fifty-year-old man.

After witnessing so many bad things, fear of Islam has become my PTSD. Now I am afraid of anything and anyone that resembles those bad memories.

I know it is not logical. I know it is wrong. I know I am considered intolerant by many. But I can't change it. They say you can't control your feelings. And it's true. It has become an automatic categorizing and boxing instinct. And I don't like it.

The instinct to categorize can easily be used and abused. It's easy to make all the bad guys in the movies or in the news look and talk a certain way, and make all the good guys look another way. It takes only a few movies for our brains to start categorizing and placing certain features and faces in our fear boxes. Government and societies can easily manipulate this natural instinct and make us fear a whole group of people for no reason.

As I tossed and turned that night, I realized how I had lost my fear of Afghani men. The only way I was able to shift the negative association was by meeting new people with the same features and re-categorizing them!

I wondered if I could heal and unlearn the other fears that trauma had installed in my psyche. Yes, I must! I decided. It wouldn't be easy. But I must do it because I don't want others to fear me because of how I look.

I promised myself to continue to meet as many diverse people as I could— washing away all the past exposures and experiences by diluting them with new ones. I would undo my fear boxes one at a time.

The next morning, I walked through the streets of downtown Munich.

Suddenly, I was startled by the loud sound of Quran, or maybe it was just Arabian music coming from a traditional Arabic store. The hairs on the back of my neck rose. My heart started pounding. I stopped and decided to go inside the store and buy something, anything! I needed to force myself to interact with "those" people. I stepped towards the door and saw several young men standing there talking Arabic. One smiled at me and stepped aside for me to enter, but the others looked me up and down in a heart sinkingly familiar manner. The probing judgment of their gaze made my heart beat faster and faster. I took a deep breath to calm myself. Suddenly, I remembered the red welts on my friend's back from the merciless lashes she'd received when she did not obey the Islamic rules. I tried telling myself these men might be atheist and the song might be a love song. But I couldn't control my feelings.

I closed my eyes for a second. When I opened them. I realized I was not ready. I walked past the store. Maybe I will try again tomorrow.

Our Connection, Part 2 (The Origin of Solo and Queennandi)
Queennandi X

I met my Prince almost 30 years ago in the L's, aka the Tenderloin, while hanging out with our folks. Some of us were doing what poor kids had to do, and that was hustle up some coins to help take care of our impoverished families, and some just wanted to chill with "the big dogs."

Our profile consisted of African- and Cambodian-descended children who shared a common thread of ignoring stereotypes and refusing to kiss society's ass for acceptance. Our "semper fi" bond was tight.

When I first met Solo, I looked upon him as a little brother. But I did not have "lil brother" feelings for him exactly, but more of some kind of weird crush that I questioned and was in denial of, because he was only 14 and I was 16, I shrugged off the feelings that maybe I was digging this "Manchild," I thought this was a fantasy I had made up in my head, so I kept all genuine feelings I had for him to myself.

I remember I used to chase him around the parked cars in front of 270 (Turk Street), attempting to take the cigarette he was smoking away from him. "What'cha doin' smoking!?" I scolded as he ran from me, usually getting away.

I always felt the need to look out for Solo and would lecture him on things—he was like the "baby" of our clique because he was the shortest—but he was a strong kid that played by his own rules. That is why I gave him the nickname, "Manchild."

He challenged the "alpha males" and it did not make a difference if they were relatives or not; he would tell it like it was without blinking or backing down. To keep it 100 (real), one of the attributes about him that I found to be attractive was his ability to take charge. I had never worked up the courage to tell Solo how I truly felt about him, and this cowardly act may have intercepted my future with him in a way that still haunts me to this day....

After leaving an abusive relationship, I went back to the safety of the streets. My brothers, Chet and Lace, along with Solo had looked out for me during the time when my ex was having a hard time taking NO! For an answer. Even after Solo moved in with me as a protector, I still continued to hide how I felt about him, mainly out of fear of having another failed relationship and possibly ruining a good friendship.

As time passed on, I could not help but to grow closer to him and him to me. I believe that if we would have stayed to ourselves and not allowed for the "party animal" lifestyle to infiltrate our happy home front, I would not have lost him.

But I was hard-headed. I did not listen to my Mama and sister Ronnie, who were the only two people telling me it was a big mistake to sacrifice my family to cater to fools' opinions about how it will never work out between Solo and me. I allowed that "It wasn't meant to be" or "He doesn't really love you" crap-talk to enter my mind. After we broke up, I realized that once our union was severed, everyone who ever had a negative vibe towards our love disappeared out of my life.

I had hurt my Prince to the core! What stupidity on my part to take life, love and a home away from a man who had done nothing but look out for me!!! Why did I care about what other suckas thought about us?? My Mama and sister may have been in his corner, but what did it matter if I wasn't?

The Prince's outlook on life was somewhat bleak after that betrayal; and since we are all human, no one has the right to judge how a person reacts to his/her heart being hurt. With that said, I feel that had I kept my beautiful family together, the white folks would have never gotten him and kicked him out of his home.

For years I was told that he was dead after being deported to Cambodia in 2001. Though life went on, I have always carried a 2-ton slab of regret and guilt in my soul over this man whom I truly loved and adored. I mourned him and I resented myself for my foolishness. Every horrible experience I had with a man, I would accept as a form of punishment for not doing right by Solo. I felt as if I deserved it, so I ended up living the life of a single Mama that was isolated, unloved and traumatized.

Although alone, I would keep getting this vibe of "feeling" someone's presence. I was hearing someone call out to me, but I would brush off the thought as being nuts. Then one blessed day in October of 2016, I ran into Solo's brother Flint, and when he told me that my Prince was alive, I made a promise to every God and Goddess who listened that I would find this man and make amends because I still loved him so much. "I don't know where I'm going, baby, but I'm coming!!!"

Without a clue to his whereabouts or anyone that was willing to assist me in my mission, I made the trip to Cambodia for the first time in 2017. I decided that I would start my search in Phnom Penh and take it from there.

About 30 minutes before landing I heard a strong heartbeat out of nowhere and I thought to myself, "Solo!!!???" Yes, I was sure that was him, he was alive,

71

but he was not in Phnom Penh because I heard his heartbeat BACK THERE!!!!
—somewhere before landing in Phnom Penh. It faded out as the plane landed.

I had no idea where "back there" was. At that moment, I realized the "Operation Solo" was going to be a long journey that had just begun.

I was ready to tell this man how sorry I was and finally share with him my honest, well-hidden feelings. I cried during the first trip after a fruitless connection, but after praying at the top of Chisor Mountain, I restored my faith. I vowed that the next trip to Cambodia would be successful.

And I still didn't have a clue other than his heartbeat….

Queennandi X. Born 'n' raised in the Fillmore. Daughter of Carolyn X, granddaughter of Our Lady Saint Lillie Mae Brantley, grandniece of Our Lady Saint Beverly and niece of Queens Janet Brantley and Nikki Swan, for without them, there would be no "me." Raised by the "Black Sheep" Queen in the concrete jungle of SF's OCP housing complex, Queennandi is a survivor of poverty, betrayal, brutality, and death. At a very young age, she chose the pen as her weapon to defend her community, her existence, and all who are suffering from oppression on Mother Earth. She is a strong voice for the voiceless—a motivational speaker, poet, author, actress, and revolutionary thinker.

Joan Osato, "Ashara Ekundayo," *The Black Woman is God* series, 2016.

Joan Osato, "Karen and Malik Seneferu," *The Black Woman is God* series, SOMArts Cultural Center, 2016.

Portraits by Joan Osato

Joan Osato has played a pivotal role in local and national theater for well over a decade and has been an indispensable part of Youth Speaks since 2001, serving as Youth Speaks' Managing Director from 2001-2007 and Producing Director of The Living Word Project with Artistic Director Marc Bamuthi Joseph. She produces Youth Speaks festivals and performance events, as well as LWP works for stage. She has brought her multiplicity of production and design talents to Living Word Project Repertory works such as *The Break/s, Word Becomes Flesh, Scourge, Tree City Legends* and *Mirrors in Every Corner.*

She began her visual arts practice as a photographer in 2008 and has been considered for the Prix de la Photographie, and awarded an exhibition in Bay Area Currents 2009. Her work has been exhibited at the Meridien Gallery, Ictus Gallery, Intersection for the Arts, and Yerba Buena Center for the Arts in San Francisco and featured in the *San Francisco Chronicle, Houston Chronicle,* and *KoreAm Journal,* and ArtSlant.

The Informant
Li Miao Lovett

Wang Xiaodong was comfortable in his middle age, with a good wife and two sons and the respect of comrades. When the first edict came out from Beijing, Wang was glad that the remaining capitalists would be accounting for their past sins. The front page of the paper depicted their great leader Mao extending his hand to the masses; all of China's youth had arrived for his declaration. Wang's hand quivered and he nearly dropped his ceramic teacup. Beneath his spilled tea the mosaic of ten thousand gaping mouths and little red books melded like tea leaves. He was relieved that the stain had not tarnished Mao's face; he was the Party Secretary of Chang'an county, but he would have to report it to his superiors.

The denouncements spread like weeds. Shrill voices echoed from loudspeakers day and night. Old landlords and capitalists were dragged out of their houses, and the youth rebels would force their victim to wear a long dunce cap that tipped to the ground like a fishing pole. Wang wondered at times if the punishment had surpassed the crime.

The orders trickled down that no stone of dissension would be left unturned. Reports from his informants came diligently by telegram each day. One, who went by the code name Twilight, went beyond the perfunctory spying in his town of Guangshan.

THE HEADMASTER OF THE LOCAL SCHOOL HAS BEEN SENT TO A LABOR CAMP. NEED REPLACEMENT. WIFE HAS TRIED TO KILL HERSELF; SEND A MONITOR. SHE MAY KNOW TOO MUCH.

Wang Xiaodong sent a young woman to monitor the headmaster's wife, following her through the course of the day, even sleeping in the same bed with her.

Guangshan was an unlikely place for such intrigue. The town had been a poet's paradise, where the elderly sat under willow-lined streets along the central canal. Centuries-old lore had made the town famous. A Song dynasty hero once slayed a white tiger by riding on its back, but the fame bestowed by the emperor had gone to his head. To this day people still say this about the seductiveness of one's desire, Qi hu nan sha. "When you ride a tiger it's hard to get off." It seemed to Wang that the fever of revolution could be as treacherous as that tiger.

Wang figured that the headmaster's wife was involved in a ring of corruption, until the next telegram arrived from the informant.

EX-HEADMASTER'S WIFE TALKS IN HER SLEEP. INVOLVED IN CONSPIRACY TO TAKE DOWN SENIOR LEADERSHIP IN GUANGSHAN. CLAIMS TO BE IN POSSESSION OF ADULTEROUS PHOTOS. SEND YOUR WIFE.

Wang wasted no time in sending his wife Li-lian to talk to the woman. She would coax her to give up the incriminating photos, or threaten her with the same fate that had befallen her husband.

A week later, Li-lian could turn up no trace of these photos. The woman said, "If I am caught uttering such blasphemy again, then you can cut off my lips."

Wang was beginning to doubt the reliability of his informant, but the next telegram from Twilight was more urgent than ever. YOU MUST COME IMMEDIATELY. ONLY YOUR INFLUENCE WILL SAVE THEM.

He decided it was too great a risk to let the matter go. Half a dozen of his friends had been thrown into prison in recent months for minor infractions.

When he arrived at Guangshan, Wang was surprised to find no signs of mass agitation, no banners decrying the leaders in bold black and red characters, no parade through town with their arms pinned back and their heads thrust down. Not a whiff of danger in the air, only the sultry fragrance of Cape jasmine filled the streets. His comrades were smoking in their offices.

"Want a smoke, Wang? They're Havana cigars, the finest."

"Me, I like the bootleg British stuff. So what if they're capitalists."

Wang shook his head, looking furtively from one face to another. He was furious. He spotted the chief of the Public Security Bureau, and pulled him aside. "My informant has sent me chasing after feathers in the wind. Tell me, who is this man calling himself Twilight?"

"He's an odd fellow," said the chief. "Keeps to himself, but never misses a beat on his paperwork." A report dated two years earlier revealed that Twilight's brother Lu Shaoming had been sent to a labor camp in Mongolia.

"I know that man's name," said Wang. "I reduced his sentence from twenty years to five. All he'd done was barter surplus rice for grain."

"You ought to watch your back, my friend," said the chief. "Stick your neck out for someone, and you could find yourself on the firing line."

Wang was about to return by train the next morning when an assistant showed up, bleary eyed and breathless, insisting that he stay put. "It's dangerous for you to go home, sir. The entire town is on a manhunt for you. They've set fire to the books and furniture in your office, and they were headed over to your house when I left last night."

It was true. The radio announced a full-scale campaign to cleanse the country of Capitalist Roaders and Western sympathizers. The seat of Chang'an county was ablaze with bonfires, men and women shouting slogans and marching through the streets.

"Down with Wang Xiaodong, enemy of the Republic!" The litany of voices crackled through the radio receiver.

His comrades urged him to go into hiding immediately. But Wang insisted on finding out where Twilight lived. Did the fellow know this was coming? Why else would he have concocted such stories to lure him to Guangshan?

When they arrived at his house in an alley behind the fish market, Wang and his assistant found the door open. Inside, the alley cats had made their home, leaving fish bones strewn across the living room, where a single kerosene lamp illuminated a desk made of old planks. Wang called out the informant's name. One of the cats meowed in response, craning its neck in search of the next meal. All they could find, behind a portrait of Twilight with his brother, was a poem scrawled inside his copy of Mao's little red book:

In these difficult times,

when black is painted white,

only the conscience of a few souls

will strangle—or save—the republic.

First published in *Stanford Magazine*, December 2011.

Li Miao Lovett grew up in San Francisco's Chinatown and in San Jose. She stopped being a good Chinese daughter in her twenties, quitting a corporate job to turn to public service. During her two-decade career in education, she has worked on the struggle to save City College from a corrupt accreditor and defend union workers. Li has written pieces for KQED, *San Francisco Chronicle,* and *Making Contact.* Her novel, *In the Lap of the Gods,* is a tale of love and loss set in China amidst the rising waters of the Three Gorges dam.

Opposite: Lucien Kubo is a Sansei, third generation Japanese American, who grew up in the Bay Area and attended SFSU after the struggle for ethnic studies in late 1960s. She worked with San Francisco and Los Angeles Japanese Americans concerned about "urban renewal" and the future of the community. She continues to create art, and actively participates in resistance work.

iii. ALL American

Lucien Kubo, "Are You an American?" assemblage, mixed media.

Civil Control Station: Registration - Ann Muto
—San Jose State Campus /Men's Gymnasium, May 23, 1942

Acrid tang of sweat tinged the air.
Katsuro and his brother, on bleachers,
waited to receive further instructions
as persons of Japanese ancestry.

At the table, he gave his full name:
       Katsuro Satou.
When the identification tags touched his hands,
32165E stood in his place.
       Family Number 32165 - Third son.
His older brother 32165C exhaled,
       "It's happening.
       They're gonna
       move us out."

Stunned, Katsuro wanted to run, hide,
disappear. Words flashed before his eyes:
       evacuate by May 30
        bedding, clothing
        essential personal effects
        no pets
        2 suitcases
       report to trains at San Pedro Street

Voices pulsated through his head:
       We're citizens!…7 days…
       who will feed Smokie?…not
       much room for baby sister's diapers
       …the *butsudan* won't fit either…
       tomatoes already planted…would
       Sumiko be on the same train?

Posters on poles assassinated his aspirations.
His life careened toward a desolate void.
Stripped of his name, reality
cascaded around him.
       32165E
            No union job
               No farm
                   No home

A Raw Truth
Ann Muto

Why would my parents share
something flawed
something ugly?
How could they bequeath
something shameful?
They closed off
parts of themselves—
To shield me from the ugliness
they believed lay inside.

They held their silence
not to hurt
nor diminish.
They could only move forward
by shutting out the past.

I could not know
Their love lay beneath
an avalanche of fear
the rubble of self-doubt.
What I heard in their silence:
I am ugly.
I am something flawed.

Ann Muto, Cupertino Poet Laureate 2016-17, continues to investigate her personal history and pursue her love of nature through her poetry. Her book *Open Passage* was published by the Japanese American Museum of San Jose. Her poems have appeared in *Japanese American Internment During World War II*; *Dancing on the Brink of the World*; *Point Lobos Magazine*; and *Inspiring Generations: 150 Years, 150 Stories in Yosemite, Generosity of Spirit*.

Left: "Civil Control Station: Registration" is based on an interview of a former incarceree when he and his brother went to the San Jose State gymnasium to register as directed on posters tacked onto telephone poles. The names and family numbers were changed at his request.

butsudan - Buddhist shrine

Tamiko
Ann Muto

She is small,
curly black hair
tied with a bow.

She stands still,
Blue Bird skirts and red vests
sweep and swirl around her.

She searches for the safety of
warm brown eyes, honeyed skin;
of knowing she is one of them.

She yearns to hear
chotto matte, gomen kudasai,
sumimasen, arigatō gozaimashita

She steps away,
slips into a box
which spins away into space.

In her box she wonders:
maybe the blond ones
know something she doesn't,
maybe she is the odd one,
the out-of-sorts one,
maybe she should
be more like them.

---

chotto matte - please wait, *gomen kudasai* - I'm sorry
sumimasen - excuse me, *arigatō gozaimashita* - thank you

Next page: Judy Shintani has exhibited in the USA and internationally including in Santiago, Cuba; Fresno State; JFKU; Springfield College, MA; University of Pittsburgh; Station Museum in Houston; Santa Fe Art Institute; Peninsula Museum of Art in Burlingame; ArtXchange Gallery in Seattle; and the San Francisco Presidio. She earned a Masters in Arts & Consciousness, Transformative Art from JFK University and a BS in Graphic Design from San Jose State University. She also attended San Joaquin Delta College in Stockton.

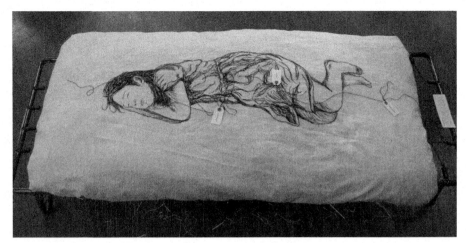

Innocent Dreamer - Judy Shintani

The sleeping girl on the straw mattress cot was created to remember the children and families—7,800 that were made to live in horse stables at the Tanforan Racetrack in San Bruno, CA. They were there for 8 months before being transported to official incarceration camps. It is hard to believe she was considered a threat to national security. It saddens me that incarceration of guiltless children is still happening, this time to Central American refugees.

Illuminations (below) are personal reflections of the Sansei—descendants of those who were incarcerated. The phrases are "word clouds" from a survey I conducted. They express some common feelings, and in addition show the breadth of the responses. I used Facebook and email to survey descendants of internees, asking questions such as "How does this history affect your life and what would you like to ask your family members about their experience?" I quickly received over 200 responses. It became apparent that 3rd generation Japanese Americans have much to say on this topic.

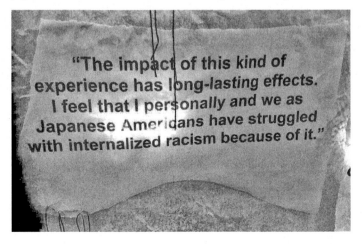

"The impact of this kind of experience has long-lasting effects. I feel that I personally and we as Japanese Americans have struggled with internalized racism because of it."

Little Jimmy
Thomas Robert Simpson

["Little Jimmy" is part of a larger solo performance work entitled *Still Headin' fo' da' Promise Land*. This scene takes place outside in front of his house. He is talking to a passerby. He is engaged in some age-appropriate activity such as coloring, playing with a toy, blowing bubbles, etc. Experiencing child-like innocence, pride, and amazement is of essence to this piece. Although written as an early 1960s piece in the American South, its message is still relevant today.]

* * *

Me, my mommie, an' my daddy gon' be movin' soon! We got's to, so dey can fix up our neighborhood. My mommie says our block is gon' be da first one dat Urban Denewal fixes up. Dey gone sell us a new house real cheap. Mama says we finally gon' git to da promise land.

The man came by an' tole my daddy an' mommie an' me all 'bout dey plans to tear down our house. Den dey gon' tear Mrs. Dories' house, Mrs. Franklin's house, Mr. Franklin's house, Mrs. Plusey's house, Mr. Bass house, da house on da corner, an' da ole grocery sto' an' da barber shop an' da dry cleaner place an' the Bar-B-Q joint.

Den dey gon' put in some new streets and sidewalks. You know why dey gon' put in da new sidewalks? So when it rains, we ain't got ta walk in the mud no mo'. An' dey gon' build some big new buildings for us to live in. And dey won't cost much!

But we got's to move out of the neighborhood till dey git done. My mommie say's I'll gon' git my own room. We gon' git a new kitchen and a new baffroom, an' everything is gonna works!

An' dey gon' mak' a bran' new school fo' me an' my friends to go to. It's gon' hab' new chairs and desks. An' none of the windows gon' be broke. An' dey gon' make dis brand new playground for us to play on.

An' he say dey gon' make dis big street. Dis street is goin' to be so big dat three cars can go one way, an' three cars can go da other way. All at da same time!

You know why dey gon' make us dis big street? So ebberbody's daddy can git home from work befor' his supper get's cold.

Den', dey gon' make dis big sidewalk up in the sky. Dis sidewalk gon' be so hi' dat you can walk over dat big street. You know why dey makin' dat big sidewalk? So us chullen ain't gots to run in front of all da cars to go see our friends.

But we gots to move out for a little while. Dey gab' my daddy an' mommie a whole lot of money for dis ole house. I think we's rich! My daddy says, we got's to sab' some of it, so's we can buy da new house when dey finish.

There's a man down da street who don't wanna go. He sa' dey should gib' him mo' money fa' his house. He say's dey just tryin' to git rid of us colored folks an' tak' our lan'. Ebberbody say's dat man crazy! He been walkin' up and down the street, with a sign, tryin' to talk folks out of sellin' and movin'. He say's, "Ebberbody should stic' together an' fight to keep their lan'." But since he's crazy, nobody listen to him.

He say, if dey build dat big street, he goin' to go up on top of it an' throw things down on dos' cars. He says dey ain't got no bid'ness makin' no big street like dat in our neighborhood."

Da city condemn'd his house! I don't know what dat means, but my mommie says, "His goin' to be the first one dey tear down." He say, "Dey gon' hab' to tear it down 'round him cause he gon' sta' right there in it.

You know why dey fixin' up our neighborhood?... Cause now we got us a King! And our King, all he do is walk up and down the streets wid' a whole lot of colored folks. He's done walked in Sama, Burningham, Nashbill, Destroit, an' lots of other places! If he don' like what he sees, he tells da white man what's dey gots to do to make it better.

Like, he told dem we wanted to ride in the front of da bus and eat anywheres w'se wants to. 'Cause he's da King, dey had to do it! Ebberbody knows you gots to do what da King says do!

When he came an' walked in my neighborhood, he did not like what he sees. So, he say's to them "fix up dis neighborhood" an' dey say, "Yes Sur, Mr. King." So dey gon' fix it up.

Oh, oh, oh, dat's my mommie calling me. I gots to go. But you can come back in…three months an' visit me when we gits our new place. Okay? Bye… Bye.

Thomas Robert Simpson is an actor, director, producer, and writer. He is the founder and artistic director of the award-winning AfroSolo Arts Festival, now celebrating its twenty-fourth season. Noted for his acclaimed one-man show, *Still Headin' fo' da' Promise Land*, Simpson writes and performs solo works about the African American black male experience. In recent biographical works based on the lives of black men, he portrays three-dimensional individuals choosing to live to the height of their ability. For more info, visit afrosolo.org.

Queen Bees
Julie Nicholson

I wonder if she remembers me, the white girl with dirty blond hair among the many shades of mocha colored children in our Queen's neighborhood.

Our favorite game is Queen Bee.

In the three-foot gap between the edge of Cookie's garage and her neighbor's gray slatted fence, hundreds of yellow and black honeybees shimmer through a veil of honeysuckle. They stagger around us punch drunk on nectar like cowboys stumbling out of a saloon. They buzz cloud our ears—wondering about what kind of flowers these girls might be.

Our friends tell us we're crazy.

"You crazy! You're gonna get yourselves stung!"

We invite them to play but get no recruits.

It's just Cookie and me standing amid the honeysuckle like statues, one carved from ebony, one from marble, the sun dappling, then burnishing our skins. We synchronize our breaths. We hold forearms; weaving a bridge for the delicate wings and tiny feet to crawl over us, tasting skin, slick and salty.

Neighbor kids singsong:

"'BEE' warned! 'BEE' CAREFUL!"

Cookie's mother says, "You girls watch out, you're tempting fate."

But no one stops us and we just keep going.

We get bold and start catching bees in rinsed out peanut butter jars with holes pricked into the lids.

The one who catches the largest bee is "Queen Bee"—for the day.

We are generous.

"Yours is bigger! You're the Queen!"

We keep the frantic bees in the jars only a minute, their tiny yellow and black bodies slam up against the hot glass, their smooth buzz now full of ragged rage—until we release them back to their hive.

Starting from pre-school, Cookie and I play Queen Bee every summer.

Then, around my seventh birthday the news comes from my parents.

We are moving to Manhattan!

My first question: Can Cookie come with?

Manhattan is a totally different beast from Queens. Cars zip down large streets; lumbering busses unload hulking, greasy groups of teens. Some grown ups rush by clutching newspapers while others sit on stoops smoking cigarettes or drink from paper bags.

The biggest change is where we live, a newly constructed, 19-story building where the door from the street is always locked. You have to be buzzed in. To get out you have to walk down a long fluorescently lit hallway and pass through a series of doors. No longer can I shout, "I'm going to Cookie's!" and let the screen door bang behind me. There is no slatted fence next to the gap where honeysuckle grows.

I beg my father to go and get her. I beg and beg and…finally he does.

Her front tooth has started to come in. She is dressed up in a way I've never seen her. Gone are the shorts and cotton tank top covered in the grime of play. Now, she's wearing a blue dress and little patent leather shoes. In Queens, Cookie could be impish and playful, or rough and tumble. In Manhattan, she is shy and polite. My mother offers her the tuna fish sandwiches I know she loves, but it seems she has to choke everything down.

We run around the halls of the building but the antiseptic feel of new construction, the lack of trees, all conspire against us. We bump into some neighbors—white kids, who snicker when I introduce her as "my best friend." I don't know any of the Puerto Rican kids who live in the projects across the street.

I also don't know the word "surreal," although that is what I feel. The sinking feeling that something that you are so confident of is giving way, turning into something else, not honey from nectar—but the opposite, dim and murky.

I remember the moment when we said goodbye. I walked her to the corner where my dad waited in idling car and watched as she trundled into the back seat. She looked out at me through the window, placed her hand, the hand I had held so many times, on the glass. I stood on the corner, the white kids on one side of the street and the darker kids on the other—all witnesses—as I watched her slip away.

Julie Nicholson is a solo performance artist, poet, and clown. She has performed in San Francisco at The Marsh Theater and Studio Shotwell. She has journeyed through in-depth improvisation and storytelling workshops with Sheila Rubin, culminating in live performance.

Next page: Tony Aldarondo is a Puerto Rican writer, actor, and poet. He has read and performed his work at La Lunada in San Francisco, Nomadic Press's Speaking Axolotl and Get Lit series in Oakland, El Comalito Collective in Vallejo, and Lyrics & Dirges in Berkeley. Tony is also a S.A.G. union actor and voiceover artist who humbly admits to falling in love with poetry.

A Bad Memory
Tony Aldarondo

At the age of eight
The police broke down our door -
With a battering ram
And pointed guns at my papi's face…

Wearing thick black
Bullet proof vests…
Then i heard their walkie talkies say -
"stand down!"
"disengage!"
"we've got the wrong address!"…

I can remember, after that day -
Both my parents were a mess…

Papi used to say, "mijo, many of us -
Are used in the U.S.…
That's why… many of us -
Are confused in the U.S.…
But that—
They'll never…confess…

Now let me get this off my chest…
(sing these words)

In this land, called our country…
I can't believe the things i see…
So much police brutality…

So much police brutality…
Police in blue i speak to thee…

Serve and protect…
Please don't beat me…
Serve and protect…
Please don't….
Beat me…

when the cops pulled me over with Sergio
Grey Rosado

We're spending the day together
little brother and i
little brother was assigned to me through mentor program
chicano, 8 years my junior with decades more life
little brother got his first tattoo
at 5
his father,
dying,
shared needles,
picked a clean instrument
for his only son
poked a gang sign
onto brother's left hand
pain and confusion
and forced to choose a side
before he could articulate things
like want vs need vs marked cattle
little brother
has done every drug under the sun
tags buildings
with a manic monkey
and teases me relentlessly
if i do anything laughable
he chuckles under his breath and says
"white girl"
chiding me for my orthorexia
his pet name for me
is Salad.

Salad and White Girl. interchangeable.
We're spending the day together
little brother and i
what were we doing downtown
we were going to the flower shop
to buy a bouquet
for his auntie
his auntie
who hated him
who had him under the roof by force

by law
as nearest kin
because dad was dead
remember
and mom peaced out too
later
when his cousins started to beat him
when his auntie started to beat him
i called the state
and they took him away
his mom turned up
in colorado
and decided she was ready to raise him
bitch: at 17 he raised himself
and fuck you for cashing in on his forgiving spirit
he wouldn't have told anyone he was getting beat up
but he told me
he didn't want me to do anything about it
he just had to tell someone
and Salad he could trust.
until Salad called the state
and they took him away
His mother is dying.
At least, says little brother, I'll get to see her for a little while.
He turns 18 and I know it's his birthday because the date is tattooed on my ribcage
because i'm thankful, i say, that you're here. with me.
because you matter, and if you hadn't been, if you ceased to be, i'd miss you so much.
I wrote him a poem and it made me cry
because all my raw shit makes me cry
and he was so shocked
that Salad could get so real
he cried too
he hugged me
and said, "i love you"
i said, "i love you too."

back to the flowers
downtown
LA's flower district is a secret delight
but LA traffic is a fucking monster

the phone says "turn right"
but the sign says "don't"
little brother eggs me on
there's a man in the crosswalk
gesturing, "no, don't"
i turn right
and a cop
perched to kill
pulls me over
i gather my ID
and little brother locks down
i've never seen him do this
having walls up is one thing

but this
this is a child sealed up in armor
in a bomb shelter
waiting for the ceiling to cave in

ticket written
i drive away
little brother is silent
exhaling
"you ok?"

brother's empty stare
pierces the window
lost

"you're lucky"
he says
and white girl
is ashamed
of how free she is

Grey Rosado is bad with names but still wants to know yours. They write poetry, prose, short stories, and handwritten letters. They have featured at Quiet Lightning, Red Light Lit, Get Lit, You're Going to Die, and more. You can enjoy some of their published work in *sPARKLE + bLINK, Buddy, Rag, Be About It*, and the *East Bay Review*. They live in Oakland and love their 3-legged dog more than most people.

Miguelito
Roji Oyama

It fluttered and circled high above the table twice. Eiji readied his weapon, a cigarette lighter. Zap! Spooked by the flash of light, the moth fled into a dark corner of the kitchen. Eiji got up to replace the duct tape that covered the tear in the screen door.

More moths clustered outside, drawn by the single bulb that hung from the kitchen ceiling. A police helicopter flying low over their house broke the silence. Its searchlight flashed through the windows, bathing it in blinding light for a few seconds. Eiji turned towards Emiko. Their eyes locked as they wondered what it had been like for their parents in 1942. Sirens. Searchlights. Curfews. As the roar of the chopper faded, they were suspended in a long frozen moment before they shook their heads and sighed in resignation.

"Shoganai nai, what can we do?" They quietly smiled at each other and tucked into the stir-fry that Emiko made weekly from all the odds and ends in the refrigerator. Tonight's was a mix of cabbage, carrots, cut-up hot dogs flavored with soy sauce and sake. They didn't have it easy, but they counted their blessings.

The old house still had fixtures from when Eiji's parents bought it in 1935. Old Christmas and birthday cards were taped along the wall underneath the kitchen cabinets. A faded and yellowed Buddhist prayer was tacked above the kitchen sink. Photos of the children and grandchildren covered the refrigerator.

Flowers from Emiko's garden brightened a mason jar on the kitchen table. An old bed slipper and a folded catalogue leveled two of the legs on the sloping floor.

The living room television blared in the background, announcing stepped up I.C.E. surveillance here in East Los Angeles. Emiko shook her head in silence. Eiji took a long sip of his beer. The creaky fan only pushed the hot air around without bringing relief.

As the heat of the day gave way to the windless heat of the night, the old house groaned and creaked as if settling down for the night. This house has been home to the Nagarumas for over eighty years if you counted the three-and-a-half year gap when they were illegally and forcibly taken to an Arizona concentration camp. They had a home to return to because their neighbors, the Mendozas, had their relatives move in and take care of the place. The rent had covered the mortgage and taxes with a little left over to help Eiji and his dad get started again after the war.

Eiji fanned himself with an old newspaper and scanned the room for that moth as Emiko said, "Those I.C.E. goons were snooping around at Murakami's store asking about Mr. Gomez. He came here legally back when they needed Mexican labor to work in the fields."

Eiji slammed his beer down. "They are a good, hard-working family! They earned their right to be Americans!"

In the 1950s, Eiji had worked for the Farm Bureau in the Imperial Valley town of Brawley. He'd helped process and settle many families like the Gomezes. "History is repeating itself, Emiko. They're rounding up and detaining immigrants today just like they did to us in 1942. Same old thing; just different excuses!"

They sighed. Many of their friends had moved out of the area. Emiko and Eiji considered it, but resigned themselves to staying, as they barely got by every month. Besides, many of their friends were close by, resting peacefully at the Evergreen Cemetery just down the block.

Just as Eiji was dropping off, Emiko prodded him, "Time to take out the garbage." Eiji quietly obliged. He headed to the back door off the kitchen. He paused at the landing. He could see the beams of police helicopter searchlights in the distance. The muffled engines went silent as they disappeared over the horizon. He silently shook his head as he headed down the rickety steps towards the garbage shed.

As he slid open the door to the shed, he saw the garbage can stir for a moment. Thinking one of the neighborhood cats had made its way inside, he slowly lifted the lid off and peered inside. Then he dropped the lid and jumped backward in shock. His heart racing, he approached the can and peered inside a second time.

A pair of eyes peered back at him. "Por favor señor, no llame la migra! Please mister, do not call I.C.E." His hands trembled as he raised his arms above his head. Eiji lowered the can onto its side. A young boy in tattered clothes emerged. "Me llamo Miguel, soy Salvadoreño, tengo siete años" My name is Miguel, from El Salvador, I am seven years old. Eiji cautiously looked down to the street and back at the yard to make sure no one was around. He gestured to Miguel to stay silent and follow him into the house.

"Who were you talking to?" Emiko asked. As she turned around, "Who on earth is this boy?"

"This is Miguel. He came from El Salvador. That is all I know. He looks hungry and needs a bath." Emiko smiled warmly and took him to clean up.

Emiko prepared a plate of food for Miguel. "I saw lots of cuts and bruises on him," she remarked. "I wonder how they got there?"

"I also found this note with a picture in his pocket" Eiji read it. The moth flew right in front of him, but he was too dumbfounded to notice.

"It seems he left home with his little brother Carlos. The note wishes them God's speed for their journey." Emiko's eyes brimmed with tears.

Miguel beamed as he gestured for more food. Emiko obliged and gave him a large second helping. His little hands reached over to hold Emiko and Eiji's, "Ustedes son tan amables y generosos, que Dios los bendiga!" You are both so kind and generous. May God bless you!

As they looked at Miguel, they were dumbstruck by the new information about his little brother.

"I will go down to Murakami's store tomorrow and ask Señor Gomez about where we can seek the right advice and not get Miguelito arrested, there are good people who can help find out what happened to his little brother."

Suddenly, a helicopter approached from above and hovered over the house. The searchlights scanned the perimeter of their house, lighting up the whole kitchen for an instant.

All three of them froze motionless. They thought a visit by I.C.E. was imminent. As suddenly as it had arrived, it gained altitude and flew off into the night. Silence had returned to the hot steamy evening.

They smiled at each other in silent relief. As Miguel returned to his food, Emiko said, "Eiji, we have to take care of Miguelito until we find safe haven for him."

Eiji nodded. "Yes, it is the right thing to do."

Roji Oyama was born in Japan to Japanese American parents who returned to the U.S. when he was 8. He became a student activist at San Francisco State in 1968 as a member of Asian American Political Alliance, which helped form the first Department of Ethnic Studies in the U.S. He earned a BFA in filmmaking from the San Francisco Art Institute. He lived in Japan in the 1970s, and now lives in San Francisco. He volunteers with Japanese diasporic community groups in San Francisco and in Latin America. He had a supporting role in the 2014 film *East Side Sushi* (2014).

Maria's Plight
Carole Chinn-Morales

Fierce knocking on the door
Grabs me frozen
Heart pounding wildly
in my throat hard
Whispering maniacally, La Migra!

Jumping up in the middle of night
Jorge hurries to the door, ears
straining
Children begin to stir, Abuelita
comforts them

I fumble with the packet of papers
Where's my cell phone, hotline
number
My voice trembling, hands shaking,
I call

Ask for a warrant
Be s-u-r-e to ask
Tell them, Slip it under the door
Photograph it. Has a judge signed?
Be sure a judge has signed

Don't panic
Resist opening the door...DON'T
OPEN
Don't answer questions
5th amendment...Remember

The officer identifies himself
Miguel Martinez

Speaking in Spanish, gruffly, with
authority
"Abre la puerta" Open the door
Pounding again, harder, more
insistently
"Abre la puerta"

Dios Mio!
What have we done?
Got a job
Cared for family
Sent kids to school
Paid taxes
Paid rent
Bought food

The DUI comes back to punish us
The terrible journey has begun...

Trump will have his way
Separating us. La familia
The border wall will divide us
Impenetrable barrier, Trump gloats
He tweets, "Keeping America safe"

We will manage through our tears
Children will keep growing
Fighting to flesh out their dreams
With or without their father
Be strong, ninjos! Be strong, ninjas!
Don't give up, persist
We will help
Dios les bendiga

Written after signing up for ICE action rapid responders team

---

Carole Chinn-Morales, a former teacher, was born and raised in San Francisco's Chinatown. A mother and grandmother, she remains part of an active, close-knit community at Cameron House. She came to writing only after retirement. Taking a series of workshops offered by her neighborhood YMCA, something new was ignited within her, as she discovered her voice through poetry.

NTA. Notice To Appear
Carole Chinn-Morales

A traumatized
Three-year-old dark-haired boy
A toddler
Torn ruthlessly from his family
Is asked to appear in a courtroom
To testify at his own deportation hearing

Given a list of attorneys
Though he cannot read
Unaware of what a lawyer is or
why he should need an advocate
Not knowing what a legal proceeding is
What deportation is
Not English-speaking
Unable to say in English
"I need to go to the bathroom."

Enters the dark wood paneled courtroom
Alone trembling not looking up
A room bigger than his whole house in El Salvador
Filled with strangers he has never seen before
Directed to sit down by a gruff foreign sounding voice
Sit down! Sientate!

Climbs onto a tall wooden chair
Awkwardly without help
His tiny feet dangling
Looking up at the judge
With wide inquisitive eyes

Oversized earphones meant for adults
Are placed gently over his tiny head
as if the child
will comprehend accurately
If he hears the Spanish translation

The judge peers down over the side of his desk
asking his first question
"Do you have a lawyer?"

Puzzled, the child moves his head slightly
Looks around the room
Eyes widening lips trembling
Legs continuing swinging
Only faster
Then suddenly bursts into tears

The judge, looking exasperated
Trying to maintain decorum
Sighs
Adjusts his glasses
Picks up his pen and
Wonders if this is justice
His third child so far this morning

Leon Sun, "Parents Not Prisons," from *Faces of NOpression; Faces of Truth, Love and Resistance*, a photo series taken at the Families Belong Together March and Rally, June 30, 2018, San Francisco, California.

Leon Sun is a San Francisco-based photographer, printmaker, graphic designer and writer.

untitled
Carole Chinn-Morales

The forlorn little girl
Dark curls surrounding her face
Stares down at her lime green tennis shoes
Much nicer than the white ones
She wore on the 2000 mile trip from her home
In Guatemala
To the border

Her dimple intact
Her shy smile still there
What's missing is her mother, su madre
No hugs and kisses and loving words:
Tu Es mi corazon
You are my heart

Nothing to be happy about
Not the new lime green shoes
Not the clean pink t-shirt they gave her
Not the peanut butter sandwiches
Cold milk
Oatmeal cookies

What has been taken from her is
her core
her center
her mother, su madre

Forcibly snatched from her without a word
No goodbyes
No smiles
Only tears
Loss
Trauma
Feelings of abandonment

S-e-p-a-r-a-t-i-o-n
INJUSTICE
In human ity
When will her mother come?

iv. Rooted, Uprooted

Lorraine Bonner, "Merciful Tapestry," clay, snakeskin, dreadlocks, rhyolite lava, 2014, 21 x 12 x 15 in.

Black Mother - Emancia Amore

Black Mother
remember you came
from a solid foundation
your mother and father's love
conquers everything on earth
they were
and are
and will be
your guiding stars always.

Their ways are unique
and rarer than the most
exquisite treasure on earth
and nothing can compare to their
home life which was built upon:
love, trust, communication
respect, truth, and hard work,
genuineness, companionship,
discipline and kindness to home.

Their home was a place
where true belonging dwells
where peace, harmony and tranquility
wrap around each other and
embalm the atmosphere
like the sweet sweet fragrance
from the Balsam tree
that stood beside
that dear old house
when the wind blew and
released its precious scent.

Black Mother
Remember that you came

from a source of strength,
goodness, and wholesomeness
in which you were taught
value, respect, discipline,
hard-work and togetherness.
You were taught to build
using various skills in the
quest for survival.

But most of all
treasure is that
which was bestowed upon you:
the love and the nurturing that
exceeds everything on earth.

You have a power
house of healing
flowing from the
true source within
you, so—
take a few moments today
to tap within this source
to help you face
the daily challenges
that you may encounter
in the struggles of survival.

My mother's and father's hands
touch me, console me
bath my wounds
and heal my pain
My mother's and father's hands
are the healing balms
of the Caribbean.

Black Child - Charlie Amore

Black Child
remember you came
from a solid foundation
your roots
route
back to times
darker than
your most darkest

Black Child
remember lavender
embalming your
child senses
placed into
your bathing water
or under your
nose to rouse
you back to life

Black Child
don't fear
your hybridity
lean in
and find the rope
that made it possible
for you to
be here

Black Child
remember how good
it feels to dwell
on what she gave
you than lament
what she could not

Black Child
the slavery of your ancestors
is only a testament
to their strength
and your purpose
don't let their
survival be in vain

Black Child
remember when despair
tried to convince you
that you would never
know her again?
Today has entered valiantly,
to tell you:
that is not your portion.

Charlie Amore is a Jamaican British Queer Non-Binary Writer. They were born and raised in South London and currently live and work in San Francisco. They write about queerness, relationships, trauma and grief—with trickles of humor. Their work is informed by personal experiences, as they strongly believe in owning your story. Find them on Instagram: @wordsofcharl.

Emancia Amore. I was born in Jamaica but currently reside in London. I am a mother of six who discovered the beauty of expression through writing during difficult times. I write about black familial love, lifestyle and nature. This poem is dedicated to all my family, with the deepest gratitude to my beloved mother and father, whose loving relationship anchored my family and serves as our beacon of love. Special thanks to my daughter and sons who took the opportunity to help me release these words. Nuff love and respect.

Twisted
Lyzette Wanzer

It was just my third day on the job; I was still learning to use the fax machine. A coworker who'd been on PTO my first two days appeared in my office, introduced himself via nutcracking handshake. He made small talk, then business-speak, back to small talk. Only so much to be said about the weather, the traffic, and the mayor. A column of silence rose between us. His gaze alighted on my head. "How did you get your hair like that?" He reached across my desk and ran his fingers through my hair.

I gripped his arm mid-arc, squeezed it just hard enough to signal my spirit, and flung it away. "If you want to touch my hair, you ask first. And when you do ask, I'll say no."

Shock and puzzlement leaped through his features. He flushed several shades of red, pivoted, exited.

~ ~ ~ ~

1980s: Braids and dreadlocks are prohibited in the workplace.

Atlanta Urban League, Chicago Regency Hyatt, downtown D.C. Marriott Hotel, Washington D.C. Metropolitan Police Department. In the U.S. Army, African Americans could not wear braids until 2002. And dreadlocks? Still not allowed.

~ ~ ~ ~

> Everything I know about American history I learned from looking at Black people's hair. It's the perfect metaphor for the African experiment: the toll of slavery and the costs of remaining. It's all in the hair.
> —Lisa Jones, 1994, *Bulletproof Diva*

~ ~ ~ ~

"Do you wash those?"

She, a fellow straphanger, blonde, on the uptown Lexington Avenue express.

"Wash what?"

"Your braids."

"These aren't braids."

"Yeah, they are."

"No, they're not."

"What do you call them?"

"Dreads."

"Dreads?"

"As in dreadlocks."

"Do you wash them?"

"Of course I wash them."

"I didn't know you were Rasta."
"I didn't, either."

~ ~ ~ ~

I can't remember her name; I can't remember the year. I recall she was in Boston, and I know it was the 1990s. She tended the front desk of a tony hotel, the kind of place with pearly shampoo bottles in the bath, sumptuous, pressed robes on the door hook, pillowed gold-foil Godiva squares. She wore ornate braids; had been for a few weeks. Guests traced her glimmering plaits with their eyes; they complimented her. Management did not. Management was alarmed. Management, in fact, demanded that she remove the braids, return to her perm, a style befitting a post at the lacquered mahogany station.

~ ~ ~ ~

> Race men and women may easily have straight, soft, long hair by simply applying Plough's Hair Dressing…in a short time all your kinky, snarly, ugly, curly hair becomes soft, silky, smooth, straight, long and easily handled, brushed, or combed.
>
> —Ad in *The New York Age,* 1919

~ ~ ~ ~

> The United States Air Force has a regulation, AFI36-2903 DRESS AND PERSONAL APPEARANCE OF AIR FORCE PERSONNEL, which in part, discriminates against African-American women serving in the Air Force. The code was recently updated to include a ban on…"dreadlocks." Female personnel with neat, clean, professional well-kept hair are being forced to choose between cutting their hair and treating it with chemicals to conform with this regulation…. The regulation itself does not define "dreadlocks." This leaves women with hair that is in no means a distraction or a detriment to their duties, subject to disciplinary action.
>
> —Treasured Locks, website

My stylist, the soothsayer. Sugarcoater, not. She pulled no punches, warned me outright about the beginner phase, the in-between phase, the neither-here-nor-there-yet phase. The need for patience. She ushered me in one January, and we began. While we began, she shared stories about schisms amongst stylists who wear natural hair and those wearing weaves and perms. Within the natural collective, additional rifts cracked along client lines: if you service natural clients, but wear a straightened style yourself, you were a preachy poser whose hands were out of synch.

~ ~ ~ ~

Ms. Boston was fired. She left her braids in. Dismissal followed. She sued under Title VII. I can't remember her name, and she wouldn't know mine, but the night her story aired, I began growing out my relaxer. I chose Senegalese casamance braids, standing in solidarity with her, sister to sister, shoulder to shoulder, across the frequencies, yoking the miles.

~ ~ ~ ~

> from dread + locks. The style supposedly based on that of East African warriors. So called from the dread they presumably aroused in beholders…also has a sense of fear of the Lord."
>
> —Online Etymology Dictionary

~ ~ ~ ~

My stylist smiled. I couldn't quite cannonball, so I stuck a toe in: braids out, spartan crop of Nubian twists in. Strangers, all races, on streets and in trains, in cafes and on elevators, commented.

"I see you're just getting started."

"That'll take forever. Did you know you can get instant ones?"

There were many paths to dreadlocks, including the immediacy of instant techniques. I wanted not just the style, but the journey. The quest. Short-cut methods would excuse and exclude any trial attending the passage. I needed the complete compass.

~ ~ ~ ~

United States District Court, S. D. New York.
Renee ROGERS, et al., Plaintiff,
v.
AMERICAN AIRLINES, INC., R. L. Crandall, President of American Airlines, and Robert Zurlo, in his capacity as Manager, Defendants.

~ ~ ~ ~

> Blacks selling [merchandise or services] to whites should not wear Afro hair styles.
>
> —John T. Molloy, *New Dress for Success*, 1988

~ ~ ~ ~

Rastafarians or others with dreadlocks made eye contact with me, nodded, smiled, sometimes spoke, in book stores, post offices, theaters, street corners, shops, trains, festivals, restaurants, libraries, galleries, parks, airports, clubs, and at Kinko's. I hadn't noticed them before, nor, as far as I could tell, had they ever noticed me. Assumptions spurred their spontaneity. My political, philosophical, spiritual stance? They never asked.

~ ~ ~ ~

"Plaintiff is a black woman who seeks…damages, injunctive, and declaratory relief against enforcement of an American Airlines grooming policy…that prohibits employees…from wearing an all-natural hairstyle."

~ ~ ~ ~

For weeks, my coworker distanced himself from me, until the day we boarded the same crowded elevator. Our eyes met across the grid of heads and hats and helmets. Neither of us blinked. He gave a small nod, small smile, touched the brim of his Derby. I nodded back sans smile. When we alighted we walked single file in silence. As we passed the vending machine, he spoke.

"Nice day today."

"Yes, it is."

"Supposed to rain tomorrow."

"Is it?"

"What do you make of Giuliani's plan for Times Square? I think it sucks."

"I agree."

"It'll turn the place into a Six Flags for tourists."

"I hope not.

"Worse than the Vegas strip."

"I guess we'll find out soon enough."

"Well, here we are. Another day, another dollar." He dashed ahead to open the door for me.

"Thank you."

"You bet. Isn't today the building's ice cream social?"

"Think so."

"You going?" He spoke to my back as I headed for my office.

"Maybe. Depends how much work I get done."

"I'm going."

I slid the key into my door lock.

"Might be a good way for you to meet other tenants in the building."

"That's a thought." I turned the knob.

"Well, have a good one."

"You, too." I shut my door.

~ ~ ~ ~

It takes care and attention and time to handle natural hair. Something we have lost from our African culture are the rituals of health and beauty and taking time to anoint ourselves. And the first way we lost it was in our hair.

—Harriette Cole, in *Hair Story*

An earlier version of "Twisted" appeared in *Guernica Magazine* in August 2014.

Lyzette Wanzer, MFA is a San Francisco author, editor, and writing workshop instructor. Her work appears in over twenty-five literary journals and books, and she is a contributor to *The Chalk Circle: Intercultural Prizewinning Essays* (Wyatt-MacKenzie), *The Naked Truth, Essay Daily*, and *San Francisco University High School Journal*. She is a two-time San Francisco Arts Commission, and a three-time Center for Cultural Innovation grant recipient.

OSMOTICS The Stealth of Oppression
Brenda Usher-Carpino

PART I: *Defining Oppression*
Although oppression can be defined in few words, its weighty footprint has left, and will continue to leave behind, one of humanity's basest legacies.

- A departure from the right of every human being to freely live life as meets their needs without harm to others.
  - Whether by choice or by force of nature…

Perpetrators descending to cruelty…
Subjects of cruel/unjust treatment.
Mental pressure or distress to which OPPRESSION subjects [v] its *subjects* [n]…

- Intergenerational trauma
- PTSD
- Ancestral trauma
- War, *iteratively*
  - Class struggle…
  - Racism
  - Action and consequence in springy sticky spirals of moral v immoral
  - Children wrenched from the arms of parents desperate with distillates of survival at our southern borders, risking…

Withholding humanity that shelters and nourishes and clothes
  - Lack of empathy
  - Genocide of Native and systemic murder of African Americans
  - Then indentured Chinese immigrants and Japanese American internments
  - Now Muslims
  - And anti-Semitism all over again
  - *And* the Mental Distress experienced by these (and all) oppressed ethnicities and their cultures.

In your face stealth—it was always there or you didn't see it coming.

PART II: *Living Oppression*
When growing up in a Black neighborhood in San Antonio, Texas, there was a small grocery store owned and run by a Chinese family. At our young age we would walk to that store several blocks away to purchase items that we needed between visits to Herbert E. Butts, a large grocery store chain at the time. I mostly remember the wife who was a gentle woman, probably around fifty at the time; I only observed that, with her graying hair, she appeared older than my parents. She stooped, and spoke softly, and always offered me a candy from a jar she kept on the counter before I left.

Don't ask me how I remember certain things, but I do…distinctly. I may have been seven or eight. She asked me if I knew about the Holocaust. What the German Nazis had done to the Jewish populations. It sounded disjointedly familiar. I knew that "holocaust" was a big word. And I knew that what we had nicknamed our older sister, whom we deemed the ruling tyrant when our father was away, was somehow related to this Nazi history of the extermination of Jews. We had nicknamed her "Little Hitler." We even knew about Mussolini. We would gleefully intone the naughty ditty—

> *"Whistle while you work. Hitler is a jerk. Mussolini bit his weenie. Now it doesn't work."*

I credit my parents and the village for educating us. Little black-ass kids. But…

—That is oppression. It seeps and stirs and seeks to spread and inseminate with systemic sepsis.

At the time that the Chinese store owner asked me about the extermination of European Jews, did I know the word "oppression" or even understand that I was living in the middle of such? Probably not. But I knew that white people did not like me for the color of my skin. I knew there were places that our Blackness was not welcomed, having seen signs that said "Whites only" and "Coloreds" placed over water fountains and bathroom doors and in window fronts. I knew that our physical world was restricted, and encompassed tight boundaries that included Mexican neighborhoods.

Racism seeks to oppress.
Racism is a function of oppression is a tool of racism.
I had experienced overt racism when a child in Texas:

- Being judged illiterate because I was black (I could read before ever going to school).
- Being mocked by white adults—"Can you count to ten?" I knew basic math when I entered first grade.
- Having to enter my mother's place of employment through the back door, although the owner really liked us—respectable and law-abiding Coloreds.
- Hearing my father complain of being called "boy" on his job, even by much younger white men. Which drove him eventually to join the tail end of the Great Migration in 1957, and to move us to Berkeley, California.

PART III: *Covert Racism is Insidious Oppression*
Wide-eyed with seeming opportunity to move about freely in society even if constantly aware of the color of my skin that darkened even more under

the California sun, to integrate into places and spaces where I had never been welcomed while in the Lone Star State. Those eyes eventually opened to covert racism. Some of today's micro-aggressions.

Tunneled and funneled and planted doubt where self-confidence used to reside.

Moving to Berkeley, California, initiated an understanding of the insidious expression of covert racism:
- Liberal California.
- Uber-liberal Bay Area.
- California, the iconic West.

Texas claims Western sensibilities, although it is one of the most racist states in the Union. But California is home to many white liberals who would gladly notarize their non-racism if it were to prove anything.

It was in Berkeley, California, that I learned that covert racism had its oppressive foot on my tender black neck. It was then I realized that racism would do all in its power to hold me back from potential success, both educationally and economically, since, oftentimes, the first supports and guarantees the latter. It was then that I was given to understand by white educators that I was inferior. Yes, this was the educational system in Berkeley in the late 1950s. And I suffered greatly from this covert, systemic, institutional racism. To be offered in junior high school a Hershey's chocolate bar in front of the entire class instead of the "A" I had earned, along with the B+ (just not quite good enough) that I was given. (My parents did not stand for it; they donned their Sunday Best, and confronted the authorities. The grade was changed to an "A.") Or, during classroom primetime, to hear a riddle that resonated like lead about Willie Mays, newly acquired Giant centerfielder—"What's black, runs across a field and catches flies?"

I knew it was abuse because it *singled out* and it *hurt*.

Not to be informed that one could study for the P/SAT exams, for which white kids had tutors. *Tutors?* An ignorant little black girl, because that is how they meant it to be. That is racism that oppresses.

Having had my wings clipped by a nation built on the backs of Africans, I feel as though I have not soared as high as I might have, even though I hold three graduate degrees, one of which is the loftiest in the land bestowed in 1978 by Stanford University.

African Americans have been oppressed for 400 years and counting in this stolen land—raped, flogged, incarcerated, burned alive, and hanged in hopes of robbing us of all humanity while profiteering and thereby subduing and culturally appropriating our gifts to humanity for however long the thrill should last. There were African empires before there were European ones. But so few people are aware of this because history is written by the conqueror (stealth), and in our day and age the conqueror is European. His reign will end. The mental, emotional, psychological, and physical distress of being African American in this country will pale some day.

Hopefully.

The sorry truth is that, should that ever happen, the oppressive nature of humanity will have moved elsewhere. But if I were to be around by then for some magical reason, I guess I hope to be holding the short end of the stick again, and doing what I can by wielding the mighty word.

Brenda Usher-Carpino is a playwright, short story writer, poet, essayist, blogger, actor, and lifestyle model. She hopes someday to add novelist to the list (the only book she has written is a 300-page dissertation, in French, which she speaks fluently). She is also a medaled veteran international race walker, an ex-figure skater, a classical vocalist, a lover of sports and of foreign films. She is the proud mother of a public defender, a truly gifted litigator, in San Francisco.

Joan Osato, "R. Defina Kuficha and Zoe Belle," *The Black Woman is God* series, SOMArts Cultural Center, San Francisco August 6, 2016.

Twice as Hard
Tehmina Khan

Your grandfather knew, in 1963,
that he had to work twice as hard
as any white man to make it half as far.
So he did diligent research
that boosted the work of established professors,
while he raised his family
on poverty-level stipends
from one post-doctoral fellowship
after another.
In 1974, he took an industry job
to make a stable home for his daughters.

Being a brown girl,
I knew I had to work
three times as hard,
but I didn't want to do it.
I wanted to dream.

He took me to his lab
and showed me liquids
in beakers and test tubes
and dry ice
evaporating into a white mist.
I was never very good at chemistry.

Obama is the son he never had, your grandmother
told me, when we hoped against history.
The man of color who worked twice as hard
and got to be president,
and still, we know, only got half as far.

The president, a father of daughters,
who said, *If I had a son, he'd look like Trayvon.*

He'd look like you.

Your seven-year old self
saw your own face in the face of the president.
Your fifteen-year old self

sees your face in the faces of the dead.
And now you face a face of one
who worked half as hard and got twice as far.
A face that disparages your face,
your name,
the direction of your prayers,
the four boxes you check
on your ethnic identity forms,
the fusion meals, hot and spicy,
you cook without recipes.

And your bargain is the same as your grandfather's.
Work twice as hard.
Go half as far.

His hard work travels with you
in your veins
under your skin.

Martin Revolo, "Berenice's Tales to Her Unknown Father (II)," photograph.

Multi-Hued Humanity Meditates on Black and White
Lorraine Bonner

Sacred Black, dark heart of womb and soil
Where all of life first takes its form,
How have You become the stench
Of evil and subservience
Rumor of contamination
Black degraded by small minds
Bent on domination
Small minds
Addicted to White

But mind unshackled leads us past
These weary scuffles for food and higher stance
The stoney laws
The rivers dammed

Quiet as a seed we breathe

As exhale is to inhale
So Black is to White,
So Death is to Life

Heedless of all judgement
Our world embraced
In their vast eternal dance

Lorraine Bonner, "Multi-Hued Humanity Meditates
on the Balance of Black and White," clay, 2015, 20 x 13 x 9 in.

Cut a Hand From a Hand - Tongo Eisen-Martin

"if you reverse the car any farther,
you will run over all the scenes in the back of your mind"

I never cared for teachers…just the pattern of fainting spells induced by wall art.
Propaganda is courage, man

The price sticker hid my tattoo
-I treasure my problem with the world

"My mother becomes from Brooklyn first thing in the morning"
—a proverb around these parts
        proverb or peasant entrance password

Writing short notes to famous Europeans
On the backs of post cards
With ransom requests

They reply with a newsreel or cigarette announcement (I can't tell the difference)

        —Noble dollars then you die inside
        (but only inside)

"They call it, 'sleeping deeper than your stalker.'
And stalker is all that badge makes you,"
says a great spirit dressed in the
bloody rags tuxedos became

        meanwhile my punch is feared by no one
        "Proud of yourself?" I ask the fret hand

        "Porch Lights" is what they call our guns

        I've seen this house in a dream
        I've seen this chair on behalf of a dream

I believe a trumpet was the first possessed object to fly

        "keep going," she cheers

the draft in the room becomes a toddler

obsessed with the altar
the altar becomes a runaway train
  got a thousand paintings cascading down my skinny arms
    Dictionaries piling up to the window bars

      —a reminder to the population that
       your blanket can work with
        or against you—

human reef/
we will be a big human reef
for concepts that finally gain a metaphysical nature
and they will swim around our beautiful poses

      we stop being flashbacks
    then stop being three different people
   then I was alone [the pistol is one city away]

one of the drug triangle's lines runs through my head
tap the bottle twice and consider the dead refreshed
"don't you want to rest your bravery?
don't you want to be a coward for a little bit?"
—back and forth to a panic attack with no problems nor fears

a man gets a facial expression finally
a Friday finally goes his way
his life is finally talked about happily in his head

      I can't possess the body of a hermit
      I must be the last of his smoke
     Now running away with three blocks of alley
      Tucked under my arm
       You ever see a man
      get to the bottom of his soul
   in a car ride down a missing cousin's street?

Half step to the right
I mean I took the whole car outside of history
Half step to the right
I mean a whole pack of wolves stepped to my left
"road marker" is what I called the light bulb we had for a sun
    a whole civilization might slink to the sink
      chain gang shuffling next to a sucker
—the long look in the mirror

a stack of money starts talking from four cities away

Rage
Charlie Amore

Driving home through Sycamore
the cyclist yelled nigger through your window
At home you tremble in the kitchen
minutes
before he walks through the door
you want to tell him
you need to tell him
because you've come to understand
that his rage is acceptable and
your rage will not be understood
your rage will stay a string of beads from
your larynx to your stomach
You let the beads show up at the
entrance of your mouth
Feel them poke as you say:
he called me a nigger
His swallow is a door closing
A dial tone mid-sentence
He rambles words like
police, reporting, face recognition—
practical words for a practical world
You wonder what that world would look like
And gag at the absurdity.
You're nine years old again
His words float around your glazed eyes
he can't see where you've gone
The only thing that travels back with you is his buzzing drone
In your ear as you stand at the doorway of your neighbor
Looking in, staying out
Another neighbor approaches and
you move aside like a bystander
when he stops you meet Rage in his eyes
The Rage that will follow you like a bad smell
for the rest of your life
but you don't know this then
Instead there's a feeling of ants
inside your skin—inside your bloodstream
In school they called you names like
driftwood and half-caste

In school they asked you to pick sides
Asked you which side you most identified with
Asked you to lessen yourself to be part of the divisions
But they were your peers
your own age
Could it have been a shade of that Rage?
His gaze triggers the flight in you
you monkeys need to go back to where you came from.
Onions sting
You burn
There's burning inside and your body
gives water to soothe the shell
but the fire's within
Before you realize it, you're at your own front door
yelling into the walls to find a piece of
yourself you lost so quickly before.
Later in bed the words dance in the dark and refuse
to let you rest; the flame flickers and the wicker burns a little more
And as you stand in the kitchen, brought back by his droning,
it dawns on you that he will never know this burning
You turn and walk coolly to your room; close the door;
stick your fingers down your throat and quietly purge your rage

First published in San Francisco City College *Forum* magazine, Spring 2018.

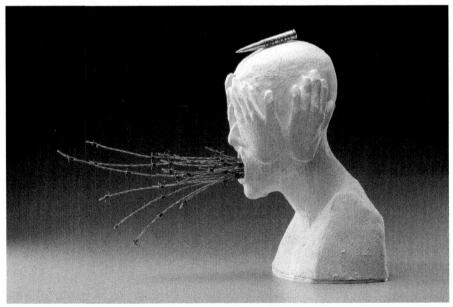

Lorraine Bonner, "Privilege," clay, bullet, barbed wire, 2009, 17 x 14 x 12 in.

Bridges, Not Walls
Nicole Henares

I keep thinking about what is in my heart—Who or what I love and why, and how this love goes beyond the physical, but nonetheless animates my daily actions. How is love, like freedom, like resistance, like survival, a verb?

It is now 2019, and I am astounded that it is really spring again. I ask for bridges not walls. I wonder how long I can keep believing in the transformative power of love.

This land was never ours to begin with.

How many times did our grandparents tell our fathers not to cry? Even at their father's funeral, my father and my uncle were not allowed to cry. We were always told to never let anyone see our tears: Tears will never matter.

A refugee child at the border remembers her tia's sparkly shoes and phone number— She calls her. The rest of the children cry and cry; they are kept in cages, separated from their parents. A man's voice in the recording mocks that their cries sound like a symphony. Someone, he laughs, should be a conductor. He is sadistic, not indifferent. I am not astounded by his cruelty. I was always told never to cry, never to let anyone see my tears.

Never cry because there are those who will enjoy seeing us cry.

Our bodies are our own, no matter what they say or do to us.

Never cry. Our tears will not matter. It will only give them pleasure.

Some nights I just want to eat an orange under the wide mouth of the night sky so my heart can feel like an island in the infinite silence of water while the moon and her hundred identical faces hover over the world, over those who still dream of sleeping the sleep of apples and point their tongues towards the west wind.

"Never forget that you are an American," my father has told me. It is what his father told him.

"But also never forget that you are Andalusian American," they both said.

Translation: We were once bad hombres, anarchists, rojos, from a shit-hole country that the United States closed its borders to, and a part of Spain that is technically not part of Europe, but the borderlands. In 2003, my grandfather's funeral mass was said in Spanish. I could only mourn in English, and did not understand the political statement behind the mass being said in Spanish, much less the symbolism of red carnations. All I knew was that we were instructed not to cry.

I navigate the diversity of San Francisco and the Bay Area under a veil of liminal whiteness. Serena Williams is and always will be a black woman, a champion. I moved to the Bay Area to become a teacher and poet and find a cohesive self-narrative and wholeness as a human being. I had to find voice for the ways Andalusia shares a coast with Africa and has the most mixed race people on the planet. I had to keep listening and to keep reading, and I have had to always keep a flower in my hair: Every poem has been a suicide note, and in order to survive, I have needed to understand more than be understood. I had to not just face my pain, but understand it as a way to more deeply understand others, and in doing so understand the ways privilege connects to voice. Sometimes I have made mistakes, huge mistakes. I have had to apologize, and learn to do better.

To keep striving to do better has required me to face my pain, and then step back from it. What I experienced as a child in no way can compare to what some of my family members have experienced, especially the immigrants in my family who worked in the canneries of Cannery Row when Spain was another "shit-hole country" the US had closed its borders to. Every immigrant group to some degree became "enemy aliens" during WW II—some worse than others.

What I experienced in no way compares to the conditions that forced my family to leave Andalusia in the early twentieth century, before the Guerra Civil. They were "human freight" on ships that were 3,000 passengers above capacity for the sugar plantations of Hawaii. My father has always told me that I will never understand that level of poverty, that level of shame. "Think of Calcutta," he has always said. What they experienced is not the same as what Serena Williams's ancestors experienced. What I experience is not what Serena experiences whenever she walks onto a court, or what Sandra Bland experienced, or Jessica Williams, or Nia Wilson. Nonetheless, I have to keep looking for the threads that connect us and stay in the present, though the past is never dead.

In the Bay Area today I pass, but I am not white. I do not want to be white. I take it as an insult to be called "white." I am a US citizen and, at least for now, my passport has not been revoked—so I am going to keep talking about how not everyone in the history of my family, on both sides, had legal immigration papers. I am going to keep on asking how and why "Americans" and human beings are regarded so differently, and human migrations are considered aberrations?

Labor has not changed, but our relationship to it has. Oh, our grandparents worked in the fields and the canneries. It hurts to remember their hands, the way the cancers ravaged their bodies. Do we really know what field work means, the way the fruit sticks to the skin and the chemicals go into the blood? Some did this work so their children and grandchildren would not have to—Did they intend for us to turn around and hoard and hate and base the value and potential of our abilities completely upon test scores and grade point averages?

Recently, it has been said to a crowd that students should bring their conservatism to their school campuses and not let their "loser teachers" indoctrinate them into socialism. I am a teacher and I am a storyteller and the only ism I am interested in is pluralism. What is it Whitman says in "I Hear America Singing" that Julia Alvarez responds to in "I, Too, Sing America"? I do not know how vast I am, but I do contain multitudes. Some might look at my book, shoe, and dress collection and say I could never be a true socialist. But I love my books, I love my whimsical dresses, and I love my sparkly shoes. The spirit defines the object, not the other way around. The love I have has no bounds.

Nicole Henares lives, works, and writes in San Francisco.

Shizue Seigel, "Sleeping Child," digital photograph, 2018.

The Name Poem
Wei Ming Dariotis

I. I feel conflicted
only sometimes
when someone asks me what my name means
I'd like to wait a little while
before skinning myself, that way

in Earthsea the wizards know
true names hold power
to name a thing is to control it
to own it

but my mother named me to free me
and to love me
[and to love herself through me]

II. an injustice, her naming
Shun Fan, she told me, meant only "Good Mother,"
but you *are* one, I reassured her
passionate on this subject at five years old
Even then she did not mince words:
I was disappointed, she told me, that my mother only thought
of my role in the family   never   never saw me as a person in my own
right
she didn't care what my name was—I was just a girl

said another way, Shun Fan sounds like
"Sour Rice"

once in boarding school in Boston
my mother was named twice / her teacher saying
you need an American name, your name is
too hard to say. You look
like a Sally, she insisted, and called her that,
from then on.

III. My name is not "Mom" anymore
my mother said, impatient with my whining
I won't answer until you guess

my real name
don't you know it?

IV. she wrote a poem
a treasure map
to find my name
"Ming" is a combination
of the sun and the moon, together
they are the brightest
things in the sky: "Shining Brilliance"

"Wei" is common in nuns' names
topped by two trees, a scroll
holds the middle hanging
above a bleeding heart
she tells me it means to have understanding or,
she says, to know your heart

Never let anyone call you
a nickname or anything that diminishes
your name, she told me

if you tell a child she is stupid
every day
she'll believe that
I want you to believe that you are
what your name is

You grow into that, you *will* love yourself

Wei Ming Dariotis is Associate Professor of Asian American Studies at San Francisco State University, with a PhD in English Literature from UCSB. Her research interests include race, gender, and science fiction; Asian American literature and poetry; critical mixed race cultural and literary studies; and educational leadership. Projects include *War Baby/Love Child: Mixed Race Asian American Art* with Laura Kina (UW Press, 2013), *Fight the Tower: Asian American Women Scholars Resistance and Renewal in Academia* with Dr. Kieu Linh Valverde (Rutgers 2019), and special issues of *Asian American Literatures: Discourses and Pedagogies* on mixed heritage Asian American literature (2012) and *Aiiieeeee! An Anthology of Asian American Writers* (forthcoming).

Public Transportation
Kimi Sugioka

When I was 6 or 7
and wore my hair in braids
I became part of the spectacle
in Boone, North Carolina
on the Tweetsie Railroad
Wild West ride;
along with tanned & buckskin clad
actors waving tomahawks
as the train passed by
All the little alabaster kids
ran up asking,
"Are you an injun?"

> A spider parachutes
> on a puff of wind
> that carries it from tree to tree
> or across oceans
> weaving a singular strand of silk
> connecting past and future,
> and you to me

Above the BART platform
a jelly-faced waxen man
calls down
to 3 cinnamon princes
He throws them a bill and yells,
"It's great to see you guys
dancing on the train
instead of killing and
robbing people"

> The lodgepole pine, among others,
> can only reproduce
> when fire melts the resin
> in serotinous cones
> that release its seeds

At the San Francisco airport
I wait for a plane

with Jesus who,
while walking through a
restaurant,
almost drops a tray of dirty dishes
shoved into his belly
by a stone-eyed Texan

> We carry the vision and
> wisdom of our ancestors
> like seeds deep beneath
> our skin,
> try to embrace a
> middling existence,
> climb propitious ladders
> that lead to storm drains
> beneath the feet
> of the elite,
> hoping for a glimmer
> of human recognition

A mourning dove hued father
cries about the times
he has witnessed his adopted
mahogany child walk into a corner store
to buy candy
as the shopkeeper
bristles and growls
as though the little boy has
already committed a crime

> Like rabbits
> in a field of low grass
> We seem too terrified
> to meet the gaze
> of the being
> beside us
> despite our familial
> solicitude

An ashen-skinned poet tells me
that I'm not any more Japanese

than he; that my heritage has been
bleached from my skin
through assimilation
Never acknowledging the generational
scars left by persecution, incarceration
and silence

      The proliferation of
      seedlings
      can only be cannily
      awakened
      by the purifying
      flame

On the train, the guerrilla dancers
flip and tumble
in gyrating double-jointed
grace
They are carnival joyous,
just shy of raucous
knowing their place
all too well

      Remember
      the spider's
      audacity,
      and the strength
      of her
      filament

Kimi Sugioka is a poet, songwriter and educator who counters the current and historical political, economic, and societal exploitation and subjugation of women, and all oppressed people, with word and song. She is informed by her experience as a bi-cultural mother, public school teacher, and human being.

Next page: A version of Sandra Wassilie's "Skin In the Game" was published in *Naked Bulb Anthology* 2016, Naked Bulb Press, 2017. Her bio is on p. 246.

Skin in the Game
Sandra Wassilie

Skin is the body's shore
where the ocean alights
then slinks away
returns on a roar

or a sigh,
not at all weatherproof
though it holds within limits
a while

no, not protective
but semiotic
signaling a state of being
one color out of

a particular spectrum
from the translucence of mica
to the depths of obsidian
each skin an earth tone

obvious
if you but look
and perceive
how each grain of sand

carries its origin,
the fragment refined
signals
a state of being

despite its glint
the weather changes
erosion shows its hand
the one that wins

but for now
you might want
to sink into my sand
play on this shore

Bone Song #9
Gail Mitchell

Her mother said she had a gypsy soul
But what she meant and could not say out loud was
She was frightened by the darkness
and afraid that all the light she could see in this child
would be diminished by the world and the church
Her prayers were for her daughter's survival,
Her fear deprived her of joy and left a hole in her stomach
and made her gnaw at words and bones
and fold and refold her hands in her lap
Misgivings and twisted history binding her
While this daughter fought and pushed abandoning those boundaries
She might be called lawless
In another time and found dangling
Please dear Lord let this one make it through…
She prayed silently as her daughter split verbs and spit words
Spilled blood and rage are the spike and hammer that renew the spirit
Her daughter's saints all played guitars
She wondered how her baby stayed sane
When all around was darkness, pain and endings
How could she pick up and move forward
And try again to believe,
When Eve and lies lived together in the same word

In the beginning was the word and I've drawn on it, to map the internal terrain and make sense of the external world, to investigate life and death, traversing a language that leaves me spellbound.

Gail Mitchell is a poet living in San Francisco. The author of *Bone Songs*, she received her MFA from San Francisco State University.

This is not a jump rope song
Gail Mitchell

Under their skirts
Within their veins
History's trace
Leaves a blood red stain

The power of fear
Torture and greed
The lash on skin
The weals that bleed

So many lost
No last names
Sold to fields
In bondage and Pain

v. No More!

Victor Navarette, "La Prision," collage. Photo by Martin Revolo.

untitled
Tawny Porter

The world is quiet
I can hear myself think
Brings me back from the brink
Of madness
Sadness
I'm vexed
How did I let all this time slip?
Who have I been and where'd I go for all those years?
Preyed on by fears
Buried in my own doubt
Letting others tell me about who I am when I knew they were wrong
They claimed to reflect back who I am, but instead they showed who they are

Life is hard for a girl without a father
One who couldn't be bothered
To give a shit about his daughter
Giving me change with a smile on his face
He thought it erased
Years of abuse
Misuse
Mistreatment
Telling me
Can't you see that you're worthless?

Since you were a little girl, they said
Just
Talk less
Think less
Breathe less
Be less
Agree with every misguided line that they say
And maybe someday you'll be worth something to them
Don't ask, don't tell
Don't stand up tall
Because aren't we all just bags of shit trying to get by?
So why try
Why not just lie
Back, make things easier
No one likes a girl who isn't easy

Easy to love, easy to
Fuck
Easy to tame, easy to
Keep down
So refrain from running your mouth
From pretending you know
Anything about anything
Don't you know
You know nothing about nothing?
That your only worth lies in the person you're
Fucking?

And when they're done with you
They can run from you
And you never say a word
Just stay quiet
Acquiesce
Say yes
When you don't mean yes
Undress like you feel sexy
But really you're thinking
"Get me the fuck out of here.
Let me feel anything but this."
But instead you lie back and wish things were different

It's time to make things different.

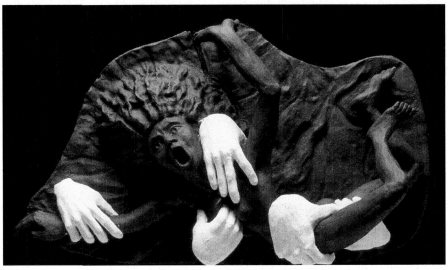

Lorraine Bonner, "World Trade," clay, 2002, 8 x 30 x 20 in.

untitled
Tawny Porter

An open letter to my young self:
To the little girl with the big heart
Who was beaten down too soon
Quieted down too early
It was never about you
Your Daddy couldn't love you
Because he didn't love himself
He hated your spirit, your smarts, your quick wit
Because it reminded him of the things he lacked
He tried to make you smaller so he could feel big
It was not because you were not worthy
But because he felt worthless
That he treated you with such unkindness
Do not take it personally
It was never about you

Your Mama loved you deeply
But didn't know how to protect you
Because she couldn't protect herself
She tried at first, but he shut her down too
She lived in a cocoon of her own self-doubt
Waiting for someone to free her
She didn't want things to be this way
But she didn't know how to change them
So she left you at his (non-existent) mercy
Little girl, you were brave from the moment you were born
You were beautifully and wholly yourself
You fought back
You stood up
You had the courage that the grown-ups around you lacked
You were honest and gentle and kind
While you were surrounded by liars and brutes and bullies
Even while these tormentors were your own family
You did not give up
You did not give in
You kept standing up and asking questions
Because the world around you didn't make sense
Their actions were not based in logic
You spun in your brain trying to figure it out

And came to the conclusion that it must be you
You were the problem
You were the failure
You needed to change
And for a while you tried
But that mask never fit quite right
It would break over and over again
Your inner self trying to get free
Pounding on the walls
Shattering the ceiling with your cries
And then blaming yourself for the mess
Little girl, the mess was never yours
The burden wasn't yours to carry
Even when they strapped it to your back and watched it drag you down
You were the only sane person in that place
You managed to live through the fire and walk away with your humanity intact
With your true self buried deep inside
Protected from the flames
You, my girl, are magnificent
Fucking extraordinary

You deserve it all
You carried all that pain and did not let it break you
Did not let it take away your voice, your strength, your beauty
You walked through the ugliness while people clawed at your feet
And came out the other side
It is not that you didn't get burned
Because oh, honey, you did
Your flesh melted and clung to your bones
It is that you didn't let it consume you
Didn't hide the scars
You wore them with pride
They are a badge of honor
They make you who you are
And have nothing to do with who you always have been
You are adorned with beautiful burn marks
They show what you went through
They show what you survived
And still, you have a fire lit deep inside.

untitled
Kimi Sugioka

Supreme travesty
The wail of injustice
howls in with the king's wind

I explain to my son
when I used to visit men
that I didn't know well.
I listened for the voices of roommates
and if, we were alone, I always kept
my back to the wall,
estimated how long it would take
to get to the door
noticed if it was locked with a bolt or
a key

I was never fully conscious of these
strategies but
when I talked to him
they came rushing back to me
in full detail

I had never considered
how oblivious men are
to the defensive posturing
that women are constantly
practicing
in their presence
It is just what I did,
what we did, what we
do

May not have ever mentioned it
if Christine Blasey Ford had
not testified publicly.

I know
that she told the truth
because this is the way it is
for women every day
Almost every woman I know

has been raped
or evaded
rape

It is tiring to think that
these events are
questionable
contested
derided
disbelieved

It is as ordinary
as putting on your shoes
to go to work,
a party,
a doctor's appointment,
grocery shopping
It is so ordinary
and so invisible

Martin Revolo, "Berenice's Tales
to Her Unknown Father (I)," photograph.

CJ Grossman, "Me Too/Her Too - Hung Out to Dry," 2018, 18 x 6 x 4 in.
Bra with mixed media

CJ Grossman created 120 bras as book covers for an art installation, all of them different, all of them painted or dyed, stuffed, lined, decorated, and containing a book called *Me Too/Her Too - Hung Out to Dry*. The book discusses information about the Me Too movement and includes the mention of two women who were killed. Additionally, there are personal accounts of sexual harassment, abuse and molestation of women faced by the author and some of her friends.

Petals
CJ Grossman

There was only the blade
of the sun's rays
the merciless wind
and the inevitable
premonitory threats
smacking lawn furniture
across the yard
like rusted leaves

fear's perspiration
dripped slowly
under her little curls
hands no bigger than a peach

innocent petals
blew from the tree
bruising as they hit the ground
where she lay
holding herself motionless
looking up only once
begging the sky to save her

CJ Grossman. In the early 1960s, still in my early teens, I became an activist in the Civil Rights Movement. Over the years, I also was active in the anti-war movement, the Third World Strike at San Francisco State College, the feminist movement, grass roots politics, and many other struggles. Perhaps because I am Jewish, and now consider myself an art activist, I feel most compelled to fight against racism, misogyny, homophobia, anti-Semitism and Islamophobia.

The Ambivalence I Loathed: How I Overcame Military Sexual Trauma
Dr. S

"Hey sweetheart, why don't you sit on my lap," the grizzled veteran taunted, his war hat pinned with jangling medals.

Most women would have laughed it off, or joked back, or ignored him. I verbally handed him his ass with indignant teeth bared, then crawled into a corner to cry quietly. Being a woman veteran is complicated. Being a survivor of military sexual trauma is even more so.

Anne Lamott once said, "You own everything that happened to you. Tell your stories. If people wanted you to write warmly about them, they should have behaved better." This is the story I own.

While the media flashes imagery of veterans in wheelchairs overcoming their plights, groups playing basketball together, laughing faces supporting each other, I hide. When people expect you to show up for this meeting or that event, I avoid. When the anthem plays, I salute proudly, but as the drum rolls, so does one tear.

I am not proud of my service...and I am at the same time. Occasionally I remember feeling like a dynamo, commanding swaths of airmen, working together in well-oiled synchronicity. My discharge was honorable, but in my dreams, I still hear whispers of "whore" and "slut" pulling at the vestiges of my dignity. While other veterans swap war stories, I clasp my shutters tight. While I keep in contact with a choice few from active duty, I mostly purged the rest from my memory.

The walls close in. The musk of people invades my nostrils and my heart races, but I know I need to accomplish tasks in these places. I cannot abide the rooms with no windows, with no link to the soothing sky. The city which allows me to make a living also surrounds me, creeping closer, waiting to sink its claws into my frazzled mind.

I was once an indomitable lioness when I was a fresh recruit. No obstacle could stand in the wake of my intent. And then they smashed it. Or I let them smash it, whichever is more accurate. They tell you not to apologize in one breath and punish you in the next. It is impossible to escape the guilt that accompanies the smashing. My body, my confidence, fragments of my soul, leached away like bones bleaching in the sun with every leer, every insinuation, every denied opportunity. I fought the current to stay alive, attempting to rebuild, and it sucked me under time and time again. The stigma of being a victim followed me into my life after active duty. Eventually I had to leave behind my entire career, regardless of my education and skills.

I found myself again in three ways. I started a business working with dogs. Dogs are the keepers of my confidences, the guardians of all that is wholesome, and unassailably trustworthy. I found in them the battle buddies I could not in my fellow veterans. Soft, musty fur comforts as it tickles my cheeks. My service dog sits at his post, diligently watching for any intruder…squirrels. I found my voice in sharing with others the joys of dogs. My karma rebuilt as I rehabilitated dogs who no one wanted. I could relate to that feeling. As I taught aggressive dogs to calm their violence, I discovered a power I wish I had earlier in life.

I learned to skydive. I unearthed the lioness and found her to be, in fact, a griffin with wings ready to soar. I no longer heeded those hissing whispers in my head telling me I was too clumsy or too this or too that to be able to jump. With the discarded doubts, I discarded the plane, and plummeted to Earth over and over again. Gravity also became my friend, providing me with a childish glee, something adults too often cannot recall. I found new friends who shared my love of the freedom of the sky. As I shed my old skin, my new one took to windy heights. Though they had tried—oh, they had tried—to break my wings, they remained unbroken, temporarily tucked away.

And I traveled. In wandering, I experienced for the first time going somewhere simply because I chose it. The heady power of it sunk into my bones and made me hungry to see more. I drank in the sights as if I could die of thirsting for new adventures. I watched…watched the people so far from my homeland, watched the strange animals and even more bizarre plants, watched the stars shifted askew across the dome of the sky. The quest for knowledge stirred in me the desire to continue my education, so I started my doctorate. Through the program, I found opportunity to expand both my mind and my experience. My travels fueled my schooling which in turn spurred more travel in an ouroboros effect for my hungry, healing soul.

Through these three avenues, I reemerged anew. I was not the same as I was before my trauma, but something evolved. Something new. Something hardier. Something wilder.

I am not the picture-perfect veteran, if there is such a thing. I am not medals, stories, slaps on the back, and apple pie. I am not what they want to think about when they picture "veteran." An uncomfortable reminder of something swept under the rug. But still here I am. Saluting.

Dr. S bio on p. 138.

Friendly Fire
Dr. S.

They are magazine glossy
And I am crumpled notebook paper
Tossed away for a better idea.
#MeToo
Was too late for me.
Gunned down
By proverbial friendly fire.
Whore, slut, bitch.
The contrived machinations
Of those who washed their sordid hands
Of the expendable ones.
My sisters and I fought a war on two fronts.
Your allies on one field,
Might be your enemies in the next.
When I hear the anthem,
Ambivalence swells with the salt slick in my eyes,
Not just for America and pride and pie
And all the shit you think is real,
But also, my innocence gone
Vanished in a deluge of unwanted memories,
Nighttime torrents threaten to pull me asunder.
But I claw with wrenching fingers,
Painstakingly wresting my life back from the abyss.
Because as hard as those abusers tried,
They could not take pride
Away from me.

I mourn my sisters who did not emerge
From this unexpected ordeal.
For them I sing,
I stand,
I salute.

Dr. S would like to remain anonymous. She has a PhD and owns her own dog training business. She travels and skydives in her spare time as well as writing in a variety of genres. She just published her debut novel.

How Goddess & Activism Got Together - R. Sridevi

I had never put the two together: "goddess" and "activism." Both have been influential and integral in my journey from girlhood to womanhood and continue to be as I move forward. But in my psyche, "goddess" and "activism" each resided in a distinct realm. One is personal, and the other is public. One is intangible, and the other is corporeal. One is on the celestial plane, and the other is on the physical. Both, however, deeply touch my spirit.

Goddesses have always been a presence in my life; they're "normal" to me. As a Hindu, I revere the Divine in both masculine and feminine forms. Beautiful pictures, paintings, and statues of gods and goddesses graced my childhood home. Myths animated the divine beings and made a real-life interaction with them a possibility. After all, the stories showed them regularly incarnating on earth and mixing with people. Much of my religious education was through the medium of mythology. Perhaps that lent to my strong passion for story.

Goddesses are a vital and crucial part of Hinduism because they are Shakti, the Divine Feminine principle responsible for all creation. Without Shakti there is only Sunya, a void packed with potential and promise. Women, by extension, are believed to also possess shakti, creative energy. So wouldn't it be reasonable to assume that goddesses and women are esteemed in Hindu societies?

Why then are there more temples devoted to gods than goddesses today? Why is it that a book on Hindu deities will predictably dedicate a separate chapter to each god but lump all the goddesses into one...and usually at the end? Why is it that in many depictions of divine couples, the goddess is considerably diminished in size? The goddess doesn't seem to be appreciated as one would expect.

Real life women don't fare too well either, not in my experience. Cultural norms subtly and blatantly preach that males are more valuable than females. According to social customs I, by virtue of being female, am expected to constrict myself and privilege males. Countless times I have been prohibited from various things such as staying out at night, going to certain places, and traveling alone. Each time I was given the same, standard, nonnegotiable, and final explanation: "because you're a girl/woman."

Sexism ignited my feminist consciousness. Sexism motivates my activism. My mission in life is unequivocal: work to create an equitable society for girls and women.

In this endeavor, I question culture and its contradictions concerning girls and women. I wrestle with religion and its repudiation of goddesses and women. I wonder, "What's the story behind all this?" Aha! A key question indeed! What IS the story? My query led me to seek out and reveal the narratives behind the "norms."

Myths are synthetic constructions, possibly based on truth, created to inform and influence society in specific ways. In the Hindu world, cultural perspectives and ethics have long been taught through the powerful medium of mythology. Mythology is inescapable as it is at the core of Hindu ritual, art, dance, and arguably, life. In a Hindu context, mythology is sacred story.

Riane Eisler, author of *The Chalice and the Blade*, discusses societies in terms of the domination and partnership models. In the domination model, one half of humanity ranks over the other, and in the case of patriarchy, men/masculine dominate women/feminine. Eisler declares that the subordination of certain stories over others is intentional. She explains, "[The] work of constantly fashioning and refashioning normative oral and written literature did not simply follow social change. It was an integral part of the process of norm changing; the process whereby a male-dominated, violent, and hierarchical society gradually began to be seen as not only normal but also right." Persistence of a sacred text or myth often parallels the continuity of structures of domination. The two mutually validate each other. In Hindu culture, the correlation between the status of goddesses and that of women is an example of this dynamic at play.

As a Women's Spirituality scholar, I hypothesize that the Divine Feminine in mythology was deliberately switched from "goddess almighty" to "good little wife" in order to sway cultural attitudes toward the subjugation of women. My research is a hunt for alternative narratives about goddesses that have been, perhaps intentionally, thrown into the margins. I aim to empower girls and women by exposing stories and presenting interpretations that demonstrate the goddess asserting authority and self-agency in a range of personalities. I offer my work as a catalyst for the reevaluation of modern-day values, particularly around girls, women, and the feminine.

I no longer separate "goddess" and "activism" in my mind. The two came together through my scholarly research. My "goddess activism" entails revitalizing the Goddess where patriarchy has diminished her and in so doing, empowering girls and women. Jai Ma!

R. Sridevi is devoted to empowering girls and women through relevant and revealing education that speaks to the mind and the soul. (Continued p. 141)

The word *quarry* has two meanings.

The first is an excavation or pit from which stone is obtained. This definition applies to several gravel pits that pockmarked my neighborhood of Sun Valley, Los Angeles' dumping grounds. At least one played-out pit, partially filled with groundwater, formed a pond, which locals called Quarry Lake.

The second is one who is hunted or pursued, or any object of search, pursuit, or attack. This definition applies to me. Neighborhood rumors that I was gay pursued me for years before I came out. Some guys whispered, "I don't want to sit next to him." Other guys begged, "Can I sleepover, please?"

Pariah by day, magnet by night, I reflect on an event in May 1984 as a confluence of two definitions of the word quarry. Ever since then, I've dug to unearth what happened when three white teenage boys with a BB gun approached a black gay man.

The teens (for the purpose of my essay, I'll use their initials), M, A, and F, were my younger brother's friends. They had played hooky from school and come to my bedroom window, asking for a drink of water. I noted M held his Christmas gift—a BB gun—and appeared to be the best shot of the three when they target practiced on cans placed on a basketball court fence pole. I passed them cups of water through the torn screen. No longer boys and not yet men, the three resembled beautiful monsters. I observed the way their faces transmogrified into those of inchoate adults and their sneakers stomped the earth, as if in a rush to own the world. Cigarette smoke billowed from their maws and drifted into my room. I turned on the fan to blow smoke back in their faces.

"Want to go fishing with us at Quarry Lake?" M asked.

Bare-chested, I rolled my tongue around my cheek. A necklace of the Mask of Benin rested above my nipples. The face of Queen Mother Idia looked serenely at the boys.

The stone excavation meaning of the word *quarry* comes from the Vulgar Latin word *quadraria,* a place where stones are squared. While no one squared

---

Through Story Digs (www.storydigs.com), she leads workshops based on her research of mythology and folklore. She also co-founded and co-facilitates the "Diversity Circle" in Oakland, California. Sridevi presented on Hindu goddesses at the 2015 Parliament of World Religions. She is also profiled in the book, *Birthing God: Women's Experiences of the Divine.*

stones at our gravel pit, I tried squaring the stone of M's invitation, which didn't add up to six sides. The trio hid something from me. They always called me *fag* and *gay*, and I rebuffed the sexual advances of two. Now they got a gun and invited me fishing. *With a gun?*

Four years had passed since another neighborhood teen tried to kill me with a railroad spike. I stalled for time, "Well, guys…" I had just turned twenty, while the oldest of them was sixteen. As minors who skipped school, they risked getting in trouble if police caught them carrying a realistic rifle on the streets of L.A. *How about giving the rifle to an adult to carry?* But how long would I live after police respond to a 911 call about a black man "holding white boys hostage" and "threatening" them with a gun?

Perhaps they wanted to carry the gun and walk behind me, but I felt uncomfortable about three armed white boys walking behind my swishing black ass. I thought of the Nazis rail-transporting my Hungarian Jewish aunt to Auschwitz. I thought of Night Riders tying my great-great-grandfather to a boxcar and setting him afire. Sweat formed beneath my Benin necklace on my chest.

I continued, "I'm sorry, but Quarry Lake's notorious for illegal chemical dumping. Any fish caught there is toxic."

A grabbed M's rifle, stormed out of view, shot, and returned, holding a wounded lizard by its tail. He placed it on the basketball court for M and F to shoot until it stopped wriggling. F dug a grave in the dirt below my window, and A crossed two Popsicle sticks atop the mound.

The birds and squirrels the boys shot were strewed on the sidewalks throughout the apartment complex for disgusted pedestrians to step over; the lizard had a grave until F kicked it. Now the twisted corpse baked in the sun, and I cannot help but imagine myself as that BB-riddled lizard had I gone to Quarry Lake with the boys.

Quarry's hunting association comes from the Old French word *cuirée,* a derivative of *cuir* (a hide), because hunters fed their hounds the kill's entrails placed on a hide.

André Le Mont Wilson was born the son of poets in Los Angeles. He began writing his own poems after his parents' deaths in 2012. He honed his skill at telling five minute stories at Moth StorySLAMS in San Francisco and Berkeley before switching to writing essays. "Quarry," his first flash nonfiction, was first published in *sPARKLE + bLINK 98* in 2019. He was nominated for a Pushcart Prize for poetry in 2018.

The Thrift Shop
André Le Mont Wilson

I was sixteen in 1980 Los Angeles, when I decided to visit the last thrift shop along my record scavenging route between school and the bus stop. The shop resembled a converted house with its pitched roof and small space. I opened the screen door, exited the light, and entered the den.

"Ha, ha, ha, ha, ha!" The thrift shopkeeper laughed at a daytime talk show on homosexuality. I never paid much attention to shopkeepers, but this one stood tall, big, old, and white to this sixteen-year-old black boy. The shopkeeper rested his head on his hand as he sniggered at the television set on his glass counter which contained jewelry and medals. He stopped laughing and shifted his eyes from the queers on TV to the one who walked in his door.

I asked, "Do you have any records?"

He answered, "Right over there," pointing to cardboard boxes on the Persian rug.

"Thank you."

I knelt at my first box. My nose inhaled the aroma of old vinyl. Hands searched the records. Flip. Flip. Flip. Fingers found the motion picture soundtrack to Jesus Christ Superstar. It was a double album! My oldest brother took me to see this movie musical in 1973. I have watched it on TV every Easter since.

I next found The Carpenters. This 1971 album put the brother and sister duo on the pop charts with their hits "Superstar," "For All We Know," and, my favorite, "Rainy Days and Mondays (Always Get Me Down)"!

I was on a roll now. If I found these gems among the albums, what gems awaited among the singles? I raised my head from the last box of albums and asked the shopkeeper, "Do you have any singles?"

"Right over there." He pointed to a record rack which stood in the middle of the aisle like a Christmas tree.

I rushed the rack. I browsed the records. Click. Click. Click.

A voice behind me warned, "You steal any of my records, I'll shoot you."

I turned. Behind the glass counter, the white shopkeeper aimed a gun at me. The thought flashed my mind, *Is that gun real?* I saw his eyes and knew. *The gun is real.*

My Mama never gave me THE TALK, the talk many African American parents give their children about what to do when confronted by a person with a gun, but I instinctively knew not to talk back nor to make sudden moves. I also instinctively knew that I could do everything right and still end up dead. I could do nothing at all and still end up dead. Too scared to run, I continued to browse records. Click. Click. Click.

Waving his gun, the shopkeeper hurled insults. "You Verdugo Hills boys suck. Your people are always coming in here stealing my records!"

Click. Click. Click. My hands shook as I slid a single from its sleeve. I was unable to focus on the artist's name, the song title, the single's condition. I told myself, *Andre, whatever you do, don't drop the record, because you'll have to make a sudden move to pick it up.*

Finding I would not flee and confirm his suspicions that I was a thief, the shopkeeper struck up a one-way conversation with me at gunpoint. "I have a son. He's in college. He's the quarterback on the football team. Now, he has a colored roommate who's his bodyguard. In fact, all the colored boys on his team are his bodyguards. They make sure no one messes with him on or off the field. Them mothers got shoulders this big." Gun in hand, he stretched his arms wide, and then returned the gun to aim at me.

He said this as if I should be proud that "my people," black bodyguards, protected his white son. By aiming the gun at me, the father let it be known that if black bodyguards protected his son, a black gun protected the father. More interested in The Carpenters than in quarterbacks, I feared he would shoot me if I failed to show enthusiasm for his story. I squeaked, "Wow." I examined every single on the record rack without wanting one.

Nodding his gun, the shopkeeper demanded, "Aren't you going to buy more records?"

Is he forcing me at gunpoint to buy records? "I did not find anything I like," I lied. I feared he would shoot me if I did not buy something. I made my first of three dangerous moves. With Jesus Christ Superstar and The Carpenters tucked under my arms, I walked towards a man holding a gun at me. "How much for these albums?"

"Two-fifty."

As much as I dared as I glared at his gun, I protested, "Two-fifty for this? Look at the cover. It's worn around the edges." Actually, I only had two dollars on me. I feared he would shoot me if I returned one of the albums.

"All right, then two dollars."

"It's a deal."

But we did not shake on it. I then made my second dangerous move. I reached into my pocket to pull out my wallet. The shopkeeper leaned back from the counter, his gun leveled at me. I placed the ones on the counter. "Thank you."

"You're welcome. Have a nice day now, you hear?"

I made my third dangerous move. I turned my back on a man holding a gun at me. I walked toward the door. My back arched. I waited for the bullets, the pain, the loss of consciousness. I prayed, *Please, don't shoot me in the back. Please don't shoot me in the back.* Nothing happened. I left the man with his TV and his gun as his only companions. I exhaled when I walked outside.

Of all the things I remember, I recall the peculiar quality of the sunlight found nowhere else in this world. The white stucco walls and gray concrete sidewalks reflected sunlight I thought I would never see again. I blinked at the sun and thought, *I'm alive.*

A version of "The Thrift Shop" was first published in the online journal *Not Your Mother's Breast Milk.*

Peskador aka Pancho Pescador is a self-taught visual artist and muralist from Chile. In 1995, he immigrated to the Bay Area, where he developed a passion for street art. Soon, he began working on public art projects, mostly murals. He's

been an active member of Community Rejuvenation Project (CRP) since 2009. He is also part of "Los Pobres Artistas," a collective of painters and muralists, mostly from Chile, that founded and organized the "Bay Area Mural Festival" as an ongoing annual event. He lives in Oakland, California, where he develops his "Guerrillas Visuales."

Pancho Pescador aka Peskador, "Bayard Rustin." Photo by Edsel Rivera.

to those in blue
Tommi Avicolli Mecca

you think you can walk
into our neighborhood
set up your little card table
hang a banner
shine your shoes and buttons
press your uniforms
paste on a smile
and all is forgiven?
you think we don't
remember the decades you
smashed windows and heads
spilt blood on the sidewalks
it's still there
the rain
the amnesia of a community
desperate to be accepted
can't wash it away
the man one of you murdered
still roams the streets
death couldn't take him away
justice wasn't blind
it was strung out on Twinkies
don't you hear the cries
of those entrapped by
your vicious vice squads
that sought us out in cruising areas
rest stops
the men carted out in bar raids

who lost their jobs
families
apartments
when their names were published
in the newspapers
because you didn't get your payoffs
you feel no shame about the
informants you sent into our meetings
you spied on us
as if we were criminals
because we dared to take
to the streets
now you put up a good front
recruiting from the community
marching in pride parades
you expect me to believe
you've changed
I don't
I've seen the reports
especially from queer and trans
people of color
and what about the murder of
black and brown people
the abuse of the homeless
the poor
you want me to welcome you
into the community
but I'd rather welcome
the devil himself

Tommi Avicolli Mecca is a southern Italian queer writer, musician and activist whose work has appeared in over 50 anthologies and journals. He is author or editor of several books, including *Smash the Church, Smash the State: The Early Years of Gay Liberation*. His most current theatre piece, *The Old Brown Jacket*, was recently featured at Monday Marsh and Solo Sundays.

To My UAC (Unaccompanied Alien Child) Client
Eddie Jen

Dear Brynner,

ConDRAGulations on winning your asylum! Do you know this word, con-DRAG-ulations? As your attorney, I would like to gift you this word. When I try to describe how wonderful and magical America is, this word is a part of my vocabulary. So, conDRAGulations—and breathe a sigh of relief. Your life will be easier now that you have legal status.

By the way, do you know what drag is?

Did you know any drag queens in Guatemala?

I met you when you were just thirteen, and, my, how much you've grown in three years. You're a teenager now! One day you'll be an adult and you'll understand the sentiment: kids, they grow up so fast.

And we've won! I wish I was there to open that envelope together with you. When your dad texted to say a new letter came, and asked what should he do, I immediately thought of Trump; I was prepared for bad news. They held up your approval for over a year after our asylum interview. It was highly unusual. So I immediately had your dad take pics of the letters and text them to me.

I read it. Then I squinted at the pic harder, deciphering the meaning of the words one more time. Then once again to make sure.

Only then, did I call your dad and say, "Congratulations, Arnolfo."

You were my first—and only—client, ever, in fifteen years of practicing law. I literally YouTubed videos on how to make a court appearance. Those times we went to court together? That was your attorney playing a cross between Ally McBeal and Dylan McDermott from *The Practice*.

Now that we've won, I've been composing acceptance speeches. I can't help it. Have you ever won anything? I've won drag beauty pageants. It took me three tries, but your attorney is also Royalty.

Did your family celebrate?

Looking back, I think we should have gone for a meal together afterwards. I would have liked taking you to my favorite Chinese restaurant for you to try their dry-fried chicken wings. I would like to share with you the happiness of my immigrant experience. Because we never had our "moment," did we?

We never had our close-up.

Here I am, savoring my hero-slash-celebrity worship from all my liberal friends on Facebook, and I'm coming to terms with the fact that you've never looked me in the eye. We never made eye contact. Not once in three years.

My hazy memories of law school have me asking, what duty of care do I owe a 13-year-old child who has been traumatized and is clearly with PTSD? For starters, I should not have grown exasperated with you when you couldn't repeat back to me (what you literally just told me) when I was taking your declarations. Patience is a virtue, and I'm always learning.

Or maybe I should have just instructed you to look me in the eye. Teach you like the way my Chinese mom taught me: you have to look people in the eye; otherwise they think you lie!

Because when we had our asylum interview—and you started replying "I don't remember" to all of the asylum officer's questions—I froze. We went over your declarations. It's your story. You know this story. Just say what happened. Tell your story. That's all you had to do.

Do you remember the asylum officer getting frustrated? She said something to the effect of, I need you to focus. Your declarations make very serious allegations.

(In the interest of full disclosure, you should know that she probably said this because your declarations read very well. You have an attorney who takes pride in his sentences.)

She asked you one more time if you could remember anything else before you finished your testimony, and that's when you said it.

I heard the meaning of your words through the voice of the translator. That helped absorb the shock.

You never speak up. To hear your shy mumblings, you coming out of your introversion, actually volunteering information about yourself.

He said he was going to kill himself.

We went through six months of preparing your declarations, and not once did you offer this information! But it came at the perfect time. In drag, this is what we call the reveal. On the main stage, before the judge who will literally be deciding for your life!, Chantay you slayed. The energy in the room changed. It was so unexpected.

I knew what happened to you, but until then, I never really grasped what it would be like to have both your parents gone and being raised by your 17-year-old sister whose husband beats her in a country where the laws won't protect her.

Until you said the words, I didn't realize that he would probably kill your sister.

I'm sorry. I forgot my client is a child.

Don't take it personally.

If it's any consolation, I'm this way with my friends, too.

You remember all those strange and different translators who called you and texted you but you've never met? They were mostly gay men. And because they're my friends, they like dressing up in women's clothing and lip-synching to Lady Gaga. And I'd like for you to meet them. We should go to San Tung's and sneak a bottle of tequila into the teapot. My friends are like cartoon characters. These bitchy friends of mine who volunteered their time for a stranger they've never met. Would you like to thank them in person? It's what my Chinese mom would make me do. I think you can relate as a Guatemalan. No matter how foreign you see me (your dad always referred to me so reverentially as "Mr. Lawyer), we share commonalities as people of color.

We eat the animal parts white people don't.

In the interest of full disclosure, I would like to make one more confession: I tried getting rid of your case right after I signed up. I got assigned to a work project in Phoenix, and the reality of what I signed up for finally hit me. I emailed the attorney who assigned me your case and politely explained that my employment had taken me to another state; I asked to be transferred off the case and be reassigned when I returned.

He never returned my email.

And, from that point on, your case became the exam I must pass. Don't worry: Chinese people are born test-takers. I never took seriously law school or the practice of law. But it was different now. I had a child whose future depended on me. Failure was not an option.

Had I been able to communicate with you, this would be the message I'd try to impart. We are descendants of dragons and pumas and leprechauns and the OG Queen herself. You have the strength in you. You made it here, didn't you? As an eleven-year-old, you fought your sister's husband when he kept beating her. And you still have that scar in your hand from where he cut you with broken glass. You got balls! And then you made it here, over 3,000 miles through foreign cities and foreign countries, to find yourself with a drag queen attorney with magical powers. And then you won asylum.

You're special. You really are.

I'm a writer. I was an attorney only in drag. In reality, I'm a writer. I tell stories. And I want to let you know that the most important stories are the ones we tell about ourselves. And you're special, my child. You're here in America. You can be whoever the fuck you want to be.

When the time comes when you're qualified to become a US citizen, say your oath and mean every word of it. Because there will be people who say you aren't really American. They will try to make you feel like you are not real. Have a finite amount of patience for them; we are all human. But stand your ground. You may not have started life as an American, but you will die an American. These small-minded people who drove you from your country—these bullies reside in every nation. And we're not going to let these same bullies drive us from America. You're one of us now. Make it count.

We're Americans.

We're the good guys.

Don't ever forget that.

Sincerely yours,
Eddie Jen
your accidental attorney

P.S. Do not get in absolutely any trouble for the next four years—not until you reach citizenship eligibility!

First published in *sPARKLE + bLINK 98*.

Eddie Jen is a writer, drag queen, and an occasional attorney living in San Francisco. He is single and does not date Republicans.

Page 152: Alan Harris has practiced his spoken-word artistry in Los Angeles, New York, and San Francisco. He doesn't really know what he's doing, but people seem to like it anyway...

vi. Consuming the Earth

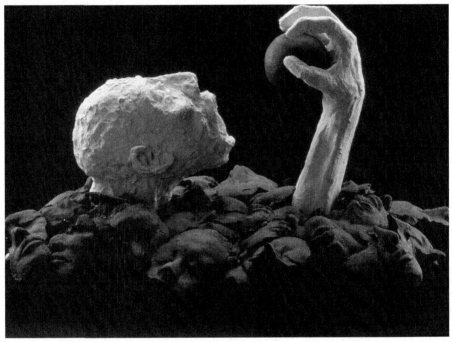

Lorraine Bonner, "Devourer," clay, 2002, 14 x 16 x 22 in.

One of Everything - Alan Harris

I got the one fork, the one spoon, the one knife, the one bowl, the one dish, the one glass, the one mug, the one pot, the one pan, the one chair, the one table, the one lamp, the one mirror, the one room. That's all I need. Just one of everything. If I was to win the lottery tomorrow, I would still want only one of everything.

If everyone could be satisfied with just one of everything, there wouldn't be the tragically ridiculous imbalance of some people living in mansions with 1500 rooms—some of which are never even occupied—while other people don't even have one room to live in. Is that really the way it's supposed to be? Is that really the way that God planned it? If so, terrible plan God, just awful. Start again.

Worldwide Minimalism. Worldwide Socialism. Worldwide Collectivism. First, gather up all of the material goods in the world and then divide them up evenly among the world's population.

Then, give everyone an apartment that will provide them with just enough room to be comfortable, so that if, for example, you're somewhat obese, then you would get a bigger place than someone who is thinner. And if you lose weight, then you would be moved into a smaller place. And if your weight fluctuates too much, well, then, that would suggest a bigger problem that you should probably get checked out. Maybe you have an eating disorder, in which case, you would probably be sent off to some sort of camp where that problem would be dealt with.

Hmmm, this is starting to sound a bit fascistic, isn't it? Maybe we should forget about that part and talk, instead, about how you very, very wealthy people probably think that this is going to impact you negatively.

Well, you have a right to think that. This is going to fuck you up big time. You're going to go from living it up in a 1500 room mansion to simply existing in a tiny Bachelor apartment in a building that probably won't even have an elevator. But don't worry. While you'll be having to make do with a lot less, compensation will come in the form of the knowledge that there is a little girl somewhere who is going to go from living on the street without enough to eat, to having a permanent roof over her head and a refrigerator stocked with healthy food.

I mean, come on, how great will that be? Won't you get an enormous amount of satisfaction out of that? Don't you think that will make up for the loss of those 1500 rooms? —Well, just give it a try…look, this is going to happen whether you want it to or not, so you might as well make the best of it…and don't give us any shit…you don't want to end up in one of those camps where they send troublemakers, do you?…oh, crap, this is starting to sound fascistic again, isn't it?…damn, this is hard…

a conspiracy of the bland
Shizue Seigel

"I can only handle a little at a time,"
you say about the news
as if reality were a substance
whose intake you must monitor.
Living on the median strip of life,
neatly trimmed, hemmed in by the
fumes of heavy machinery heading nowhere,
you work hard to block out the howling of wolves.

You set out your lawn chairs
and measure success
by your progress up or down
a narrow strip of green,
awareness restricted
to the latest diet and the coolest gadget
carrots and kale or neo paleo—
as if you could buy a solution
as if you had control.

Or…you can binge on hypervigilance—
wire your nerves to the virtual—
its constant blasts of
fear hate and lust
triggering chemistries within your cells
constricting your heart
dilating arteries
depleting adrenals
exploding your brain…
as if passion alone could
change the world.

But bland is not tranquil,
denial does not bring peace
and passion alone does not equal love.
Love is steady, alive, and awake.
Breathe deeply. Look around. Stretch
your body and your mind.
reach out a hand
to somebody real.

Warmup in the Wind
Jerry Geffner

People say that global warming it isn't so bad
at least right here right now the water feels pretty good

But folks who believe that
are the most lost
the kind of lostness that many Germans and Jews had
when they said
things can't get any worse

They did not get that Hitler had written a very long play
and this was the first part of the first act
just a warm up

This act is called "warmup in the wind"
and we can look
right under our beds and in the area
between ears
to get what the temperature really is

We are all in the soup
and we know they are cooking us alive
and those of us that see this way
know that it is not easy to get out of the pot
know that the first act is going on a long time

cooking us alive and trying to keep the lid on the pot

Those others think they are sitting in warm mineral springs
or at least an expensive spa or
an adult Disney movie

The film rolls on and we are outside in some grand valley
with the most delicious air
and the water covers us and we let go in mindless bliss
while things warm up
it feels so good to sink into a stupor,
lost at the edge of a pool our eyes get blurry
and we see double

Some are sitting higher up
much closer to the lid
it is always hotter there so
SOS to those that still can't read the smoke signs
don't know that the cooking works best when the heat is turned up real slow
this leads to the lowest chance of escape
to the lowest incidences of rebellion
to shove the lid off and
remove the pot from the oven

Jerry Geffner, son of a holocaust survivor and a mother from a poor Russian village, was raised with progressive values. He got involved in the civil rights and anti-war movements in the 60s and has actively supported the rights of women, LGBTQs, Palestinians, and immigrants ever since. As a social worker he was on the front lines during the AIDS epidemic and in efforts to serve communities in need. He is now involved with what he calls creative resistance.

Shizue Seigel, "What Endures," digitally altered photo, Albany Bulb.

Just Breathe
Susana Praver-Pérez

A solo scrub-jay perched on a wrinkled orange tree
　　　calls out dawn like nails
　　　　　on a chalkboard.

I can still remember mornings like symphonies
　　　and plump oranges
　　　　　on glossy green.

Oakland wakes to a grey brew
　　　of pollution and soot.
My sister can't stop coughing
A wheeze planted its rusty roots in her
　　　once pink lungs.

Pesticides drift,
　　　settle on a withered hibiscus.
Birds fall, bees die.

Monsanto—Not <u>my</u> saint!
Monsanto dances with the devil
　　　on a bed of crushed wings,
　　　　　dollars jingling in its pockets.

I recycle, reuse, reduce, but what can I do
　　　to curb corporate cravings
　　　　　that shoot up towns and rainforests,
　　　　　　　greenhouse gases spurting
　　　　　　　　　from exit wounds?

Who would imagine we'd take to the streets and march
　　　for air to breathe
　　　for water to drink?

Thousands strong, our chants rising like ravens, we march
　　　for a future
　　　for this sacred Earth.

We march in the too hot sun
      so sweetgrass may always grow.
We march lest we leave our children
        a fractured sphere
      and to our grandchildren, nothing
          but prayers.

"Just Breathe" was first published in *Still Point Arts Quarterly*, June 1, 2019.

Shizue Seigel, "wrong path," photograph, Albany Bulb, 2014.

Maria and the Home Village

Cris Matos captured the tranquil beauty of his childhood home in Utuado, Puerto Rico, in the 1960s.

Cris Matos, Bay Area musician, songwriter, poet and photographer, grew up in Utuado, a small village in central Puerto Rico. He and two of his children returned with supplies immediately after Hurricane Maria ravaged the island.

He later reported to friends in the US: "We spent seven days in Puerto Rico seeking out family members, and helping others along the way. Your encouragement, prayers, and donations literally carried me the whole trip. I felt your prayers as if they were the foundation of our mission.

"We brought six suitcases of food, flashlights, batteries, water filters, plus four generators, and were able to get a vehicle and gas to get around the island.

"My home town of Utuado was one of the hardest hit areas of the island. There was no electricity, no communication, no clean running water and limited food. The area was continuously pelted by pouring rain. The roads and homes in the area were being washed out with nowhere to go and no way to get out. People are dying of water contamination. It is dire. It is still dire."

Above: What's left of a house overlooking Caonillas Lake. The owner said he shouted a warning to his family after he felt the house rumble. They and their horse managed to escape before the house collapsed down the hill. Below: another home and horse in Utuado. Photos by Cris Matos in Puerto Rico after Hurricane Maria, September 10, 2017.

When the Lights Come On
Guy Biederman

You go to Bali to write a book and do anything but. You want to tell the story of the fishermen's wives in Sri Lanka, made widows by the tsunami, whom the priest tells you about, introduces you to. They are Muslim, feel threatened, and keep to themselves. They welcome you slowly. They ask what your life is like—a nurse, a psychologist, a mother, a wife. You ask what they need, how you can help. They say they need lights. At night. You nod, thinking they want to read, share stories, weave. At night, they say, village men enter their tents and rape them. The air leaves your chest. The world leaves you remote and horrified and spinning, and when you regain your upright balance you go to the village priest. You arrange for lanterns and kerosene and the priest, a manic thin man on a motorcycle sees that they are delivered. On your last day in country he says there is something he wants to show you and he takes you to the tents at the edge of the sea. At dusk the lights come on. And you see the glowing rows, the brilliant light cast against the darkness and dangers that come out at night and you are overcome.

So you go to Bali to write, a widow yourself now, and you do everything but. You fall in love. You swim daily. You get hit by a motorcycle and it breaks you up. Badly. You come home to your daughter's—a floating home where every day you rise and fall with the tide. Your brain floats in a pool of blood. Your head begins to heal. Your hair turns beautiful silver, more silver than you are old. The love of your life gone. Your daughter goes to work each day. The coffee is strong. The light on the water moves in strange and gentle ways. You sit by the window in a chair with a cat, a journal, a pen you don't own, and turn on the floor lamp. Smell kerosene.

Guy Biederman served as a Peace Corps volunteer during a civil war in Guatemala, has worked as a gardener, publisher, and writing instructor. He offers drop-in Writing Groove sessions at Marin City Library and hosts *The Floating Word* on Radio Sausalito, featuring the work of local writers and promoting open mic opportunities throughout the Bay Area. He's the author of *Soundings & Fathoms,* Finishing Line Press.

Skid Bid - Tongo Eisen-Martin

Lord, here comes the tap water whistling through the windows

Institution tile under the brake pedal
           Matching the white watch
                      Painted on my palm for smash and grab recollections

people who are related by ballad:

        a hotplate failure fishing for proletarians
        and
        the matchstick that is a draft card
                (by the time the loner finishes sweeping the train)

also related by ballad:
        under-paved streets hanging like strips of film in thin air

                Brother, I miss the carpentry more than the religion

        I tore the tattoo out of my uncle's picture and lent it to my friends
                        one left cross at a time

                    —life mimed behind my back

the child would do better upside down:

the child's cake party is in the precinct / mainstream tune playing upside down
        a t-shirt with their face printed on a cop's thumb

twenty-eight hours later, a headrest will do

the city rain feels like clientele
I dozed on the back of a bus and
woke up in the mind of a three-story man

"God wants you here with that crowbar in your hand…all of the world is a
third floor."

                    seasons invent themselves
                but we invent the underground

—cause and effect is nothing but a casual venue I once played—

he decided not to kill me like giving loose change
don't teeter now, tall man
nobody at point blank
nobody finally again

lung first I fell

a love
then
a rule
then
a hate

dance moves within murder attempts within dance moves

"Lean back and be celebrated by small people," he said. The clothes on my life teacher needed new patches. *"Sit back and disrespect it all"*

"I've given up on counterrevolution," I said
"Well then here is your weapon, Little Bank"

—That's our father you are writing graffiti on—

Horn players beat me up
and everyone left the altercation a better person

"knowing what you know now
would you still have written fortunes
on the bottom of church shoes
and put them back on the rack?"

"How does everyone think that a rich guy is their twin?"
—along with other tantrums is my cue

fortune teller half sleeps while talking about a mayor treading all over the posters in my childhood room and how cold calculation mothers nothing and a vision of chess pieces in chains......

"Then you will have fear. Then you will have form."

untitled
David Erdreich

Yes I am stuck in this body.
For 65 years I have identified and differentiated birds.
Field guide is my bible.
My life list is my death list.
I mark down each new species sighted in a book with
short abbreviations, personal reminders.
I remember most first sightings of a species vividly.
Each a talisman on my life path.
Many become old friends, their various behaviors
heartwarming curiosities.
Others I see only once.
They bring different habitats to life.
As often as possible I mimic their speech—
An insufficient attempt to understand (like Solomon)
what they are saying.
Different species converse.
Their parliament was revealed by Attar.
His perfume still resonates.

When the prairie breeze speaks to the trees
   You do not know it.
When the pebble laughs and becomes the water's staff
   You do not know it.
Salt of the earth you are
   and yet I do not sprinkle you on my salad.
There are more than a hundred ways to solve the problem
   Yet only one will do
For you are not alien intelligence
   The Canada Goose is magnetically tied to the earth
From the supernova's cauldron burst and set the golden flow
   Every chemical element shows a trace in your electric body
You do not know it
   You are too busy taking a selfie

Do not mistake anger for poetry
   Can bravado interface grace?
Central casting is but a wormhole
   Or a worm butt hole
A tube masquerading as a point of entry

for an hourglass with a pinched expression
A compost layered and loved in absinthe absentia
    stench smothered by hay sitting in the odd fallows home
Shroud and winding pole pitch a night sky
    Roaring borealis sprinkles rarefied propellant
Heat striking the center of de-composition (my writing),
    Spore support says yes to shiitake grown at home,
but cannot tame wild Chanterelle.
    Western science will never document every snowflake shape
Yet eternity is knowledgeable as idiot's delight

David Erdreich has worked as a psychiatric social worker, day care owner, house parent in a half-way house for youth, senior meals program, street vendor, airbrush artist, truck driver, and gardener. He sings with two semi-professional choruses, plays alto sax, bird watches ,and presents an annual poetry/jazz show, as director, composer, arranger, producer, singer, horn player, roadie, fool.

Photo by Shizue Seigel.

His English Name was Aaron - Carole Chinn-Morales

A homeless man helpless
Was murdered
Next to a historic
community serving agency
in Chinatown
Beneath a six foot cross

A cruel violent act
Carried out viciously

Last Sunday morning
Quang Tran, a homeless man
Our neighbor / Lay prone on the ground
in his spot on Joice Alley
Wrapped in his blood soaked sleeping bag
while unaware church goers drove
Into the parking lot as usual a few feet away
Lenora noticed

So senseless and horrendous
The mind reels helplessly

Was it drugs, alcohol psychosis
an act of revenge
We may never know

Countless souls like Quang Tran
Wander the streets of San Francisco daily
Hoping for a single restful night
Without danger

In shadowy doorways / Dimly lit sidewalks
Under freeway overpasses
Shivering in the penetrating cold
All over the city alone
Quang Tran was one of these

Our eyes have been opened
We will never be the same
The wound is raw and gaping wide

CONservatorship: The New "Ugly Laws"
Lisa "Tiny" Gray-Garcia

"This (conservatorship law) sounds like slavery to me," Memphis, houseless poverty skola reporter for POOR Magazine's RoofLESS radio, reported after a terrifying town hall on SB1045, the new anti-poor people legislation that was just signed into existence by Gov. Jerry Brown and will be enacted as a "demonstration" law in San Francisco, Los Angeles and San Diego.

It used to be a crime in this country to be disabled. Now it's a crime to need help.

"SB1045 expands who can be 'conserved' in three counties in California," said Susan Mizner, an ACLU disability rights lawyer who spoke at the town hall on this law held in San Francisco earlier this month. She went on to explain the target of this law: "It is targeted at homeless people with psychiatric and/or addiction issues."

Beginning with the turn of the century "ugly laws," which made it illegal to be unhoused and disabled in public, legislation in the US literally incarcerated people for being poor, for not having money to pay illegal taxes to the rich and/or for having outstanding debt (a reality which still exists in many cities today).

These violent anti-poor people laws were an extension of indentured servitude and the enslavement, rape, murder, and land theft of First Peoples and stolen African peoples. But then as you travel down the violent path of paper violence, politricksters and what I affectionately call Lygislations, you end up with the conservatorship programs adopted into law across the US and completely related to the supposed care—read forced treatment—of disabled children and adults and elders supposedly unable to care for themselves.

Like most of the colonizer laws, the Conservatorship laws enable and support the buying, selling, stealing, and pillaging of poor people's assets, bodies and homes. They are rooted in western hetero-patriarchal, ageist, ableist diagnoses of mental and physical health, while at the same time, providing an ongoing population and need for a multi-million dollar industry of elder ghettos, group homes, nursing homes, mental hospitals, etc. And through the Conservatorship law already on the books, poor elders and their families can lose their only assets, lose their ability to take care of themselves, and owe the state thousands of dollars which follows them to the other side of the spirit journey.

So now in 2018, in addition to the hundreds of laws already in place, which make it illegal to sit, stand, sleep, lean, lie, put a backpack down, put up a tent, or eat while houseless in cities across California, we have a new one. A new law that takes the criminalization, incarceration, and harassment of poor folks to new violent, sci-fi movie level. It's part of a national trend toward the government taking control of older people's lives.

"If you are homeless and have been taken in on eight consecutive 5150 violations, you could be subjected to this conserving," said Jennifer Friedenbach, executive director of the Coalition on Homelessness at the town hall. And oddly, just like the ugly laws, which worked with the settlement houses aka the saviors and social workers, this law is supported by neoliberal politricksters like San Francisco's mayor, who claim this is the solution to homelessness. And just like Care Not Cash of the early 2000s put into law by politrickster Gavin Newsom, this is another way for the state to steal aka "Conserve" poor people's resources, because once you are CON-served, every asset, belonging, thing you have will be seized by the state, ensuring that not only you will be incarcerated for being seen, you will also be unable to survive outside of the institution. "Does this law expand the Lanterman Act which gives services to disabled peoples in California?" my brother and revolutionary in disability and economic justice at POOR Magazine and founder of Krip Hop Nation asked, and sadly no one on the panel could answer. Leroy worries the impact on disabled communities of this Conservatorship will weaken the Lanterman act which is the only way disabled, poor Californians get resources.

Lisa "Tiny" Gray-Garcia bio on p. 263.

Mel Waters, "Mario Woods," from *Black History Month* series, San Francisco Bayview District, 2016. Photo by Edsel Rivera.

E.K. Keith
Incarceration Academy

There are worse prisons than high school
but it's hard to understand
when you're young
and your school is a little gulag
where you endure

the humiliation
of a bathroom escort

or the small torture
of holding it until lunch

From the Window of a San Francisco Public School

Iconic skyline   jagged teeth
muzzled by a chainlink fence

Who will this city   eat next
the next teacher evicted
the next family sleeping in their car

Will it be
me

Silver tongues of freeway
lick around us
hungry

E.K. Keith is a Latinx poet who calls San Francisco home, but her hometown is Houston where she learned to write in the sprawl. She performs her poems on the street corner and takes the mic at coffee shops, bars, and radio stations. Her work appears online and in magazines on all three coasts and places beyond, and *Ordinary Villains* is her first book of poetry. E.K. organizes Poems Under the Dome, San Francisco's annual open mic celebration of Poetry Month inside City Hall. Her work as a public school librarian creates opportunities for her to make the world a better place every day.

vii. Carefully Taught

Shizue Seigel, "Blood in the Brain," etching.

Boys in the Soot
Hussain Abdulhaqq

At thirteen, I had just hit my first growth spurt. I walked to and from junior high with friends. I walked the same path every day with the same four guys. One sunny spring afternoon on our way home, a police car came from nowhere, jumped up on the curb, and blocked us off on the sidewalk.

Shocked, we were stiff with fear when the two large armed and armored men stepped slowly from their squad car. Both white and clean shaven as usual, they both had their hands already on their guns. They told us to stand against the wall. A couple of us tried to ask what was happening or what we'd done. They didn't answer; they just kept asking, "Where's the pipe?"

In the midst of our confused denials, they grabbed us one by one and searched us, spinning us around and turning out our pockets. When the man got to me, I had no idea what to do. He kept yanking on me and saying, "You know the routine," over and over.

A couple minutes later we'd all been robbed of more than our money, and two men with guns on their hips had us lined up in broad daylight facing the wall of a store that still had a dingy Woolworth's Five and Dime sign above its new awning. Not much could be more public. In Atlantic City, New Jersey, it was where everybody walked, it was the "avenue" on a spring day, just after school.

The cops said three teens had broken a window with a stick. They said it must have been the four of us.

Daryl asked if they'd found a pipe or a stick or anything that had broken glass on it. He asked if there was any broken glass on us or in our shoes when they had us take them off. He was ignored.

One of them stood a ways back. Whenever anyone tried to turn their head, he barked, "Keep your eyes on the wall! Keep your hands where we can see them!" I could feel the grit of the sidewalk through my socks. The other cop paced back and forth behind the four of us and talked about how they were the biggest gang around. He told us they had the best cars; he told us they had the best guns and they were the biggest gang in town, so we'd better know our place and stay in line.

Eventually, they backed off and took their car with them. We put our shoes back on, gathered our things and refilled our turned-out backpacks. We grumbled and griped to each other and walked another two blocks to the public library. That was where we introduced Daryl to Dungeons and Dragons for the first time. We escaped into imagination.

* * *

For most of my youth, my mother was an administrative professional in our school. I spent a lot of time in her offices while she put her nose to the grindstone. I liked to read and to draw, and I was quiet and well behaved enough that I went unnoticed by many.

But then there was a month during eighth grade when there was a mandatory rotation of sports.

The sole immigrant Indian girl in my grade and I found ourselves happily playing badminton and finding a way through the language barrier to cheer and keep score and offer soft condolences for wide misses. We were a lanky gangly pair. At least for a few weeks I enjoyed gym class.

That growth spurt sent me up like a beanstalk. I noticed certain people began to treat me differently. Not all people, but I noticed a specific pattern.

When I was small, white women used to pet me. They would tell me I spoke so well and they were amazed with all that I had learned. I only really saw white women in the offices where my mother was working, and it was always pleasant to see the working women she got to know well, as they were always kind to me.

But now that I was thirteen years old, something changed. They didn't talk to me anymore. They pretended they couldn't see me. They even seemed a little afraid when I approached them, too. Now, they'd known me for years, but it was no longer the way it used to be. Strange, but I wasn't pushing the issue: this was my mother's workplace and that's what was important.

On the other hand, sports people who used to ignore me now all got excited when they saw me. Never before had gym teachers and coaches greeted me with such wild eyes and active handshakes.

I ran with the nerd crew. Everyone knew that me and my buddy Rob had started the chess club after school. We were the only members for a couple months.

What had changed? My height. I was no longer a little boy but a very tall boy. Rail thin and always with my head in a book, but I was now as tall as a man. My face looked the same, my voice had not changed yet, not yet, but that was coming as well.

Perhaps these few people, sports coaches and fair-skinned office women, had an insight as to what was happening to me. Perhaps they knew that I was…

Becoming the monster!

I knew I was different well before I was an adult.

I had learned, both from parents who tried to teach me the tools to deal with this world and from the men and women who reacted so oddly to me, that being Black carried a lot of cultural stigma, much of it undeserved. The history of our nation and the place people like me held was never hidden from me, but I had somehow thought that in 1992 it simply "wasn't a thing" any more or that I could just "keep my head down" and let it pass.

It was not that I was becoming some mythical dark shadow monster, but I was certainly growing out of being a child. I was no longer benign in their eyes; I was the threat they had feared and now I had appeared.

Rob told me that his family had told him about Black people all his life. Funny, they were afraid of the same things I had been told to fear about white men. The first real discussion I had with my first all-white best friend opened both our eyes. The real threat was silent ignorance.

Since the age of six I've experienced many watershed moments that told me how I am seen by others regardless of how I see myself.

Today I stand a Black man proud and strong, with as many stories to tell as the boys who grew up alongside me. Despite all this, I remain that small, eager, smiling, and thoughtful boy. Deep within me, I feel we all still are…or at least we should try to remember the time when we were.

Hussain Abdulhaqq. I am an urban garden educator, a naturalist and a Black man. Raised in a family of soldiers, artists and teachers who expected every child to learn to do all three, I value a family so large it quickly encompasses all of humanity even if I only get to meet a few. Be more like the bees than the butterflies, work more like ants than roaches.

Just Across the Street
Shizue Seigel

Malikah was the brightest kid I met in Avalon Heights public housing. At five, she could oversee her younger sister and cousin, listen in on the neighborhood gossip and pore over picture books at the same time. She was the kid everyone sent to the corner store for milk or bread, though she could "forget" to give back the change until asked for. She looked forward to starting school in the fall. In 1992, I was as hopeful as Malikah. I was sure she had the spirit, the smarts, and the curiosity to break out of the poverty around her.

From the top of Avalon Heights, we could look past "the projects" and the decayed industrial base of southeast SF to the bay and the hills beyond. It was a jack-the-giant-killer view, a seven-league-boots view. On a morning like today, the sun transformed the cloud-paved sky into hammered silver and set the bay aglitter with a thousand points of light. But just how far did that light penetrate into the heavy concrete apartments that stepped down the steep hillside? During the three years I worked on an HIV prevention project in the mid-1990s, I found out.

Just across the street from Avalon Heights were a public health clinic and an elementary school. The school turned its back on the housing, barricaded itself behind tall white retaining walls topped with cyclone fencing

The school's impact showed in the sullen faces of neighborhood kids; most hated school and thought they were stupid. Their mothers, "educated" at the same school a generation earlier, were reading at 2nd to 4th grade levels.

In contrast, the low-slung health clinic next door, designed with community input, was warm, brown, and linviting. It sat level with the street, with large plate glass windows so residents could easily stroll over and scope out the waiting room before walking in for help.

I'd been hired by an experimental HIV/AIDS prevention project funded by the Centers for Disease Control. I was supposed to gather stories from real women, and turn their condom experiences into educational tales about safer sex (with names and details changed). The resulting flyers would be passed back into the community by the project's outreach workers. When I was hired, the program was months late getting going. The office was tense and arguments frequent. The white, educated management didn't trust the judgment of outreach workers hired out of the community. Mandy, Tamika and Roxanne knew what would work and what wouldn't. They chafed against directives designed without their input, but their thinking was dismissed because they spoke Ebonics.

I agreed with the outreach folks. "How do you expect women to walk into a strange office and talk about their sex lives to a stranger?" I asked. "They have to meet me and decide whether they can trust me."

"You can't go into the neighborhood without training," the bosses said. But they could design programs without stepping foot in the neighborhood, I thought. I fought for training in community health outreach, and got it. Soon I was out in the neighborhood, wearing my funkiest clothes, with African beads, leaving my denture at home to reveal missing teeth, bonding around kids, food stamps, and disappointing relationships. I was Asian American, but poverty was as familiar to me as my grandma managing a skid-row hotel in Stockton.

One of the first to volunteer her story was Charise. The other young women looked up to her. She was "too cool for school," but underneath her lizard-like calm, undercurrents of anger flickered and flowed. A hard, world-weary air made her seem much older than 18. The stories she shared off the record were anything but safe—knife fights that scattered her face with scars, a stomach wound from a jealous rival during a dance, having a child at fifteen, long before she was ready to stop partying…

But the words she allowed me to print under a pseudonym were disappointingly facile—safe and predictable mouthings calculated to satisfy authority figures. "I didn't plan to have my daughter, but now that she's here, I'm raising her the best way I know how. And she's happy. I'm happy. I didn't get much support like mothers give their daughters. I've had to figure out my life on my own."

Her flyer created a positive buzz in the community. More women stepped up, and stories began to roll out. Still, I was surprised when LaRhonda volunteered. She was Charise's sister and Malikah's mom.

She was not talkative in the best of moods; sometimes she could be positively catatonic—as if a rhino's hide were her only defense against the world. When I knocked on her door, she took so long to answer that I was sure she'd changed her mind.

LaRhonda was slower to speak than Charise, but what she said came from the heart. "People think I'm stupid, but I ain't. I never done good in school, 'cause I had too much on my mind. I was worried about gettin' food, about getting' jacked up. I grew up in foster homes—got beat with a broomstick, wore my clothes 'til they were ragged…. One time my foster mother got drunk and cut my face with a knife.

"Now, I got two sweet little girls that I'm raising by myself. At first when the outreach workers started talking about condoms, I was like 'Ummhmm, yeah,' and then I'd forget about it. But when my sister's story come out, it really hit me where it hurts.

"I started thinking, 'Who's going to take care of my girls if something happens to me? My stomach about dropped out. My head started pounding because I know what can happen with no momma around. I don't ever want my daughters to go through what I've been through. I'm going to do all I can to make sure they keep their momma.'"

174

LaRhonda and her sister were about the same age as my own daughters, but they hadn't received the support my children got on the west side of town. They could barely read, they did not understand impulse control or school readiness. I didn't doubt that LaRhonda and Charise loved their children, but they lived in a desolate neighborhood without parks or playgrounds. They and their children sat inside all day, shades drawn, watching TV—channel surfing for people who looked like them. They were mesmerized by the worst depictions of their world: *Cops*, *America's Most Wanted*, and *Jerry Springer*. And I was not the one to tell them to do different. If my own daughters didn't listen to my advice, why should they?

I continued to visit Avalon Heights long after the job ended. Malikah started kindergarten with bright-eyed eagerness. By second grade, she started hating her "mean teacher." LaRhonda passed her GED and then sank deeper into depression when she couldn't get the day care she needed to keep a job.

Malikah stopped saying hello. She began fading into doorways with a haunted look. LaRhonda was too depressed to answer her door, no matter how long I knocked. Then Miz Jean told me that Child Protective Services had taken the girls. LaRhonda's boyfriend was molesting Malikah. The next year, LaRhonda was stabbed to death by her next boyfriend.

I felt pierced through the heart. LaRhonda had said in her story: "I don't ever want my daughters to go through what I've been through. I'm going to do all I can to make sure they keep their momma." She did the best she knew how. Why doesn't society know how to support damaged young parents so they can heal themselves and nurture their children?

As for the school just across the street, it transformed itself again. By hosting a Chinese language immersion school as a magnet, it pulled itself from the fifth rank—the lowest—to the fourth. There are no African American kids in the immersion program.

Origins, Migrations and Pilgrimages
Ravi Chandra, M.D.

When I was in kindergarten, a white boy said my skin was dirty, because it was brown. I went home, and scrubbed myself, head to toe, with Ajax. After all, it made the tub white. Wouldn't it do the same for me? My skin turned raw, but stayed brown. I asked my mother, "why am I still dirty?" She looked at me, a little surprised. "That will not go. That is your skin." I went back, and told the white boy. "I'm not dirty." "Yes, you are," he said, and ran off.

My mom told me never to use Ajax on my skin again. She didn't tell me what racism was. She didn't know much about it herself, at that time. We were just a few years here, living in the deep South—Tuskegee, Alabama, where she was doing her medical training. There were public schools and Catholic schools, all mixed race, legacies of integration. In those years, school was an oasis. A large and welcoming extended family, where I sometimes called the teacher "Mom" by accident. (I held the word all too close now, all too ready. It was always on my reborn tongue, even as "Dad" receded into dark silence.) I was carried along by the friendship of classmates and warmth of teachers. At home, there was the confusing absence of my father, but in those early years, I felt wanted, and special. The pinnacle of inclusion was the 4th grade. We lived in Nashville, Tennessee, a mile from the Grand Ole Opry. I rode the bus to school, and was easy friends with blacks and whites alike. I was Cub Scout pack leader, 4-H Club president, and public speaking champion. But I knew something was wrong. There was a disconnect, and I was somewhere on the other side, able to pass at times, but inside, feeling apart, even as I couldn't make out why.

My teacher pulled a black boy angrily out of class when he smooched his lips next to a white girl. She took the paddle off the wall, and I jumped between them. "You cannot hurt my brother!" I shouted. Maybe I'd watched an after school special the day before; maybe it was in my blood, a bit of righteousness that had passed from my mother's father, to her, to me. The black boy said, "Man, you ain't my brother. Let me get my whoopin'. And don't try to kiss no white girls." Now, it's probably hard to imagine that any 4th grade boy would be allowed to kiss a girl under his teacher's eyes, but when the color line was involved, reactions were more intense on all sides.

Christina, a smart, pretty white girl, had a crush on me. In all shyness, I didn't know what to do with the attention. We sat next to each other on the bus; I reassured her I still liked her after her new glasses made her feel self-conscious; she was a cheerleader for me in the class spelling bee, and I was in awe of her smarts, looks, and kindness. One day, her little sister declared she was going to marry me—probably a sentiment her big sis had inspired in her. Their mother was not pleased about her daughters' interest, and forbade

176

them from seeing me after school. I didn't have words for it, then, but these incidents of difference-made-visible lingered. I presumed I was unacceptable because of my brown skin. There was a color line, and I started to struggle with it, internally and inchoately. Needless to say, I never tried to kiss Christina. "Don't try to kiss no white girls" became the enforced rule, rather than "stand up against racism." Racism itself was never acknowledged or discussed, much less the idea of standing up against it. My nascent bravery went unnoticed.

Some whites struggled in their own way against the color line too. The Den Mother of our multiracial Cub Scout pack was white. Whenever my own mother was on call in the hospital, I stayed with her and her family, and was treated as a son. But still, something was wrong. There was a refuge of acceptance, in the classrooms, playgrounds and homes of friends, a refuge that the adults must have known would be challenged or evaporate outright as we grew. Still, no one spoke to me of race; perhaps they were shielding me, or perhaps they were in denial. Perhaps they all had hope that our futures wouldn't be affected or defined by the color of our skins. But somewhere underneath my conscious awareness, I felt there was something wrong. There was an emptiness, a separation, larger than the still-growing disappointment with my father. I was 10 years old, being carried along by unseen forces, a vulnerable heir to histories and conditions of my adopted country, conditions that would become a disconsolate fit, a subtle shaper of consciousness-to-come. The migrations continued.

From the comfortable nucleus of Nashville, we moved to inner city St. Louis where my mother was continuing her training rotations at the Homer G. Phillips City Hospital. Here, the color line was more palpable. The year after, we would move to the North. St. Louis was a fulcrum of our American voyage, in the middle of the country, and perched between tensions. Our journey paralleled the Great Migration of Blacks from South to North, yet another thumbprint of diaspora, disillusionment, and discovery. I felt at home and part of the group in an all-black elementary school in inner city St. Louis. The teacher, an African American woman, saw a spark in me, and tagged me to go to an integrated "gifted" program in the suburbs. My walk to school turned into a ride on a yellow school bus that took me from the gritty brick buildings of the inner city to the tree-lined suburbs surrounding the Kennedy Elementary School, from a class where everyone looked like me to a class where I was only one of two non-white students. Before, I played with all the kids at recess; afterwards, there were cliques, rivalries and aggressions I couldn't understand.

It was a lift academically, but a rift interpersonally. I lost a feeling of togetherness, and acquired a daily sense of migrating to another world, a world where I wasn't sure I belonged. The inner city had been left behind, devalued. My commonality with other dark-skinned children was rent; in its place, a confusion about how I was connected to them. I felt difference more

177

than congruence with my classmates. The world had grown larger, and less understandable. My skin, my identity, my boundary of communication with the world, was in question. I was a fatherless child, and my mother's strengths didn't include a complete understanding of the world to which she had brought us.

My suburban teacher, another African American woman, tried her best to reach and engage me, involving me in the class play and trying to get me to take up a musical instrument. She also told us about how the "For Sale" signs went up all around her block when she and her husband moved into their house in a previously all-white neighborhood. "Why would they do something like that?" I asked her in all innocence. She burst into tears. I apologized, thinking I'd hurt her feelings. "No, it wasn't you," she said. But we never talked about what "that" was. Racism was still an unacknowledged force; even our teachers didn't feel free to discuss it. The force of division and trauma floated between us all, as yet unnamed in my life.

One day, near the end of the school year, I went back to the classroom of my inner-city teacher, and thanked her. Despite the problems I'd encountered, she'd created a miracle in my life. She hugged me, my head pressing against the bottom of her warm bosom. She was a mother, even at work, and she gave me another birth that year, another origin, but still one with an uncertain foundation.

Excerpt from *Facebuddha: Transcendence in the Age of Social Networks*, 2017.

Ravi Chandra, MD is a psychiatrist and writer in San Francisco. His book *Facebuddha: Transcendence in the Age of Social Networks* won the 2017 Nautilus Silver Book Award for Religion/Spirituality of Eastern Thought. Dr. Chandra is a graduate of Brown University, Stanford University School of Medicine, and UCSF. He served as staff psychiatrist and medical director of RAMS, a community mental health clinic, from 2006-2013. He blogs for Psychology Today (The Pacific Heart) and for the Center for Asian American Media (Memoirs of a Superfan). www.RaviChandraMD.com.

Speaking English
Sue Granzella

A week before the 2016 Presidential election, I was listening to "This American Life" while brushing my teeth. The featured story was of a Somali woman, attacked at a Minnesota Applebee's because she was speaking Swahili. The blatancy of the anti-immigrant violence so appalled me that I put down my toothbrush and listened for twenty minutes, perched on the edge of the tub.

The attacker first approached the Somali woman, Asma Jama, with the admonition that when in America, people must speak English. When Jama ignored her, the attacker began yelling that Jama should go back to her home country. At this, Jama began addressing her calmly, in English.

Then the attacker smashed a beer mug into Jama's face, and pandemonium ensued. As Jama's children screamed, the attacker stormed out of Applebee's, leaving Jama gashed and bleeding.

That portion of the radio broadcast ended with the words of a witness to the attack:

> Talking to other people about it, they say simple things like, 'Well, you know, she could have just been speaking English.'
> —*This American Life*, episode #600

As I wondered how a person could feel such rage because an immigrant wanted to talk to her friend, I found myself remembering another immigrant, a very young one, and the treatment he received long ago in my classroom.

When Zayd showed up in my fourth-grade class in December of 1990, Arabic became the tenth native language and the third written alphabet in the classroom of thirty-four kids. Zayd was from Yemen, a country I'd never even heard of back then. None of us understood a word he said.

Zayd was adorable, a contradiction of angles and circles. His profile was all pointiness—thin, prominent chin, long, narrow nose. Curving eyelashes ringed his golden eyes, and his hair fell in soft loops of brown. His smile was frequent and electric. Though the students hovered over him, I felt sorry for Zayd. All day, every day, to speak without response, to listen without understanding.

The classroom itself was a contradiction, too. Built in the 70s, it had an accordion wall shared by the room next door. It was designed for flexibility and community, allowing us to open up into one huge room, but the teacher on the other side of the wall was cynical and bitter, so it remained a divider between us. The countertops and cabinets were all yellow-and-white Formica brightness, but the light from outside was blocked by cloudy shatter-resistant windows, covered with metal.

The hippie-design room was not nearly big enough for the number of students crammed into it. There was hardly space for the beat-up wooden shelf, upon which I placed my similarly beat-up books from thrift stores and stacks

179

of discards from the Oakland Public Library. Besides my teacher desk and the thirty-four individual student desks, the only other furniture was a set of two small nesting tables, clunky wooden blocks with grooves carved into them by generations of students experimenting with scissors.

At the front of each side wall were two tiny alcoves pushing out like Mickey Mouse ears from the otherwise square room. Our reading corner was stuffed into one ear and I made it cozy, hanging posters of book covers and tossing plump homemade pillows across the drab patch of indoor-outdoor carpeting. The larger nesting table was wedged into the corner alongside the weary bookshelf.

One day, I heard whispering during the supposedly-silent reading time. Irritated, I traced it to the cramped library corner, and headed over for a showdown. There I found Zayd pressed up next to Dominic, their heads on the floor, jammed together under the nesting table. Their four hands clutched the cover of a book called Zoo Animals.

Dominic pointed to a page, and said, "Giraffe."

Zayd giggled. "Zhuh-duf."

Dominic nodded.

Then Zayd pointed. "Za-ra-fa."

Dominic repeated in a whisper. The two boys grinned, and flipped the page.

A few months after Zayd arrived, we were studying multiplication. The kids had piles of plastic colored squares on their desks, and they were building arrays, adding one row at a time. Even kids who usually floundered during math could move tiles and count; the kids were buoyed by success, their energy high. Amid chatter and clatter, they added rows, while I questioned them rapid-fire, jabbing my index finger at individuals.

"How many rows? How many in each row? How many squares in all?"

They cried out responses, and students cheered themselves with hisses of, "Yes!"

And then came the sixth row.

"How many rows?"

I saw it first—Zayd's face bursting into light. His hand shot into the air, his legs propelling him upward. He'd never spoken before the class. I'd never heard him initiate a word of English.

I pointed to him.

"See-eeks!"

The class gasped as one.

"How many in each row?"

His hand an arrow, straight into sky.

"Trree!"

"How many tiles in all?"

"Ay-deen!"

I put down the chalk.

But Zayd wasn't done. No one else even raised a hand as I tossed out questions and Zayd tossed back answers, number after number wrapped in the gentle curves of his voice, the voice I'd hardly heard before that day.

Until finally his words stopped, and Zayd met my delighted smile with a huge grin. Then thirty-three kids began to applaud. Outside, there were broken appliances in the creek and gunshots at dusk, the sidewalks sparkling with bits of shattered glass. But inside, nine- and ten-year-olds cheered for the curly-haired boy whose English-speaking voice, finally gone quiet, had just begun.

Excerpted from "All the White People," *The Masters Review,* March 11, 2019.
https://mastersreview.com/new-voices-all-the-white-people-by-sue-granzella/

Sue Granzella teaches third grade in California. Her writing has been named Notable in Best American Essays, and she has won numerous prizes in the Soul-Making Keats Literary Competition, a contest for which she is now a judge. Winner of the Naomi Rodden Essay Award and a Memoirs Ink contest, her writing has appeared in *The Masters Review, Full Grown People, Gravel, Ascent, Citron Review,* and *Hippocampus,* among others. www.suegranzella.com.

Pancho Pescador aka Peskador. "Tupac: They got money for wars…" Photo by Edsel Rivera.

Find Your Bubble
Dena Rod

As a child taught to fill bubbles when it came for standardized testing, one bubble over all others gave me pause. My date of birth and name were easy. Yet when it came to choosing race, I froze. I was certain that 'Iranian' was something my parents made up. After all, we had no Internet to check facts. Since I barely knew any one at my elementary school who was Iranian, I figured my parents were lying to me about where we were really from.

My mother matriculating at Bangalore University in India led her to encourage me to make friends with Indian immigrants' children at school. Our childhood experiences were similar but our foods and languages were different. Despite our knowledge of these differences, we knew there was strength in numbers and banded together. Our wacky sense of camaraderie wasn't without hiccups. Once I erred in admitting my loathing for the mid morning shift on Sunday's public access programming: all the Persian music videos, commercials, and programs turned to Bollywood for the rest of the day. When I said I hated how Iranians now only got a few hours, I inadvertently insulted my comrades' culture to the point where it was all they could talk about all week at recess.

Yet the other Iranians I knew were not at school, but in my extracurricular activities: piano lessons, swim classes, and at weekly extended family gatherings called mehmoonis. The world globe in our home further exacerbated my suspicion of my parents perpetuating a long con of where we were really from. At its time of manufacturing, North and South Rhodesia and the USSR were still nations. Therefore, Iran was labeled as Persia. Due to my ignorance of this historical context, I despaired to the point of tears when I couldn't find the Iran my parents told me existed. I sobbed for reasons I didn't quite understand. This was the early 90s. All my Barbies and other dolls were white or black, including every single catalogue model, sitcom star, cartoon character I was exposed to.

There was no bubble to fill on my standardized test that encompassed all these things. The nuanced categories of today's US census—with Asian, Pacific Islander, Native/Indigenous American, non-Hispanic White—weren't available. Forced to make a decision, I marked myself down as Asian, based on my very exhaustive research of our home globe. Iran was in Asia, therefore based on these limited racial categories, I must be Asian. After all, I wasn't white, because the suburban whiteness I witnessed was composed of boloney sandwiches, baseball, and three-story houses. With the aromatic spices stored in my Maman's cupboard, our Persian rugs in every room, and Farsi being my first language, I knew I wasn't white.

Yet, I wasn't satisfied with marking down Asian and I worried I would get in trouble. Especially since STAR Testing was considered the end all be all of tests. I raised my hand and asked my 2nd grade teacher. Her puzzled face gently corrected me. She informed me Asian meant someone who was Chinese or Japanese. She gave me examples, using my classmates. Despite my confusion, and her lack of linguistic nuance, I erased the bubble marking me as Asian and filled in the one for white. Looking back, I wonder what bubble my Indian American classmates had filled out.

Filling in that bubble for white was based on the current US Census definition for white: "a person having origins in any of the original peoples of Europe, the Middle East, or North Africa." Meaning, Morocco, Egypt, Turkey, Tunisian, Algeria, Saudi Arabia, Iraq, Iran were all effectively counted as white, despite the fact that we were considered brown in any other context in the United States. The cops pulling my father over, with his thick black mustache over full lips and his strong, connected eyebrows didn't consider him white when they heard his accent. My mother abbreviating her name to DJ so it would fit on a Target nametag wasn't considered white. None of the kids on the playground thought of me as white when I said things like eucalyptus leaves were used by our ancestors for healing. I was called ancient instead.

When I see how nuanced the conversation is today regarding race and ethnicity, with words like "white passing," "Afro-Latinx," "colorism" used daily on social media, I'm astonished at how far we have come in twenty years. These terms weren't part of the layman's lexicon when I was a child. Perhaps adults in academia in the early 1990s were familiar with intersectionality, but to elementary school kids there was very limited language available on how to express ourselves racially that wasn't black or white. The binary was very much intact, spilling over to the shades of characters in the cartoons and toys that you could get. I remember fruitlessly searching for myself amongst these representations and feeling like, if I had to pick one, then I guess I was white.

This was further complicated as I grew up because the attacks on the Twin Towers occurred when I was in middle school. I sharply learned that I wasn't white. There were more Afghanis, Pakistanis, Iraqis peppering my classes as I advanced through high school. I didn't suffer at the hands of classmates who tortured those who were visibly Islamic looking, and had more foreign sounding names. My generic sounding name meant I had another form of white passing privilege; my name doesn't clock me as someone Other. White friends brought up my ethnicity as proof of their lack of racism despite exhibiting anti-blackness and anti-Semitism.

However, in the wake of Black Lives Matters and subsequent movements, I cannot say that it's due to any inherent goodness inside of me. It has to do with light-skinned privilege. Even though I am considered white by the US census, my facial features imbue me with what Tyra Banks would call ethnic ambiguity. This allows me to move through the world in ways others easily identified as Muslim can't. My mother attempted to preserve this white passing privilege by making sure I always wore sunscreen so I didn't tan too quickly and too often, despite my summer swimming lessons.

Yet my Baba affectionately calls himself a "brown boy." He has claim to the title based on his experiences with white suburbia's reaction to his body. A lot of Iranians don't understand why the first generation of Iranian Americans often self-refer as "people of color" due to the fair complexions prevalent. This tension is likely to always be there, due to the legacies of European beauty ideals being upheld in non-Western cultures. It wasn't until I completed a survey on a visit to the Asian Art Museum that I found delineated categories for different parts of Asia that actually fit who I am. Iran fell under the category of "West Asian," separate from "South Asian" for the Indian subcontinent and "East Asian" for the examples my 2nd grade teacher gave me. Labels aren't the end all be all of identification. Yet finding the right name can help find our place in the world for those where we don't see ourselves reflected.

Dena Rod is a writer, editor, and poet based in the Bay Area. Through creative nonfiction essays and poetry, Dena illuminates their diasporic experiences of Iranian American heritage and queer identity, while combating negative stereotypes of their intersecting identities.

Shizue Seigel, "Veils," mixed media, 2009.

Remembering Galileo
Susan Almazol

"How embarrassing for Tony to lose to a colored boy."

I stopped in the crowded hallway, stunned to hear such a comment. After all, I was back in cosmopolitan San Francisco. My body turned ice cold, reverberating from a sudden memory. I watched as Stella reached for a book from her grey metal locker, flanked by two other Italian American girls. They were nodding their heads and murmuring support.

I spun around again to head to my math class but not before I caught Stella's eye. She stared back.

I was in New Orleans again in an instant. People staring, brazenly asking: "What is that?" as I walked by. I ducked into the air-conditioned Maison Blanche department store the first time it happened, momentarily escaping their hurtful ignorance and the blistering humidity of Canal Street.

"What is that?" I heard again and again during my two years in New Orleans where Asians were viewed as aliens.

I first experienced New Orleans-style racism when the junior high school counselor, all smiles, looked at my shining report cards from California. Without saying a word, she placed me in remedial classes from English to math to social studies. That's how she willfully dealt with the first non-white student in her school. I discovered what she did a couple of weeks later when school started. Even my nine remedial classmates told me I didn't belong with them. My teachers themselves quietly re-arranged my schedule so that I was rightfully in the top academic tier.

But here I was a senior at Galileo High School, back in California after my Army sergeant father was transferred to the Presidio of San Francisco.

Blending as we did once again among other Asians, we all secretly sighed with relief. We had been wordlessly wounded by the whites-against-blacks and where-did-we-fit-in racism of the South during the uncertain time when New Orleans schools were desegregated—with fierce resistance but not outright riots—in 1960.

My parents, immigrants from the Philippines, had no language, no skills to counsel us. All they could advise to do was not to drink at the water fountains marked "colored" or to sit at the back of the bus.

I had arrived at Galileo at a time of racial upheaval—in schools, the city, and the country. At Galileo, Blacks, Chinese, and Chinese Americans from nearby Chinatown were beginning to outnumber the Italian Americans. The principal, an Italian American who had attended Galileo, reminded us frequently that back in the day—his day, the 1930s—Galileo was the top academic school in the City. The subtext of his boasts was that this superiority was due to the Italian-heritage students from North Beach. And there was still the expectation that the Italian Americans would lead the way—for instance, that Tony would be president of our 1964 graduating class.

Meanwhile, the Black population in San Francisco had grown tenfold in the previous 20 years, after they began pouring into the city for war jobs, replacing the 5,000 Japanese residents incarcerated during World War II. A large housing project sprouted near Galileo, close to Fisherman's Wharf, to accommodate many Black families. Then, in the 1960s, working-class Hong Kong Chinese arrived in large numbers, taking advantage of the shifting immigration quotas.

The fight over the International Hotel on Kearny Street near Chinatown was emblematic of these times. A place where single Asian men, mostly Filipinos, could live cheaply within their community, the hotel was targeted for razing in the late 1960s to make way for a parking structure. Despite a fierce fight by a newly galvanized coalition of Asian American activists, the hotel was shut down, and its elderly occupants, in their 70s and older, were evicted. They scattered and died, many far away from their community.

I could see at once how these demographics played out at lunchtime in the school courtyard. Black students gathered in one area. Chinese, Filipinos, and other Asians and Asian Americans remained on the periphery. The Italian Americans took up space in the center.

To my surprise, I ended up actively fighting this brand of segregation, in sharp and unexpected contrast to my pained silence in New Orleans.

My activism was awakened by Patty's arrival from Washington High School. She quickly befriended me and a fellow nerd, Margo, a tall, quiet Hispanic girl. We were quite the threesome at lunch time, whispering and plotting. Chubby and nearly as tall as Margo, Patty cackled loudly. Margo tended towards quiet smiles, while my hearty laughter belied both my smallness and shyness.

Patty was a whirlwind of fun who enjoyed stirring things up. My guess is that she did a little too much stirring up at Washington. She sized up our situation pretty much the way I had and egged us on to challenge expectations, starting with the student body elections.

I don't recall what led me to run against Mia, the presumed coordinating secretary to be. The popular athletes and cheerleaders usually ran for office. It was a big step for an Asian American student to step forward, especially one taking demanding academic classes. We had no time for extracurricular activities, other than the school newspaper, and so had no following. But I was upset that my story about increasing racial incidents was shot down. Then Richard, another quiet nerd who was Black, decided to run against Tony. Maybe that's what did it for me. I wouldn't be alone in my battle for inclusion. Richard was regarded as thoughtful and conscientious, and so was I, judging from comments in my yearbook.

We won. We were not a slate. We were both too shy to run much of a campaign. We were voted in by the other students who also wanted change, who wanted a more inclusive community.

New Orleans—I remember with pain and shame. The pain of being stared at, of being talked about as if I were invisible, of my own silence in return. I squirm when I recall walking past the water fountains marked "colored" in search of the "right" fountain for me.

Galileo—I remember with pride. Was it the support of friends that empowered me to act? Did the swiftly changing times across the country buoy me? The profound changes in the 1960s, after all, were due to years of invisible shifting until we reached a turning point.

Yes, I believe supportive conditions pushed me through the concrete of pain and silence, so boldness could blossom. Over the years, I have taken brave personal stands, quit my job on principle, marched, volunteered in campaigns, participated in vigils and walkouts, and written letters and stories. More recently, I have created and exhibited mixed media installations on the lasting consequences of war, on saying yes to aging, and on the healing offered by sangha.

I like to think that my taking action when I was 17 years old birthed a larger courageous self that I have continually grown into.

Susan Almazol is a Filipina artist based in Oakland, whose media include clay, cloth, and conversation. Her ceramic sculptures and installations plumb inner realities for universal truths. Her textile creations celebrate beauty as sacred. Her dance and writing flow from intimate conversations with herself. www.susanalmazolarts.com

Experiments in Middle-School Student Solidarity
David Kubrin

In the late 1980s when I began teaching science at James Denman Middle School near San Francisco's Balboa Park, our Peer Resource teacher, Faye, mentioned that our school was the most racially mixed in the school district. I suggested that we form a group to explore race/ism. When she agreed, I proposed the name Students and Staff Concerned about Racism (SSCAR).

Faye agreed to facilitate our weekly lunch-time meetings where 6th, 7th, and 8th graders, along with teachers, counselors, and paraprofessionals, could talk and share stories about race and racism—many concerning the nearby corner store where students often bought snacks and sodas. Students complained about being immediately viewed with suspicion because of their race or the way they dressed.

A particularly moving moment in one of our first meetings was a white math teacher describing how her parents refused to meet their own grandchildren because their father, the teacher's husband, was black.

In another early meeting, Filipino students revealed that a Filipino teacher regularly used a Tagalog term akin to the "n-word" in class when referring to their black classmates. Within a few minutes, that teacher's 7th and 8th grade students had organized a small mixed delegation of students to go talk to her and explain the offensiveness of her behavior. I remember a number of teachers attended the meeting. I was struck by how little adult input was needed to organize their plan. At the early meetings, perhaps a dozen adults attended the initial meetings, but gradually their numbers dwindled.

After two years, Faye had to move on, but around the same time, I was approached by Indra, the facilitator of a new organization with a compatible but broader agenda focusing on school violence. We agreed to join forces and at our first meeting we decided on the name Helping End Abusive Language and Stereotypes (HEALS). The new organization had a budget; the meetings included pizzas, and attendance increased.

Our concerns ranged widely. A lengthy discussion ensued, for instance, when students confessed how they used to tease our Special Ed students.

We also discussed homophobia—more often than not, in my memory, an adult broached the topic. Several months into the Fall semester of our third year, I suddenly realized that I had not heard a single student call another "faggot," that ever-present middle school explisult. In prior years, I'd heard the hateful term dozens of times a day. Other Denman teachers hadn't noticed, but upon reflection, many of them agreed. I asked teachers from other middle schools when I attended teachers union meetings and a number of district-wide forums. At these other schools, "faggot" was still in regular use. My informal survey was not rigorous, but I began to think that even a dozen or so students meeting weekly for a few years could have influenced the language and behavior of their 650 to 700 schoolmates on a fundamental instance of oppression.

In our fourth or fifth year, the HEALS meeting focused on that day's *San Francisco Chronicle* report that a Japanese-American-owned shop had been plastered with swastikas and sprayed with racist messages. A public hearing was scheduled for that night. The 7th and 8th grade students arranged that several HEALS members would go across town to make a statement of our solidarity. Again, Indra and I played little role in their planning.

During our second year, the *Chronicle*'s reporter on the secondary school beat came to a SSCAR meeting to listen in and ask a few questions. When she inquired, "How has being in this group affected you?" an articulate and active 6th grade African-American girl eagerly volunteered, "There's this girl in my classes…. I really can't stand her, never have, and anyway I used to call her a 'white bitch' before, but now I just call her 'a bitch!'" Almost in unison, Faye and I turned to the reporter, "Oh, write that down; put it in your article!" It was a clear sign that we'd made some progress—but still had more work to do.

Faye, Indra, and I had built a platform on which students could express themselves on these fundamental issues of their lives. But the most important and inspirational work emerged from the students' own initiative, teaching me profound lessons in the workings of solidarity.

David Kubrin's passions are writing and dancing; he is an artist and a community organizer through his role with Mission Arts Performance Project (MAPP), as well as an activist against Empire. Forthcoming is his *Marxism & Witchcraft* (Autonomedia 2019). He has a BS from Caltech and a PhD from Cornell University. In 1960, he won a Guggenheim Fellowship for his work on Isaac Newton's alchemical cosmogony.

Mel Waters, "Frederick Douglass," *Black History Month 2016* series. Mission District. Photo by Edsel Rivera.

Judgment: The TRACKING SYSTEM
Tureeda Mikell

In the Fillmore my rites of passage begin at 12 years.
2 younger sisters and I arrive
at our second foster home in San Francisco.
I weigh 205 pounds. I have Bell's Palsy. Nerves on left side of face, dead
Left eyelid half blinks while awake, won't close while asleep
Left side of mouth droops whether I laugh, cry, talk, or eat
Severe acne covers my face, chest, and left arm
Hair short, uneven, balding in some areas
Our mother has died of Lupus, I have been raped.

Entering the front door, foster mother whispers,
"Look at her, she's pitiful. Looks like the rats been sucking on her head"

She said it as though I couldn't hear, or perhaps didn't care if I did.
No one asked us, how are you? Are you OK?
Would you like a drink of water?

My first day at Marina Jr. High School without records of my past,
Without a clue of my intellectual capacities,
School assesses my appearance
Tracks me in systems of X, Y, Z.
X 1-13 Gifted
Y 1-13 Intermediate average
Z 1-13 Special Ed/retarded

I am placed in 13Z, Special Ed, retarded.

Music teacher learns I have perfect pitch
Learns I can sing any set of notes heard in perfect sequence;
Art teacher shares with students and teachers what I wrote about the arts
They say I will make a name for myself in the arts.

At George Washington High, 1966, I'd become school pianist, and
the only Black teen to compete as concert pianist in 1966
at the Ensemble Festival at S.F. State College
Performing 5 pages of Chopin's Revolutionary Etude from memory
When 16, I'd be the first student at George Washington High,
to transpose *Romeo and Juliet* from orchestral score into piano score.

Yeah, Fillmore foster kid—Special!

¿How You Say?
Josiah Luis Alderete

Do that thing you do
Where you mispronounce my entire history using only two words—
"Moctezuma's Revenge"
It's not necesario to sacrifice flesh or corazones,
We've known that for 1000's of years
Since before Coatlicue appeared and we started calling her Tonantzin,
Pero you've never been interested in that part.
You're here because you've got that White Man's Burden itch
You're here to capture the whole thing on your iPhone
You need to have that historical selfie in front of the massacre to prove your
point,
That you can slip into the history books and say "I told you so"
That perfecto mushroom cloud photobomb
That in the end no one will see except you and your Manifest Destiny,
You always knew how to look directly into the camera
When you called this place "home"
—and really in this reality and day and age that's half the battle,
¿What else can you mispronounce for us while we bleed?
¿Will you continue to discredit her serpentes?
¿Will you continue to believe that we still have gold hidden somewheres on
our bodies?
¿You know that these days at the borders they are checking everywhere and
everything right?
You can try telling them that the razorblade underneath your tongue
is just for the language and see what they say,
See if they believe the red, white, and blue in your eyes they very well might.
¿Are you sure that that's the real name for what you do?
It's just that there's no way I can pronounce that and keep a straight face…
"conquistador" I'm used to saying…¿but this?
It's hard for me to see past these modern masks and disguises
While you on the other hand seem to have no problem at all
Drinking down an entire cultura's agua bendita
While texting AND colonizing all at the same time.
Yeah we know that you've always kept parts of us as trophies

—the hands and the ears and the scalps,
But there's also the shreds of languages dangling like strips of flesh off our backs
hanging somewheres in your closet.
There's also the blessings and milagros from our own gods
Pickled in glass jars in your pantry.
¿What else have you done to us, where else did you hide us?
¿How the hell do you think that you're going to pronounce all of this when we
are no longer around?
I have to say that you do tell me a lot with your stolen prophecies and predictions,
You use our languages with your feet, dream about our screams,
You ask to learn our curse words first and then speak them with our blood in
your mouth,
And you get away with it because, after all, talking in America is complicated
these days
Especially with all the emojis,
There are words that I struggle to forget that your ancestors stuffed down our
mouths
That still jump out of our throats, out of my voz,
Out of habit, out of reaction, out of custom,
These sustos, these palabras are always pronounced correctly
No matter how hard I try not to,
Meanwhile what you're saying may be between the lines
But it's also dangling around your neck on gold chains
It's also got heaven's own white privilege microphone pointed right at you,
So that even with all your cartoon accents
We hear you loud and clear telling everyone
That that's "us" in the back of your throat
Making those guttural noises—it's not you,
You misremember us just enough
So that we disappear but are still here
You look the other way, squint your eyes
And we become those worn out and tattered stereotypes
Still talking funny, still mispronouncing American history, still looking for
work…
You keep on doing it after all these years
And still have the nerve to call it a holiday.

viii. Sickness and Health

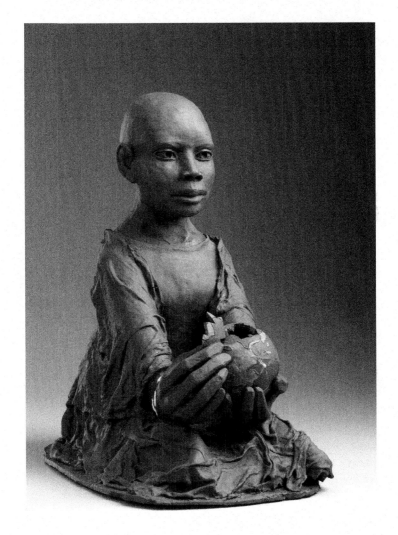

Lorraine Bonner, "Wounded Healer," clay, 2017, 19 x 12 x 16 in.

Baby Grace with her mother in front of their Los Angeles apartment.

The Gift
Grace Morizawa

My mother died on December 21, 1976, on the winter solstice, the darkest day of the year. That Christmas was numbing for my brother and me. We already had the tree up but we took down the decorations.

Maybe because Mom died around Christmas time, the season's rituals have kept us close. Though we live in different states, we spend every Christmas and New Year's together. We don't talk much about her, but we remember her as if she were still with us.

My mother was 35 when my father died, leaving her with two young children aged 4 and 7. We moved from Los Angeles to live with my grandfather in the town of Ontario in eastern Oregon. When Japanese Americans were forced to leave the West Coast, some relocated to this town just outside the exclusion zone. The mayor of the town was so favorably impressed by the hard-working newcomers that when Japanese Americans were released from incarceration in 1945, he invited them to come resettle in Ontario and help clear the land for farming. My grandfather and many other Nikkei settled there rather than return to West Coast homes.

My mother had been primarily a wife and mother before my father died. Now she worked in the fields in the summer and in the cannery and packing shed in the winter. She worked swing or night shifts so she could take care of us during the day. Once I woke up to see her scrubbing the floor at 3:00 AM after a long shift at the cannery.

She went to school to become a beautician even though she hated it. But it was a winter job that paid more than the cannery—in the summer, even weeding onions paid more.

Finally at 50, with my brother and I grown and gone, she went to nursing school in Idaho—her life-long dream.

Once I asked how she kept going, never complaining, never stopping. She didn't answer me. She just looked as if I had asked a foolish question that she didn't understand. As an adult, I came to understand. By example, she passed that same determination on to us.

In December 1976, we thought my mother was going to recover from an operation for stomach cancer. But after the surgery, the doctor told me, "It's too late." When he opened her up, he saw the cancer had spread too far, so he closed her up again. My mother must have known this. The moment she was conscious, despite the long cut on her abdomen, she was kneading the familiar lump in her stomach. The doctor didn't come after she regained consciousness to examine her or talk with her. She looked at me, and I had to tell her what the doctor had said.

Back in 1976, some people did not believe in telling people they had a fatal illness, but my mother was a nurse. Thirty years earlier she had nursed her own mother as she died of stomach cancer in the hospital at the Heart Mountain Concentration Camp. My mother's hospital was not behind barbed wire. She even had a bedside phone to talk with her brother in Chicago, and I had come from California to be with her. She was in Caldwell, Idaho, which was only 30 miles from Ontario, but not as welcoming. Looking back, I can't help but wonder if her hospital care was neglected because she was Japanese American. Even then, I thought her doctor was callous. She didn't officially die of cancer, but choked in the middle of the night after they removed the tube draining fluids from her stomach. During the day she kept vomiting, but felt better by evening. She wanted to crochet the pillowcase that I was embroidering. We took turns working on the case and finished it. That night she died.

I could be angry, but Death is death. No amount of speculation or brow beating can bring someone back to life.

Back in her apartment, I found hints on how she had pulled herself together and hung on to hope even though she saw her mother die of the same disease. In her medical book, the passages on stomach cancer were heavily marked. They described the illness in detail, and to my surprise, promised the possibility of recovery with early diagnosis. This was a change from the prospect of inevitable death from stomach cancer that had haunted generations of women in my family. Mom expected to survive. She had taken out a loan to tide her through long days of recovery after the operation. She had marked and labeled all her legal papers—health insurance, will, bank accounts—they were neatly filed in a wooden tomato crate. My father's sheet music was left on the piano as if she just finished playing it.

Practicality was her stepping-stone through her life—establishing a life in Los Angeles after camp, losing a beloved husband, raising two small kids. I thought about how we moved into Grandpa's two-room house that was barely a shelter against the harsh weather of the high desert. In the spring she planted a lawn. She didn't stop. She marked passages in Buddhist readings and scriptures and copied them in a spiral notebook. Buddhism was her shield against a difficult existence. An obutsudan, a Buddhist shrine, was on the bookcase next to her bed. She must have slept every night with the Buddha looking over her.

But she had also joined the local chorus to sing the Messiah at Christmas time. "Your dad liked to sing the Messiah," she explained, "so when one of hakujin at the beauty-salon invited me, I decided to try it."

These days, neither my brother nor I go to temple regularly, but we attend annual Buddhist Oshotsuki services on the anniversary of her death. And I look forward to Christmas and the whole commercial shebang. The lights, the carols, the brightly wrapped packages—even Macy's Thanksgiving parade on TV. Some consider it crass, but after my mother died, the brass bands and giant balloons began to symbolize the human spirit preparing to endure through the long, cold winter.

Grace Morizawa is a Sansei, third generation Japanese American. Her parents met in Heart Mountain concentration camp, Wyoming. She grew up in Ontario, Oregon, where West Coast Japanese fled to escape incarceration. Japanese Americans from Minidoka, Heart Mountain, Tule Lake, and other American concentration camps voluntarily resettled there during the war and after. Grace taught elementary school in Oakland, worked on a national school reform project, and was a principal of an elementary school in San Pablo, California. Currently she is the Education Coordinator for the National Japanese American Historical Society. She has an MA in Creative Writing from San Francisco State, and an EdD from the Leadership in Education and Equity Program at UC Berkeley.

Aleuchi
Kimi Sugioka

It's just that I don't trust hospitals
where honey skinned men are
    concerned or
manzanita women for
that matter considering
Billie Holiday
and so many
others

Killer King took one such
beautiful young man
I met when he was maybe 9 or 10
exceptionally human
and
brilliantly
alive
I
remember
the
Rodney King insurrection
his mama said he drank
so much orange soda he
got a stomach ache
and she
laughed
through the
chaos and
worry

At the age of my own
beloved son,
bicycling across the
country Aleuchi
fell sick in LA
where he was
stashed in a back room
alone with
a curable illness
No one to hold

his hand or
advocate

for the poem
of his breath
till his phone
and life lost their charge

A story
I didn't believe
was mine
to tell till
so many
years
passed
and so many
dark skinned
young men
became
the ghosts of
so many
cherished
children

so
I don't trust hospitals
or the street
or the BART police
or the cops
or this
complex
industrial
racist
prison
and together
we must
mourn and fight
for them
and
Aleuchi

Cositas
Katie Afshar

Waiting room mothers pile in with their babies.
Sometimes a man. They could all be deported.
This clinic is for them and I'm a ghost
shining light in ears, down throats.
Deep breath más profundo, alveoli puff
like sea foam.

Onshore fog tumbles into this city—a city
full of people who've abandoned their stuff.
Residents stay 18 months average, then go
someplace else. I stop plucking my eyebrows.
Give up mascara. My squirrel lashes blink in mist.

Patients shut their mouths till the third-fourth appointment.
Gold star flashes from a front tooth, laughing woman
lifts a baby in a SpongeBob onesie
while Francisco guards the door, broadcasts Happy Friday!
carries his mariachi guitar like a woman's long heavy hair.
I want to hold something like that.

When I was a girl telephone wires were ripped
from the old Sears building. We wound
lime-yellow-pink into bracelets, ten to each wrist.
In the know—we thought of ourselves twirling
in lunch lines, four square, jump-rope
with our homemade jewelry, homemade identities.

In Mexico they say brazalete, in Nicaragua pulsera.
In the Mission District bracelets are braided
from colored rubber bands.
I like your bracelet I say
reaching a stethoscope towards the little girl's heart.

"Cositas" was first published in Rabbit 26, a journal for non-fiction poetry.

Katie Afshar is a pediatrician and writer from the San Francisco Bay Area who likes to garden at night and sleep during the day. She has been published in *Rabbit Poetry Journal*, *Metonym*, *Milvia Street*, *Cagibi*, and *The Sun Magazine*.

Reverence
Raluca Ioanid

When I hear the radio and TV blaring about Donald Trump and the border wall and ICE raids and families torn apart and children imprisoned in detention centers, I always think of this story of Gustavo and Hector, eleven- and thirteen-year-old brothers who traveled 2,168 miles from El Salvador to El Paso to be reunited with their mother. Theirs is one of many stories that I have been trusted enough to be told. As a family nurse practitioner working at a community health center in Fruitvale, Oakland, most of the patients I care for are immigrants and many are new arrivals. Transnational motherhood is a phenomenon of women who are straddling two nations, hearts torn between their children back home and the lives they are building here to support their children. Often, the families I care for have mixed immigration status, sometimes the children are documented and the parents undocumented, other times vice versa. The lives of these families are marred by a complex snarl of legal processes and a constant fear of possible separation and deportation.

Ana hums quietly. Christmas songs on the radio are nearly drowned out by the sound of the conveyer belt of brightly colored tubes of lipstick at the packing plant. Ana's quick hands gather up brightly colored lipstick tubes off of the assembly line, eagle eyes inspect for defects, deft fingers wrap the lipstick in silver tissue paper, tuck it into neat pink purses with metal clasps.

The foreman looks on at the workers from a high lifeguard chair. Instead of saving them from the ocean's wild waves, he's meant to keep the workers on their toes, heads bowed, silently working the line. Ana smiles as she hums, even though it's Christmas Eve and she's far from home and still without her boys, she knows they're close and will be here soon enough. As hard as it is to imagine her babies, eleven and thirteen, spending this holiday in a cell block at an ICE detention center in El Paso, she was so grateful they'd finally made it across the border. The lawyer had promised, just a matter of weeks now before she could go down and get them out of that hell hole and bring them home. Even though this place, this cramped apartment by the Oakland Coliseum wasn't much, they'd be together, finally.

Hundreds of miles away the same Christmas, radio songs filter into the guard station of the detention center. The jowly prison guard sips hot cocoa and plays sudoku, grateful to be presiding over a facility of children instead of murderers. Gustavo and Hector shiver under their thin blankets; no wonder they call this place

"La Hielera," the Icebox. The boys can't hear the radio songs from inside their concrete cell. There are no clocks, no windows, in this lightless place where time doesn't matter. They don't even know it's Christmas Eve.

This is the end of the 2,168 mile journey, mostly on foot, across the spine of America and now there's no telling if they'll be sent back to El Salvador. Gustavo and Hector listen to each other's weight shifting in the rickety aluminum bunk bed, wishing for a sleep that doesn't come. The guard's heavy footsteps trundle past as he conducts his hourly patrol of the unaccompanied children, stacked like poultry in the detention center. The waxy lipstick smell jolts Ana's mind, snaps her focus back to the belt just in time, before the foreman will notice her attention had wandered.

Although my primary role as a nurse practitioner is to provide medical care and treatment, a big part of helping people to find health and well being is to hold space for their stories and the immense journeys they have traveled. As I listen to immigration stories that speak of fleeing peril, of dangerous migration paths, of family separation, and the unspeakable risks that people take to arrive here, I am reminded that few immigrants actually want to leave their country, their language, or their family. I know this too first hand as an immigrant from Romania. Too often it is the political and economic pressures that make "home" no longer livable, and make coming to this unwelcoming country a risk worth taking. The power and strength of people who traverse the planet to make their way to the United States into a life as new immigrants that often demands them to be invisible inspires me. I am humbled to bear witness to this power and strength and honored to accompany my patients in whatever ways I can.

Listen well.
A man feels he's drowning in his own lungs,
that it's hard to make it up the stairs to his second floor apartment.
My stethoscope presses against his papery olive skin.
I listen for the lung inflating,
feel the press of his ribcage against my hand,
the thrill and heave of his heart.

His sounds stir
tiny bones inside my ear,
I wait for the snap of each valve,
mitral, tricuspid, pulmonary, aortic.
There, listening gives the answer,

the whoosh of the aortic valve that won't open.
Pay attention.
Bodies won't
tell their secrets
to just anyone.

A woman feels "something in my head,"
as though spirits are weighing her down.
Slowly, her story emerges
of carrying five children from a rural Kanjobal
speaking mountain village of Guatemala
across the bony spine of America,
into a life of being/feeling/imagining
herself invisible.

Listening and feeling
I find my way
to the things that are told
and those that don't want to be told.

I peer with an ophthalmoscope,
red light illuminating the eye
of a young strong man
who doesn't believe in the diabetes
that is slowly dismantling him,
ravaging his kidneys, taking hold of his retina.
Inside the creamy golden universe of his optic disc,
I watch the pulsating maze of vessels.

The vital force of us is strong and wild
from the first rush of blood
through a baby's hummingbird heart
to the final hiss of breath
echoing through
the cathedral of the ribs.

We are both fragile
and fierce,
a miracle of nerves and synapses,
bone and sinew, a universe of universes.

Details have been changed to protect privacy. Raluca Ioanid bio on p. 203.

Oakland County Hospital
Sriram Shamasunder, MD

i saw you today in the emergency room of Highland hospital.
skin thin and white as paper.
blue from your veins translucent

28 years young your chart says
though now emaciated
your cheekbones sharp like elbows
your flesh a wet napkin draped over your bones

tongue large
protruding from the tracheal tube

your sister stands at your bedside
fatigued by your illness
and fatigued by years of rescuing you from yourself

your forearm
a historical map she can trace
a family history of sorrow
suicide attempts
and overdoses

i want to know you before all of this.
like morning light before it hits the window
and frays

before you were my patient
before you were anyone's patient

a snowflake before it falls into a blizzard
unrecognizable to itself

if we back up enough years
this muddy puddle gutter
surely
was a clear raindrop glistening in its glory

this dying log,
warped and burned

emaciated and fallen in a redwood forest
was once regal
how many years back must i go to find
the grey goose flying across the grey sky
before she is shot down

the rhythm of your heart must have once beaten with the
rhythm of the ocean waves against rock
or the rhythm of children's feet running down streets

if i were to see you years back i would have loved to meet
the tiger in the forest
rather than this caged tiger
sick in this caged body

i hold your hand
i hold your hand
long enough to imagine
the fire that must have burned
before this ash.

Sriram Shamasunder graduated from University of California, Berkeley and completed his residency in Internal Medicine at Harbor-UCLA Medical Center. He obtained his Diploma in Tropical Medicine & Hygiene in 2013. Throughout his career he has spent several months out of every year in underserved settings around the world including South Los Angeles, rural Liberia, Haiti, Burundi, and rural India.

Sri is an Associate Professor of Medicine at UCSF, and co-founder and faculty director of the HEAL Initiative, a health workforce strengthening fellowship working in Navajo Nation and seven countries around the world. HEAL currently has over 100 fellows over the last three years, half of whom are Native American and from low and middle income countries (LMIC).

From p. 201: Raluca Ioanid was born in communist Romania and raised in capitalist New York City. By day she is a Family Nurse Practitioner in a busy community clinic in Fruitvale serving a diverse immigrant community. By night she is a trapeze-flying writer of stories. Her work has appeared in *The Sun*, *So To Speak*, *Riverbabble*, and in the anthology *Your Golden Sun Still Shines*. She is a frequent contributor to the Bay Area Generations reading series and a co-founder of the Reverie Writer's Group.

Towards a Real Time Medicine
Sriram Shamasunder, MD

ultimately
the study of the way
hot metal rod buries and burns into
flesh
is too late
to identify again and
again on each patient
the again
the way
electric shock
penetrates
cauterizes sears again burns
again
black into black skin

is too late

bullets will always
break holes into whole skin

to only memorize the way
depleted uranium crams into
soldier bodies and rises
again
with a lump in the throat
or a lover's breast
is too late

we believe in on time
on time
right now
medicine
in bodhisattva medicine buddha
who sharpens his
ears

sits lotus position alone
still
quiet as the night
for the wind to carry
any cry or shriek

we believe in
let the witness take a stand
Dr. Wendy Orr
24 year old
South African
apartheid
prison doctor
who said enough
my scalpel cannot heal
without my voice following
cut silence
call out loud
the name
the necessary
the baton
the white police guard
the stove hot revolver
before a welt rises
like a mountain on flat skin
or another body is buried
a small lump of dry earth

we believe in
house call
great depression doctors
open their black bag
write prescriptions
for bread

we believe in
Dr. V
Indian doctor-saint
the infinite vision to
dream and do
erect
as many free eye clinics
as McDonalds
an assembly line
of sight for the poor

we believe in
doctors without borders
of commitment
Dr. Gilbert Granados
Dr. Jyoti Puvvula
who stand months
before the Federal
building in Los Angeles
in protest of the Iraq war
the doctor/soothsayers
who know war
only brings together
a community
of severed legs

blood that clots
in the throat
of
mother earth

we believe
in
Dr. Jack Geiger
Dr. Mary Basset
Dr. Joia Mukherjee
sadhus of the night
who travel mountains
and slums
to wring poverty out
in all her incarnations
repeating her name as they walk

AIDS
TB
Malaria
Diabetes

we believe in
Dr. Franz Fanon
Dr. Che Guevera
doctors who draw
the wretched of the
earth
back into the line of history

we

do

believe

> Of all the forms of injustice, inequality in healthcare is the most shocking and inhumane.　　—Martin Luther King Jr.

On AIDS in Tanzania
Sriram Shamasunder, MD

Something as simple as a pill in the palm of her hand

This Tanzanian woman
Sings as she breastfeeds

They say it was the rain
But it was always my tears and sweat
Which brought up the maize

They said the railroads
Will bring a new day
But it was always diamonds going
with the sunset
The other way

And now she dies and is dying

Something as simple as a pill in the palm of her hand
This Tanzanian woman
Brilliant orange head wrap
Red African mud between her toes
Any pill
Anything close to healing
She does not hold in the palm of her hand.
her left breast sags in
the sun.
ribs exposed
continuum with the spine of her too large wooden chair
she resembles the chair
both of them frail
twigs
ready to snap

a pill
something as simple as a pill in the palm of her hand

her hands scathed
rough as maize husk
she dies and is dying
her 5 month old
baby boy born at dawn
suckles at her dry left breast

he suckles ashes from her left breast

something as simple as a pill in the palm of her hand

Who owns this pill?
What plant or human genome extract gave birth to it?
Who cut the compound, packaged
into compact cure?
In which boardroom, what lawyers patented it?
Blue suits and leather suitcases
tucking death into the space between fine print

Who keeps the cash?
Which markets rose while she fell?
Which corporate graph will track her demise?
Who will clench their fists one over the other as she opens her hand?

This Tanzanian woman
Her baby boy born at dawn

Who will begin to ask for a moratorium on their death penalty?

Something as simple
as a pill in the palm of her hand

Who will join this standing up?
A reach to claim the pill
demand the pill
And place it in her hand
Something as simple
And good
As healing
A pill
in the palm of her hand

Do Asian Americans Need Psychiatry?
Keh-Ming Lin, MD, MPH

In 1979, after completing my psychiatric training in Seattle, I moved to Los Angeles, to live among Asian Americans. In Seattle, I'd been involved in a project studying the health and living conditions of Vietnamese refugees, and had learned much about the dislocations and atrocities of war, and the daunting challenges of starting lives anew in an alien environment. For several years I watched the refugees struggle. While admiring their resilience and apparent equanimity, I was also alarmed by the degree of distress that only surfaced during in-depth interviews. It was clear that these refugees were hurting, and they had nowhere to go for help.

To a lesser extent, other Asian groups share with refugees the stress of displacement, acculturation, and overt and covert discrimination. Yet multiple layers of barriers—cultural, structural and linguistic—exist between them and health care providers. Unfortunately, their absence from the mental health system was often taken to mean they had less need for services. This fits with the myth of Asians as the "model minority"—not making waves, and needing less attention. Few caregivers noticed that the handful of Asian patients who occasionally showed up at the emergency room had typically been extremely sick for a very long time, often ten or even twenty years, without benefitting from modern advances in medications and therapies.

The timing for my move to LA couldn't have been better. After the century-long policy of blocking Asians from entering the country was lifted in 1965, a large number of Asians settled in the region. They soon exceeded ten percent of the population. Facing such rapid changes, the County finally decided in 1984 to fund a small Asian Pacific mental health program. We found space in the city of Gardena, recruited three bilingual professionals conversant in Japanese, Tagalog and Vietnamese, and a Korean-speaking receptionist/interpreter. With me as part-time psychiatrist, on loan from my academic post at the Harbor-UCLA Medical Center, the Coastal Asian Pacific Mental Health Center was born.

The funding didn't come easy. It was the result of months of endless meetings, during which many questioned the necessity and viability of such a program. They didn't believe that Asians needed or wanted our services. They had a point, given the widely held myth of Asians' resilience and mental strength. When someone suggested that it might be more cost-effective to teach patients English instead of providing services in their languages, I was too dumbfounded to respond.

"If you build it, they will come" became the staff's slogan. We were all gung-ho to prove the nay-sayers wrong. Yet, for weeks, no one showed up, and we became increasingly worried. Could they be right after all?

Outreaching to the communities, we were further dismayed when some of the community leaders declared, "No, we are not crazy. We don't need you guys. Do you think we are that weak?"

We sighed a secret sigh of relief when someone finally knocked at our door. To this day I still remember him vividly. Mr. Woon, a shy young Korean man in his early thirties, was brought in by his anxious mother. Dropping out of college after his freshman year, he refused to go back and had not been able to find a job either. He slept during the day and ranted and raved at night. He said that Mr. Kim was after him. Which Mr. Kim? Most Koreans we knew had that surname.

It turned out this Kim was the supreme leader of North Korea, who had been sending messages to him, harassing him, coercing him to steal top secrets from the South, and from the American military. Mr. Woon resisted, never giving in, for so many years, and he was proud of it. But it had been hell. He might not be able to take it much longer…

I never figured out how our young receptionist managed to gain Mr. Woon' trust. But she did, and he never linked us with the great Mr. Kim, never worried that we might be trying to poison him by giving him drugs.

Lo and behold, modern pharmaceuticals worked wonders. Mr. Woon gradually calmed down. He was truly surprised that Mr. Kim decided to let him be. "After all, he is such a busy person. He has many other things to attend to." He started working at his uncle's auto shop. For years, he kept my car in top shape.

Patients like Mr. Woon started to trickle in, and we had good luck with them. Or rather, they had good luck with us. Gradually, our clientele expanded. Patients with depression and anxiety materialized. We had luck with them also.

We had good luck not because we had any hidden healing powers, but because the majority of them were "virgin" patients. For reasons not well understood (but much speculated about), patients without previous exposure to treatment are much more likely to respond and improve. In addition, since it took great effort for many of the patients to reach us, they were more likely to be motivated and actively participate in their treatment.

As is usually the case in starting anything new, the first step was the most difficult. Our initial "success" attracted the attention of those communities that we were not able to cover with our limited resources. "You call yourself Asian Pacific. Where is the Pacific?" Such questions made it much easier for us to seek funds to fill the gaps. Samoans and a Tongan joined the staff, and the clinic kept growing. In the meantime, my culinary tastes also expanded, so did my waistline.

Cambodians represented a different challenge. So many settled in the Long Beach area that the city was nicknamed "Little Phnom Penh." We set up a small satellite clinic there, which was immediately swamped by those who had been weighed down by horrendous nightmares and flashbacks for years.

Much more needed to be done. But how could we convince the powers-that-be that one Asian Pacific clinic was not enough; we needed two?

At election time, we realized that Long Beach belonged to a different supervisorial district. The incumbent, facing stiff competition, decided that it would be good for him to have "his own" Asian clinic. A phone call from his office made a separate Long Beach clinic a reality.

Finding qualified bilingual therapists was the next challenge. We found a Cambodian monk with PhDs in both religion and psychology. This was too good to be true, until we found out that he refused to shed his Kasaya (Buddhist monk's robe) at work. This generated a small crisis among the administrators. But he was well qualified, and he understood when to play which role, regardless of his attire. Since most Cambodians are devout Buddhists, a psychologist immersed in their spiritual world turned out to be just the right person to pull them out of the post-Pol Pot abyss.

Watching the two unique clinics emerging in the space of less than two years and quickly becoming essential components of the general mental health system, I was grateful. But eventually I came to realize that administration was not my forte. There were limitations in how far I could push for public-academic collaborations, so I returned to academia in 1986. Fortunately, by that time, the two clinics were already in good hands and they continued to do well.

Watching them from a distance, sometimes I imagine myself as a midwife who helped to bring two beautiful babies to the world. They are now mature, competent adults, providing capable helping hands to multitudes of people of divergent backgrounds. Even so, their capacity is limited—still no match to the needs of the continuously expanding Asian communities in the country. But it is comforting to know that some thirty years later, a whole new generation of competent leaders in the field are carrying on the mission. Thanks to them, today the search for care is a less daunting task than in the 1980s for those who are struggling with psychiatric problems.

Keh-Ming Lin, MD, MPH, is Professor Emeritus of Psychiatry, UCLA, Distinguished Life-Fellow, American Psychiatric Association. He was the Founding Director of the NIMH/Harbor-UCLA Research Center on the Psychobiology of Ethnicity, Consortium on Asian American Mental Health Training, the Coastal Asian Pacific Mental Health Center and the Long Beach Asian Pacific Islander Mental Health Center. His professional publications include four books and more than 200 journal articles and book chapters. Prof. Lin now lives in San Francisco, and joined the Write Now! workshops to work on an in-progress novel and a memoir. He is also enjoying the opportunities to share his work with audiences.

Beauty in Strep
Kevin Madrigal

Fuck.
…Shit.
My throat is on fire.

Today,
not because of the locally grown, perfectly roasted (but not burnt!) chile de
arbol tomatillo salsa presented at my prima Hakke's torta shop—
No.

Today,
because in my travels I was careless.

Too aloof to recognize the early symptoms of
Something greater.

Sound familiar, Kevin?

Dehydration looming
Every swallow of water
More painful
Than the last.
Streaming splinters
with no care of
esophagus lining.

But México is a country run by powerful matriarchal care.
A free consultation and 3 prescribed meds for less than $10 later
The American born tourist in Mexico
Recovers. I'm back on track.

But what would be the case if my identity
Flipped?

A turista born in Guadalajara traveling in
California (read: once Mexico)
Dies. Unable to afford care.

America doesn't give a shit about
Melatonin presenting foreigners.

The origin of foreign—Other.
But in Oaxaca, México—Otherness is celebrated.
Oaxaca welcomes you to bring your baggage
Celebrate the vibrant colors and ancient traditions that make you uniquely you.

After all,
The most delicious, life changing mole negro

Mole that opens up your taste buds to
Palate the previously unpalatable.

Mole negro that reclaims the narrative
Of white conquistadores over brown bodies.

This mole is made by the hand of the indigenous cook
With a deep, intimate understanding of the combinations of
Una cornucopia de ingredientes
Each from its own, distinct background.
Never from a melting pot
Where all are homogenized and forgotten.

Kevin Madrigal bio on p. 251.

Oaxaca students blend present realities with indigenous roots at an
end-of-semester celebration, 2013. Photo by Shizue Seigel.

Suicide Clause
JoAnn DeLuna

Back in America,
the South Dakotans—supported by the 8th US Circuit Court of Appeals
—upheld a provision requiring physicians to notify women seeking abortions that,
"abortion increases the risk of suicide."
But, what if you're already contemplating suicide?

Down in Texas, the Christian politicians
shot their rifles into the air crying,
"Victory, for safer abortions!"
as a new law passed by Governor Rick Perry
unnecessarily required abortion clinics uphold the same standards as hospital
surgical centers…
Victory!

The clinics closed en masse,
women scurried like roaches
down to the Mexican border town of Nuevo Progresso
(which, ironically translates in English to New Progress)
—seeking miscarriage-inducing pills.
$35 for a box of 28 Cytotec-branded pills.

"Some of them," said Lucy Felix, *"will wind up in the E.R."*

"My intent was not to close abortion clinics,"
State Senator Glen Hegar said, "but to increase the quality of care…………"
Victory!

The Texans made parents out of women
who admitted they weren't emotionally,
nor financially ready
to bring children into worlds
worlds without fathers,
worlds filled with shame,
guilt, / ridicule, / doubt / and embarrassment.

Those pro-lifers sure seem like the kind of folk who get shit done…
Now, if we could only rally them
to lobby the government to provide free childcare,
for the unborn children they rallied so hard for
outside of abortion clinics.

Yea baby, when it comes to females,
The U.S. Supreme Court ain't got nuthin' to do with my selection.
Unwanted pregnancies, lack of financial stability or rape?
Only if there's fetal endangerment!

Back in Ireland, Janet Ni Shuileabhain tweets her abortion:
"I cried from relief and sadness
that the first time I had been pregnant it wasn't a happy event.
It was a time of stress and worry."
#abortion #Ow #sadness #heartbreaking #WTF #TMI #brave #wow

In Spain, the women protested
by flicking thongs at the Pope
and registering their bodies as intellectual property,
thereby retaking the rights to their own bodies.

"An abortion performed without a woman's consent is considered feticide."

—But what do you call a birth
without the consent of a woman?

They call that morality,
a law,
a right to life.
But who's life?
Certainly, not a woman's.

"Human life, from its commencement to its close,
is protected by the common law."
From its commencement to its close
"Life begins when the infant is first able to stir in the womb.
Life, is protected not only from immediate destruction,
but from every-degree-of-actual-violence
and from every-degree-of-danger."
From its commencement to its close
But, who protects the women whose lives have yet to close?

JoAnn DeLuna, originally from Texas, is a bilingual journalist, poet and comedian with a journalism master's degree from Amsterdam University and City University of London. Her poetry was published in anthologies in Texas, California, and New York, where she lived for 8 years and performed at the Nuyorican Poets Café, Lincoln Center, and Bushwick Starr. She now lives in San Francisco.

ix. And Justice for...

Sandra Takashima Shaw, "All PEOPLE Are Created Equal," from
The 'AND' series, newspaper articles about racial violence in the United States,
acrylic and ink on canvas, 60 x 48 in.

California artist Sandra Takashima Shaw grew up in a small, all-white Ohio town. With half Japanese and half Scandinavian heritage, she felt like an unwanted outsider. The 'AND' Series reflects her desire for greater harmony among people and society. Her art has been featured in museum exhibitions, and is collected privately and exhibited internationally.

Ballot for a Justice Warrior Who Came Before
And for Those Who Can Only Dream (Nov 2016)
Susana Praver-Pérez

Your absentee ballot arrived
     in the mail
The Registrar of Voters doesn't know
     just how absent you are
Your name on the envelope
     jolts me
          like an aftershock

The trail of your convictions
     still arched in the air, blazing
          like a comet's tail
     even though your body had crashed to earth

I wrestled with being your hands, knowing
     each crease of your palm like my own
I weighed consequences…imagined my defense…

But your Honor, he worked so hard for a better world,
seemed a shame for him not to have a say, let it all unravel

But the tapestry is torn—each slur
     a slash in the social fabric
Each family asleep in the rain
     a stitch undone
Each soul lost to a bullet
     a thread ripped from the warp

There was no Morning After pill potent enough
     to stop misconceived ideas
          that kidnapped
          the country
          that Tuesday
Tears flowed across our fractured land
Children clung to their parents in fear
     of deportation

But democracy does not dead-end
      in a polling booth—
A radiant wave of hope flowed
      down Oakland's International Boulevard
Many too young to vote
Many Dreamers
      fighting off a nightmare
         turned real
      when Wednesday's sun broke the horizon

I wandered among them like a refugee seeking shelter
      amid their rainbow
      of placards, scribbled pleas
      for amity and compassion
Their voices, vulnerable and raw
      echoed your own passion

They, my Love, are your absentee ballot

Leon Sun, "No Concentration Camps," from *Faces of NOpression; Faces of Truth, Love and Resistance* photo series, 2018.

Election Night: What Elizabeth Warren could have said...
Dan Brady

I'd like to tell people still standing in line
All across the country
Marking ballots, casting votes, still waiting to have their voices heard,
To know no matter what happens
I want to thank you for how we worked together—
It's been a hard fight
For the House, the Senate, State Houses, and local offices
Because we've been in and are in a fight, together
For Democracy and a future where everyone
Has health care and human rights,
While Wall Street and faceless corporations
Are held to account, taken to task,
And no longer legally lie, cheat, or steal—
Nor can they bend the justice, legislative, or regulatory systems
To their wills;
We fight for a Democracy
Where people no longer die due to debt designed to disable,
Where children, teens, adults—all people—
Are free of fear when walking down streets,
Going to malls, to a yoga studio,
A church—or synagogue
Because, they're not being shot, shot at, or hearing shots,
Because there are no shootings,
Because we are pulling together,
Building a future inclusive of science
With moral obligations to protect both the truth and the Earth
And have a justice system worthy of that name,
Which no longer grinds up the poor, needy, or people of color, those
"huddled masses yearning to be free..."
Where the government is held to the rule of law

We are in a fight for our country where seniors can retire with dignity,
Social Security has been enhanced, enlarged, and expanded
Women have equal pay for equal work
And make decisions about their bodies

We are proud of this New American Dream
Proud of being immigrants or descendants of same

And know diversity is what has always made America Great
Again and again and again…

Tonight we fight for this Dream…and the Dreamers
To show ourselves as a nation
Which keeps mamas and babies together.
With a government that is, of, by, and for the people
Where the Federal Reserve has been taken in hand,
Citizens United has been dumped
And the troops are finally coming home
To help everyone here, in the Homeland
This is The Fight, Our Fight and we are in it all the way
Every donation, door knock, or phone call you made…mattered
Every step you took
Brought us all closer to a better future we are building…together
And that is something to be proud of
So, no matter what happens
I want you to know serving the public is the greatest honor in life
Having Democracy's back
Means that it will have ours
The election being over does not mean the struggle ends
It was only one day…an important day
But just another day all the same.
Keep on keepin' on…get up, stand up, fight for what is right…
And yes…let's truly remake America Great!

Dan Brady was born in New York City in 1952. When his father died in 1960, his mother decided to return to California. She managed to raise seven children and do well despite trying circumstances. Dan was the first of his family to complete a college education. He graduated from San Francisco State University in 1975 with a degree in Sociology, and in 1985 went back to obtain an elementary teacher's credential. He began teaching in 1987, and for a while writing was set aside. He married in 1989, and soon the muse moved again as he began a return to writing. Science fiction, being a long time fascination, was where he began. During that time, he also made a return to writing and performing poetry in San Francisco's open mic scene, notably at Sacred Grounds Café, where he is the current curator.

Wall of Empathy - Susan Dambroff

after 2016 presidential election

Outside the BART station
at 24th and Mission
sticky notes
line a wall of empathy
scrawled messages
in a rainbow of colors
and languages
You are safe here
Vamos a cuida de ti
phrases of resilience
Keep your head up
All are welcome
with prayers and drums
and shades of color
We are all immigrants
in sparks of accent
and orientations of love
Buenvenidos
we blaze a different imagination
sign in ferocious disagreement
No Justice No Peace
high school students walk out of classrooms
This is not my president
hands circle around city parks
We will be counted
millions of women
march on Washington
This is not our inauguration
We wear safety pins
and black armbands
We will protect each other
We will protect the planet
No Dakota Pipeline
Black Lives Matter
We will always be
a sanctuary city
Paz Mundial
Moving forward together
When they come for you, I will be there

We Will Be Seen
Elaine Elinson

I was riveted to the spectacular vision: all the Democratic women Members of Congress gathered on the floor of the House of Representatives dressed in white.

Deb Haaland and Sharice Davids, the first Native American Congresswomen in the history of the country.

Ilhan Omar and Rashida Tlaib, the first two Muslim women Representatives.

Doris Matsui, born behind barbed wire at the Poston Relocation Center during World War II when her parents and 120,000 Japanese Americans were incarcerated simply because of their ethnicity.

Jahana Hayes, 2016 Teacher of the Year, one of the first African American women to represent New England.

Tammy Baldwin, the first openly gay member of the Senate. Combat veterans Senators Joni Ernst and Tammy Duckworth.

Lucy McBath, whose African American son was shot and killed by a white man who objected to his loud music.

Asian American women from Hawaii, California and Washington. Latinas from California and New York.

"Today we stand together wearing white in solidarity with the women of the suffrage movement who refused to take no for an answer," said Representative Brenda Lawrence, co-chair of the bipartisan Women's Issues Caucus and vice president of the Congressional Black Caucus. "We will be seen!"

They brought with them a wealth of experience. They had spent years fighting for reproductive rights, voting rights, educational equity, and immigrant rights. They had battle scars from working against racial profiling by police, homophobia, sexual harassment, and gun violence. And we can presume that all of them had challenged sex discrimination, many times over.

As I watched them hugging, smiling, and taking their seats in the august chamber, it was hard to imagine that only a century ago, women did not even have the right to vote, much less run for office.

Left: Susan Dambroff is a poet, performer, and teacher. Her poetry has appeared in *Stoneboat, POETS 11 2008, Earth's Daughters, Red Bird Chapbook*, and several Holocaust anthologies, including *Blood to Remember* and *Ghosts of the Holocaust*. Her chapbook *Conversations with Trees* was published in 2018 by Finishing Line Press. She performs in Spoken Duets with Chris Kammler.

I tried to put myself in the place of those courageous women in California who fought for suffrage: their radical imagination allowed them to think of what might be—even though it had never been before. I tried to think of the chutzpah it must have taken to persuade men—the only voters in the state for more than a century—to mark the box for woman suffrage on the 1911 ballot.

The dazzling image of the women in white in Congress reminded me of the century-old photograph of suffragists in 1908, also all in white, marching in Oakland to the Republican Convention to demand the inclusion of woman suffrage in the party platform.

But the rich diversity of today's Congresswomen reveals an even more compelling story.

Initially most of the leaders in the California suffrage movement, as in the national suffrage campaign, were wealthy, white society women. But many working class and women of color played key roles, roles that have often been marginalized or ignored in our history.

Selina Solomons, an ardent activist from a San Francisco Jewish family that had fallen on hard times, bristled at the elitist club ladies who dominated suffrage organizations in San Francisco. She opened the Votes for Women Club near Union Square, where she cooked and served lunch to shop girls, waitresses and laundry workers in the downtown area. She stocked the dining room with suffrage literature. Her menu listed "three kinds of soup: oxtail, tomato bisque and clam chowder" and "salads served with mayonnaise and fresh olive oil." At the bottom she wrote, "We hope that the girl who comes to eat stays to organize for the vote."

I found Solomons' pamphlet, "How We Won the Right to Vote," in a dusty archive at the San Francisco Public Library. With wit and great insight, she documents the arduous daily organizing and deep commitment of the suffragists.

The California campaign began in the late 1800s when three hundred women went to Sacramento to lobby for the vote. They were met with ridicule by the male legislators, who told them to go home and mind their daughters.

One of those grassroots lobbyists was Naomi Bowman Talbert Anderson, who was born to free Black parents in Indiana on 1843. A brilliant young woman, her dream of going to Oberlin was thwarted when her mother died. She began speaking at suffrage and temperance meetings around the Midwest. Like many African American women in the East, she felt the sting of prejudice from white suffragists. Some of her white colleagues ran a children's home—

from which African American children were barred. So she organized her own. After arriving in California, she traveled throughout the state speaking to African American church groups and clubs. The *San Francisco Call* described her as "a new apostle to the Negroes" and a "woman of commanding and magnetic presence."

Under the influence of advocates like Solomons and Anderson, the suffrage movement became more welcoming to women of all backgrounds. "Parlor meetings" in wealthy private homes gave way to "suffrage teas" in community halls, which the organizers decorated with flowers to mask the smell of cigar smoke from the men's political meetings. Members of the Waitress Union organized the Wage Earners Suffrage League, addressed 185 union locals in the city, and rode in a "Votes for Women" float in the Labor Day parade.

Pro-suffrage messages not only adorned billboards and advertising on the ferries and street cars, but the ingenious women organizers stamped them on paper bags at grocery stores, stenciled them on napkins at ice cream parlors and even stuck them in pockets of clothing that were to be picked up from the tailor.

Sarah Massey Overton, an African American suffragist who moved to San Jose from Massachusetts, initially became a leader in the movement to desegregate California's public schools. Her efforts to unite black and white women led to the founding of the Interracial Suffrage Amendment League in San Jose. According to her obituary, she "set out at her own expense" in 1911 to encourage African American men to vote for suffrage.

Tye Leung was the first Chinese American woman to vote in the United States. Born in San Francisco's Chinatown in 1877, she ran away at the age of 12 to avoid being sent into a forced marriage in Montana, a common practice at that time. She joined Donaldina Cameron at the Presbyterian Mission where she braved vigilantes and trafficking rings to rescue Chinese girls trapped in brothels. Leung later became a translator at the Immigration station on Angel Island, the first Chinese American woman to be hired for a government job. There she fell in love with Charles Schulze, a white immigration inspector, and they bucked California's anti-miscegenation laws by traveling to Washington to marry.

Across the Bay, Clara Elizabeth Chan Lee and Emma Tom Leung were proudly photographed by the *Oakland Tribune* as they became the first Chinese American women to register to vote in Alameda County.

The suffrage movement in California was not without its race and class conflicts. An article in the *San Francisco Call* in 1902 reported that the California branch of the National Federation of Women's Clubs called on its delegates to "vote against drawing the color line." That vote led to the resignation of its president, the unfortunately named Mrs. Lovell White.

The histories of these courageous women have been sidelined by the dominant narrative. We know little more about Oaklanders Lee and Leung, except that they were wives of prominent male members of the Chinese American Citizens Alliance—women were not allowed to be members. After 1895, there is no written mention of Anderson in suffrage literature, and not much more about Solomons after the victorious suffrage initiative in California.

Yet their prescient voices now resonate in the halls of Congress, thanks to the women who carry on their legacy—who, to paraphrase Representative Lawrence, will be seen and will be heard.

Elaine Elinson is the coauthor (with Stan Yogi) of *Wherever There's a Fight*, winner of a Gold Medal in the 2010 California Book Awards. She served for two decades as the communications director of the ACLU of Northern California. A former reporter in Southeast Asia, her first book, *Development Debacle: the World Bank in the Philippines*, was banned by the Marcos regime.

Leon Sun, "Chinese Progressive Association," *Faces of NOpression* series, photograph, 2018.

Holman Turner, "Ironic Symbols," photograph.

Holman Turner Artist Statement

I am a product of what America claims to be, not what it actually is. My work reveals what I see from that vantage point. For years I attempted to keep these visual and written images to myself; today they can no longer be contained. It is not as if I must sit down and struggle to produce both the prose and visual work that now flows from me. They simply demand to have life, and I am the vessel through which they are passing.

For years, I made every effort not to look at these entities that had been created for me by what some call, "The American Dream"; because for me, it had simply been an "American Nightmare" of violence and hypocrisy.

So, as these images, both physical and written, are viewed—"I am free." For no longer am I trapped in the world you created for me; for now, I am simply, me.

Holman Turner. As an African American man who took his first breath during the days of segregation in Alabama, not a day has passed since, that I have not yearned to be "free." Free to live the life America "claims to be"; maybe for some—but not for me.

My work describes the view you have provided me. So, I will no longer pretend not to see—what "your" America has done to both you and me.

Civil Rights and Islamophobia
"Injustice anywhere is a threat to justice everywhere."
Haleema Bharoocha

In America, it is normal to wake up to a mosque shooting or massacre of Muslims. Although Islamophobia is not new to America (Turtle Island), it has increased in the last few years and has threatened the civil rights of Muslims and all settlers of this land. The Council on American Islamic Relations (CAIR) recorded a 17% increase in anti-Muslim bias incidents nationwide in 2017 over 2016. Today, Almost 1 in 5 Muslims experience discrimination regularly according to Islamophobia Studies Public Institute (ISPU). We've watched as Islamophobia has grown into its own industry—profiting over 200 million dollars from hate. According to CAIR, this industry consists of 74 actively Islamophobic non-profits, 8 major funders in philanthropy, media outlets like Fox News, Muslim free businesses that explicitly refuse to serve Muslims, and legislation like the Muslim Ban.

Islamophobia intersects with other forms of oppression. When you start to add the layers like race and gender, this is made clear. Islamophobia is rooted in anti-Blackness. The first Muslims in this country were Black Muslims mostly from West Africa who were enslaved and forcefully brought to this country. This is well documented through the stories of people like Yarrow Mamout, a Black Muslim from Guinea who was enslaved in 1752. Black Muslims established Islam in the US through the Nation of Islam and the Moorish Science Temple of America, a history which is rarely recognized due to the erasure of Black Muslim identity in the mainstream and anti-Blackness. Islamophobia is also gendered. Visibly Muslim women are more harmed by Islamophobic violence whether that is through policies like the Burkini ban or the intersection of gender-based violence with hate-based violence. Muslim women who wear hijab are disproportionately targets of Islamophobic violence due to the visibility of their identity.

It is important to note these intersections when fighting for civil rights so we can ensure that everyone has their rights. As Dr. King says "injustice anywhere is a threat to justice everywhere. We are caught in an inescapable network of mutuality, tied in a single garment of destiny. Whatever affects one directly, affects all indirectly." According to ISPU, there is an 80% overlap with anti-Muslim legislation and legislation that oppresses other minority groups. ISPU research looked at who was passing Islamophobic bills and bills that oppress other communities. They found that there tends to be an overlap in who is passing the bills. This is yet another reason why we must understand the intersections of the issues because all oppression is connected.

When we talk about civil rights, we must talk about the rights of all people, including Muslims. Organizations and advocates seeking to do equity work must include Islamophobia in their analysis to develop a holistic strategy and fight for our collective liberation.

Haleema Bharoocha. I am a young Muslim woman of South Asian descent. Before people know my name, they know my religion. I experience Islamophobia in many forms and work to dismantle it. I facilitate equity-focused workshops for advocates on topics including bystander intervention, Islamophobia, racial equity, and gender justice. I have trained over 500 people. If you are interested in my work, please email me at haleemabharoocha@gmail.com.

Lexi Bella, "I Went as High as I Could,"
Portrait of Therese Patricia Okoumou. Photo by Edsel Rivera.

227

Persist
Choppy Oshiro

Cboppy Oshiro, "Persist," cut paper, 2017.

As the rights of people of color, immigrants, women, LBGTQs and others are being eroded, what gives me strength to keep working for a just and equal democracy are people like this: "One might not have the power. But a thousand has the power," said Virginia Sanders. "Don't let anybody fool you that you don't." Sanders, 76, has been an organizer and activist all her life. She marched in the civil rights movement. She protested against the Vietnam War. During the 2016 primary, this petite black woman marched up to men in Ku Klux Klan robes to distribute flyers about then-candidate Bernie Sanders—no relation. (They took the papers, she said.) For someone like Virginia Sanders, it's not so much a political issue as a moral one. "We have to fight. Freedom isn't free," she said. "Power concedes nothing. It has to be taken."

Choppy Oshiro is a graphic designer who grew up in Hawaii and moved to San Francisco, earning a BFA from the Academy of Art. She complements her passion for creating art around community and social justice issues by providing design and photojournalism services for Oakland-based California Nurses Association/National Nurses United, and has served on the board of directors for Kearny Street Workshop. Her artwork is created with cut-paper techniques based on katagami (Japanese textile stenciling). www.creativehotlist.com/coshiro2

Por medio milenio y más
Rafael Jesús González

a Berta Cáceres (4/3/1971- 2/3/2016)
y todos los mártires de las Américas
muertos defendiendo la Tierra

Por medio milenio y más
hemos muerto defendiendo
la tierra, los bosques, los ríos
de invasores extranjeros
cegados por la codicia,
enloquecidos por la ganancia
en moneda sangrienta.
Hemos sufrido traidores
infectados por esa locura
que por esa misma moneda
venden a sus propios dioses.
Nuestros huesos siembran la tierra,
nuestra sangre la riega
y el sagrado maíz
a veces nos sabe amargo.
Pero seguimos luchando
y nuestros huesos y sangre
crecerán un nuevo mundo en flor.

Hace tres años hoy que Berta Cáceres, activista por los derechos indígenas y humanos, defensora de la Tierra y fundadora del Consejo Cívico de Organizaciones Populares e Indígenas de Honduras, COPINH, fue asesinada por su trabajo en nombre de la justicia. Y aun para ella y sus compañer@s en Honduras muertos o prisioneros no hay justicia de un gobierno opresivo apoyado por los Estados Unidos de América. (Y sus compatriotas huyendo de la pobreza y violencia en Honduras que llegan a la frontera mexicana/estadounidense buscando refugio en los EE.UU. son perseguidos y sus niñ@s separados de sus padres por ese mismo EE.UU. amigo de dictaduras.)

Pensando hoy en Berta Cáceres, pensemos en los tantos mártires como ella por toda América Central y el mundo entero, tantos de ellos gran mujeres. Pensemos en ellas especialmente este Mes de la Historia de la Mujer, este 8 de marzo Día Internacional de la mujer.

Hace mucho que he dicho que ha llegado el tiempo de que tales mujeres

For Half a Millennium & More
Rafael Jesús González

to Berta Cáceres (3/4/1971-3/2/2016)
& all the martyrs of the Americas
killed defending the Earth

For half a millennium & more
we have died defending
the land, the forests, the rivers
from foreign invaders
blinded by greed,
crazed by profit
in bloodied coin.
We have suffered traitors
Infected by that madness
that for that same coin
sell their own gods.
Our bones sow the earth,
Our blood waters it,
& the sacred corn
sometimes tastes bitter to us.
But we go on struggling
& our bones & our blood
will grow a new flowering world.

It has been three years today that Berta Cáceres, activist for indigenous and human rights, defender of the Earth and founder of The Civic Council of Popular and Indigenous Organizations of Honduras (COPINH), was killed because of her work in the name of justice. And still, for her and her companions in Honduras killed or imprisoned, there is no justice from an oppressive government supported by the United States of America. (And her fellow citizens fleeing poverty and violence in Honduras who come to the Mexicana/U.S. border seeking refuge in the U.S. are persecuted and their children separated from their parents by that same U.S. friend of dictatorships.)

Thinking today of Berta Cáceres, let us think of the many martyrs like her throughout Central America and the entire world, so many of them great women. Let us think of them especially this Women's History Month, this March 8 International Women's Day.

I have long said that the time has come for such women as she to take the

tomen las riendas del liderazgo por el mundo entero. El patriarcado ha seguido su curso por milenios y nos ha traído peligrosamente al borde de la extinción. Lo que el mundo ahora necesita es la ascendencia de lo femenino, la esencia mamífera de unir, fundación del amar, de la compasión, del nutrir, del cuidar, proteger. Y ha llegado el tiempo para que nosotros los hombres liberemos y cultivemos lo femenino en nosotros—y para que la humanidad nos unamos para crear un nuevo mundo de justicia profundamente arraigada en el amor.

Me inspiran las indicaciones de que esto esté sucediendo. Me inspiran la mujeres tales como Alexandra Ocasio-Cortez que hemos elegido a la Cámara de Representantes en los EE.UU. y las tantas mujeres líderes de corazón y conciencia por todos los estados y el mundo entero.

Rafael Jesús González taught Creative Writing and Literature at Laney College, Oakland and founded the Mexican & Latin American Studies Department. He was Poet in residence at the Oakland Museum of California and Oakland Public Library 1996. Thrice nominated for a Pushcart Prize, he was honored in 2013 by the National Council of Teachers of English for his writing and for Lifetime Achievement by Berkeley in 2017. He named Berkeley's first Poet Laureate in 2017. http://rjgonzalez.blogspot.com/

Peskador aka Pancho Pescador, "The Walls Are Ours!" Community Rejuvenation Project mural, Oakland, 2017. Photo by Edsel Rivera.

reins of leadership throughout the world. The patriarchy has run its course for millenniums and brought us dangerously close to the edge of extinction. What the world now calls for is the ascendancy of the feminine, the mammalian nature to bond, foundation of love, compassion, of nurturing, of caring, protecting. And the time has come for us men to liberate and cultivate the feminine in us—and for humanity to come together to create a new world of Justice deeply rooted in Love.

I am inspired by the indications that this is happening. Women such as Alexandra Ocasio-Cortez, whom we have elected to the U.S. House of Representatives, and the many women leaders of heart and conscience throughout the states and the whole world inspire me.

Desi Mundo (below) Desi Mundo is an Oakland-based spray paint educator, hip-hop cultural diplomat and the founder of the Community Rejuvenation Project, a pavement to policy mural organization that has produced more than 250 murals, throughout the Bay Area as well as nationally and internationally. His largest mural, the "Universal Language" galvanized the Oakland community in the struggle against gentrification resulting in $20 million in community benefits, as documented in the feature documentary film "Alice Street."

Desi Mundo, "Dolores Huerta," Community Rejuvenation Project mural, Oakland, 2013. http://crpbayarea.org. Photo by Edsel Rivera.

current
Shizue Seigel

The Buddha and Saint Francis
bum around town
trolling for wisdom along the margins
We're all in it together
us and them a hair's width apart
eyes melting with the moon
enfolding hearts clenched tight
against the erosion of hope

Love always wins
but who sticks around long enough
to find out

as the spheres sing
heaven and hell lose direction
nirvana is a state of mind
here and now always accessible
if we simply stop to notice

existence was never easy
sediment settles slowly
as we drift along in this plankton stew
of yes-no, right-wrong
minidecisions and micromoments
the answer is always yes

x. Shifting the Narrative

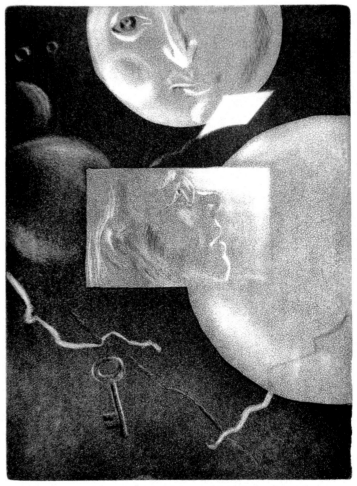

Shizue Seigel, "The Key," etching.

If history were the past, history wouldn't matter.
History is the present.... You and I are history.
~ James Baldwin

Freedom Come
Sandra Bass

Both of my parents are children of the South. My mother was born in a small town just outside of Jackson, Mississippi. For over a century, her family had lived on the same lands they had first worked as slaves and then later as sharecroppers. As members of her family sought warmer suns, they ventured to California and came back with stories of the simple yet unknown pleasures they found there. "You need to get out of this place," said one, so the story goes. "In California, a colored man can walk down the street and pluck oranges right off the tree and nobody will bother you." Shortly thereafter my grandfather went to check out this land of freedom and riches for himself. Within the year he relocated the family to San Jose. It was 1944 and they found a home in the city's Japantown not long after the forced evacuation and internment. Although it's not clear who lived in the house before them, I've often wondered if my family's hopes of securing a piece of the American dream were built on those hopes being dashed for a Japanese American family.

My father's hometown of Phenix City, Alabama, was so infamous for its long history of "wickedness" and corruption that at one point it was nicknamed Sodom. The tale of what it took to clean up the city inspired the film noir classic, *The Phenix City Story*. Dad's mother was an unmarried teen when she gave birth to him in the family's lean-to shack on top of Glover's Hill, not far from the Chattahoochee River. His childhood memories are threaded with stories of navigating through the waterfront saloons, gambling houses, and brothels in search of an uncle who could toss the family a few dollars to get by. Their California dreams landed them in Soledad in 1948. My grandmother got a job as a cook on a farm, and for the next few years, they lived and traveled with the farmworkers throughout the Salinas Valley.

Although my family had left decades before I was born, the South permeated our home. It hung heavy in the air on Thanksgiving when the stink of chitterlings would linger long, long, long, after they were cooked and eaten. It would ride in on a wave of laughter, "book taking," and trash talking when family and friends settled in for a game of Bid Whist. On Easter, it would push up against my father's atheist tendencies until he relented and took us to church to recite Bible verses before my grandmother's congregation. And on those relatively rare occasions when we would cross paths with another black person in our corner of suburban San Jose, it was my mother's Southern sensibilities that led her to always smile and "speak."

And yet, my understanding of the South was fixed in time. It was fueled by engrained customs, bits of ancestral memory, and what I learned from reading about slavery and the southern black freedom struggle of the sixties. For the most part, family members shared little of their experiences. Instead they seemed to hold on to their stories until the weight of them had lifted, or had grown so heavy that, like dew collecting on a leaf, they sagged and dropped one detail at a time. No one in my family longed for the South. Most never returned. And with each passing generation, its grip on our family's traditions loosened. A few years ago, I realized I needed to visit. In part to explore my family history, but also to better understand the region and the persistence of its imprint.

Southern air is insistently intimate. Moist, clinging, warm. It lies on the skin coaxing sweat out of pores. Trees hug highways, byways, backroads, and dirt roads. In the summer, visible heat waves emanate up from the ground, penetrating shoe bottoms and warming soles. The environmental embrace of the region is hard to escape. Visiting the South for the first time, Harlem-born writer James Baldwin observed that even though he was in a country he had never seen before "something in me had come home." And so it was with me. Something in the air, the land, the brown faces I passed on the street, felt familiar and welcoming, as if the ancestors of my blood and of my people had been waiting to receive me.

Baldwin spent several weeks in the South shortly after the end of the Montgomery Bus Boycott. He was so terrified of traveling in the region, he flew between most of his locations. Sixty years later I had trepidations as well, particularly since I was traveling solo during this time of Neo-Nazi and KKK revivalism. However I decided to drive. My road trip began in Atlanta, and ended 900 miles later in Jackson, Mississippi, with stops in Montgomery, Birmingham, and Phenix City in Alabama, and Carthage, Edinburg, and Philadelphia in Mississippi.

To reach the National Memorial for Peace and Justice in Montgomery, Alabama (better known as the Lynching Memorial), my mapping system routed me past the First White House of the Confederacy. Secessionists consecrated the house to their unholy cause in 1861 and the city has been known as the

"Cradle of the Confederacy" ever since. When Baldwin visited in 1957, locals shared that people still wandered the halls of that house and wept. Nearly one hundred years after the fall of the Confederacy, one can only guess what exactly they were mourning. Lovingly preserved by the State of Alabama and the ladies of the First White House Association, the birthplace of the Confederacy represents the finest in Italianate architecture. White, pristine, manicured, with brick red chimneys fortifying its frame.

Less than ten blocks away, the Lynching Memorial sits at the top of a gentle slope. It is massive, spanning over six acres. Tarnished steel sculptures of black men and women, chained, kneeling, screaming, pleading, rust running down their naked bodies, mark the entrance. Over 800 corroded steel columns representing the counties where lynchings have been documented hang from the structure, much like black bodies hung from trees. Inscribed on each are the names of the 4,384 African Americans known to have been murdered in the period between the end of the Civil War and the beginning of the Civil Rights Movement, although the full death toll is far greater than that. As I walked

Kwame Akoto-Bamfo's sculpture at the National Memorial for Peace and
Justice, in Birmingham, Alabama. Bamfo, who lives in Ghana,
was denied a visa to attend the memorial's opening on April 26, 2018.
Photo By Sandra Bass.

between the columns looking for the counties where my family had lived, at times I would reflexively reach out and touch a name, calling them in for just a moment. Near the end a guide asked me what I thought. "Overwhelmed" I answered. "Yeah," he said, looking off into the depths of the memorial, "It's a lot to take in." Following his gaze through the vast field of stolen lives, I had no words. Several silent moments later, "I feel you" was all that came.

National Memorial for Peace and Justice. Photo by Sandra Bass.

And so it goes throughout Montgomery, in fact throughout the South. The Legacy Museum which charts the unbroken history from African American enslavement to mass incarceration, stands within Montgomery's former slave market. In Birmingham and Jackson, Confederate monuments are minutes away from sites commemorating the Civil Rights Movement. In Alabama and Mississippi, the legacies of Confederate General Robert E. Lee and Martin Luther King, Jr., are celebrated on the same day. Historian Barbara Fields captured the significance of this perpetual contest over memory and meaning succinctly, "The Civil War is still going on…. It's still to be fought, and regrettably, it can still be lost."

From the South to San Jose, the seventeenth century to the twenty first, the war rages on. My family did find a good life in California. At times we also found ourselves navigating the minefields of race without the solace of living within a black community. Our California dreams were complicated. Reporting from the frontlines of the 1960s, Baldwin feared that all that was left of "the great dream that was to have become America" was the illusion of greatness, a narrow narrative used to justify the wanton exercise of power. Illusions rarely go down without a fight, and this one is particularly tenacious—as Trump-supporting crowds chanting "make America great again" attest.

However, liberation begins with truth telling, and that truth holds both shadows and light. It is the Lynching Memorial uncovering the brutality at the heart of the well-trod narrative of the gallant South. It is also the story of ordinary black folks rising up and facing down a centuries-old system of oppression wielding "unarmed truth," a belief in our inescapable connectedness, and faith in the inevitable triumph of justice. These are the stories of the South. These are the stories of the nation, and both need to be told.

That which weaves us together transcends time, histories, identities, and geographies. My travels through the South revealed that this holds true whether we know it, honor it, like it, or not. We can flail away in our ignorance and bump up against each other like leaves on the wind, as fate allows. We can give in to the tyranny of our darkest impulses and allow fear to flow freely through our social web manifesting as chains, bars, and walls to justify delusions of superiority and separation. Or we can embrace the inescapable truth that my liberation is inextricably bound with yours and act with courage and humility to foster a reverence for all life. We can choose. Given the challenges we face as a human community, we must choose.

Sandra Bass, PhD, promotes transformative social change as Associate Dean and Director of UC Berkeley's Public Service Center. Born and raised in San Jose, for the past decade she has lived in San Francisco.

National Memorial for Peace and Justice. Photos by Sandra Bass.

Sand Creek
Francée Covington

On my way to visit the Denver Art Museum, I encounter an art installation composed of a series of nine-foot tall bright red Y shaped towers with writing on them. The lettering lets me know that this isn't just any shade of red, but blood red, because the installation is an homage to the Native American tribes all but wiped out as a result of American Imperialism.

I stand under one and then another. The words on the second Y go from top to bottom and read:

Gold
WARS
STARVE
SUFFER

1858
YUTAHS
8000

1878
YUTAHS
4000

1920
YUTAHS
2000
RENEW

One of the last monuments I view has four simple lines—one date, three words. I stand on my toes and crane my neck to read:

1864
SAND
CREEK
MASSACRE

I think because it's so stark, the wording so succinct, that this event must have been so horrendous that it stands alone in the annals of local history or because most local people viewing the installation will already be familiar with the event and therefore nothing more needs to be said. On this day, I don't know anything about Sand Creek. Days later, when I return home, I discover through research that I am right on both counts. In the bloody history of U.S.

government and Native American relations, the Sand Creek Massacre is a singular monstrosity, a crime against humanity which makes it difficult for me to keep a dry eye as I read about the history.

In 1851 the land holdings of the Cheyenne and Arapaho were vast, and this was recognized through a formal treaty with some Indian Nations, including the Cheyenne and Arapaho. But the discovery of gold in 1858 precipitated the Pikes Peak Gold Rush and the flood of whites to the territories. In 1861, in an effort to bring peace to their people, ten chiefs agreed to cede the majority of their land to the United States government because the Treaty of Fort Wise was to last "as long as grass shall grow and the waters flow." In other words, forever. The land holdings of Native Americans were redefined and they were left with territory one-thirteenth the size of the reserve they'd been allotted by the Fort Laramie Treaty of 1851.

The first time I see the name of the man responsible for the Sand Creek Massacre, I'm confused. It seems to be the name of a close relative, John Covington. I look again, and am relieved to have misread it. It's John Chivington. In April 1864, soldiers under the command of Colonel Chivington and territorial governor John Evans started attacking and destroying Cheyenne camps, including their summer buffalo-hunting camp.

Chivington said, "Damn any man who sympathizes with Indians! I have come to kill Indians, and believe it is right and honorable to use any means under God's heaven to kill Indians." Eight hundred to one thousand troops left Fort Lyon, Colorado under the leadership of Chivington with a single goal— to wipe out the Cheyenne and Arapaho at Sand Creek. On the morning of November 29, 1864, they attacked.

When the Cheyenne and Arapaho realized that troops were descending upon them, they raised the American flag and a white flag as signs of peace and that they were under the protection of the federal government. Seeing the flags, two officers ordered their men to stand down. Those pieces of cloth meant nothing to the majority of soldiers. Chivington had set the tone weeks earlier with his admonition to the troops that every Indian should be dispatched: "Kill and scalp all big and little; nits make lice." The great chief White Antelope, who'd been one of the proponents of signing the peace at Fort Wise, ran out yelling "Stop! Stop!" Realizing too late what was happening, he sang his death song:

> Nothing lives long
> Only the earth and the mountains.

Many eyewitnesses, including scouts who had been forced to take the military to the hunting camp, came forward to tell the truth about what happened that awful day.

> Jis to think of that dog Chivington and his dirty hounds, up thar at San Creek. His men shot down squaws, and blew the brain out of little innocent children. You call sich soldiers Christians, so ye? And Indians savages? What der yer 'spose our Heavenly Father, who made both them and us, thinks of these things?
>
> —Kit Carson, Frontiersman,
> Indian Agent, and Army officer

> In going over the battleground the next day, I did not see the body of a man, woman or child but was scalped, and in many instances their bodies were mutilated in the most horrible manner—men, women, and children's privates cut out... I also heard of numerous instances in which men had cut out the private parts of females and stretched them over the saddle-bows and wore them over their hats while riding in the ranks.
>
> —Lieutenant James Connor,
> eyewitness testimony to Congress, 1865

Slaughtered: 133 Native Americans, including 105 women and children. Most of the Indians were killed by the four twelve-pound cannon balls fired upon them. The night before the attack, the soldiers had been drinking heavily and this resulted in many of them being killed by "friendly fire" during the massacre.

Some Cheyenne were able to escape and walked day and night, fifty miles to the Cheyenne winter hunting camp. A number of investigations were launched, outrage was expressed, but no charges were ever brought against Chivington and his men.

My walk among the monuments lasts a somber fifteen or twenty minutes. At that time, I suspected Sand Creek was some sort of seminal event in our nation's life, but on that day, I was ignorant about the details. I take a few photos and sit on a bench facing the monuments. My suspicions will be confirmed later when I return home and do some reading on Sand Creek. I sit on the viewing bench close by and try to sort my thoughts. As the descendent of a Cherokee great-grandfather, I'm familiar with our people's Trail of Tears, the forced march and migration from our ancestral lands—thousands of lives lost, our lands gone, our future bleak. No journey was ever more aptly named.

I close my eyes and ask God to give us more wisdom and care as a nation. That we be more diplomatic in our dealings with other people and less warlike, that we learn from past atrocities. But, of course, we have to be taught the history in order to learn from it, and Native American history isn't taught in our schools. Only the victor gets to write and disseminate the official version of what happened.

In 2007, Sand Creek was named a National Historic Site and is now preserved by the National Park Service. No matter how many times I return to Denver, it is a site I will never visit.

Author's note: During my travels, I've visited every continent but Antarctica. Mystified by the rise of the Tea Party, I embarked on a mission to visit all fifty states and meet more of my fellow Americans. It's been wonderful exploring and talking to resourceful, caring people and learning things I should have known years before. It was difficult to write about Sand Creek, but we must examine our history and continue the conversations necessary to formulate a plan for systemic change.

Francée Covington. During a successful TV career as a producer, director, and writer of news, documentaries, public affairs, and magazine shows, Francee Covington worked at television stations WCBS in New York, WBZ Boston, and in San Francisco at KGO, KPIX, and KQED. She later formed her own video production company and led it for more than twenty years. Her clients included numerous Fortune 500 companies, *The Oprah Show,* and city and state agencies. Active in the community, she currently serves on the San Francisco Fire Commission. She's retired, lives in San Francisco, and is working on a collection of short stories.

Wind River Reservation, 2007, Shizue Seigel photo.

The Haunting
Sandra Wassilie

I.

The women are leaving the village
They are leaving trauma

Trauma of ruptured tradition:
    The Old Ways simmer while
        children attend schools taught by strangers
        women work the local wage jobs
        elders lament loss of language   the dance   the hunt

    Modern demands New Ways overcome   minimize tradition

Trauma of economic change:
    Gap between TV reality and reality village
        hunters imprisoned in villages made stationary
        animals managed for sport   for cash
        diminished food for the village table

    Husbands go away for wage jobs instead of hunting—not all go
        or change

Trauma of personal despair:
    Chaos erupts when the mail plane lands heavy with freight
        the village on fire with alcohol-fueled anger
        something inside people dies

    Elders angry with youth—youth strike out at each other
        or give in   give up
    Husbands jealous of wives working   wives worried about children
        losing their way   to despair

Some sometimes hit   rape   shoot   kill   sometimes kill themselves

II.

So the women are leaving the village
    the Old Ways no longer work there
    the young thirst for New Ways

I left long ago

They are leaving for the city for jobs for safety
   they are taking the Old Ways with them
   they are mixing them with New Ways

They are mixing their culture their bodies

I mixed culture
I Outsider arrived in the village
Mixed my body with one born to the village
Wise Women wearing kuspuks spoke to me in dreams
Warned me to respect the Old Ways
To bring the Old Ways forward to bring my children
Mixed children forward into the mixed world
The mixed world is finding New Ways
The voices of the Wise Women echo in the New Ways

   to stay the hand steady the hand study
The New Ways are remembering the Old Ways

That is my work to help the remembering

Born in San Francisco, Sandra Wassilie lived most of her life in Alaska. Currently an inhabitant of Oakland, she frequently returns to visit her children and grandchildren of mixed Scottish-Irish-Mexican and Yup'ik Eskimo heritage. For more than 60 years, she has witnessed changes in the land and its indigenous cultures. She writes of places she has been and of the adaptations people make to survive loss and trauma inevitable in an increasingly crowded, often confusing, multicultural world.

  Wassilie has served as managing editor and poetry editor for *Fourteen Hills*, and cofounded the Bay Area Generations Reading Series. Her poetry appears in a chapbook *Smoke Lifts* and in several literary publications. Wassilie is recipient of the Ann Fields Award (2011) and Celestine Award (2014) for poetry.

Aquí No Tenemos Tamales
(We Don't Have Any Tamales Here)
Avotcja

The Road Kill Café
Is alive & well & open for business
In just about any city U.S.A.
Offering
A whole new menu
Complete with
Lifeless, spice-less unrefined brainlessness
And FDA approved organic GMO's
Guaranteed to be completely devoid
Of any recognizable semblance
Of natural ingredients
Scientifically approved foods
Absolutely untouched by human hands
And assembled mechanically
In quietly converted "astro-crop" fields
Fields cleansed of undocumented Farm-workers
The Road Kill Café
Offers the ideal meaningless meal
For those whose intelligence
Has been devoured by greed
And no longer have time
To deal with the trivia of anything real
The Road Kill Café
Is now serving the newest in Fast Food
For the racially untainted pure at heart
Speaking "English only" to Classrooms
In Centers of Higher Learning reserved for
The few remaining unmixed pure bloods
Who will swallow any thing
As long as their financial stomachs stay full
Intellectually bankrupt intellectuals
Who could care less about what's in their food
As long as no "unwanted Aliens" are picking & packing it
Hey!
There's a new entrée or two on the menu
Ignorance al la Carte
SB1070 & HB2281
Estupideces saboreadas de la bobería

Two more tasteless items for those who've lost their taste
Yours on the Luncheon Special
Of The Roadkill Café
No Tamales, no Enchiladas, not even a Taco
Ni un olorcillo de Salsa picante
The doors are open at
The Road Kill Café
Today en Arizona
Mañana in any city U.S.A.

Shizue Seigel, "White Bread," etching, 11 x 9 in.

Today I became Mexican like my father
Kevin Madrigal

When I was young, being Mexican meant
accepting hugs and kisses from tios and tias
that you never remembered meeting.
(They all remembered you, though)
Being Mexican meant unconditional love
for anyone that you called family.

But as I got older, my idea of being Mexican changed
especially growing up in America.
Every time I eat out, I'm confronted with my identity.
It doesn't matter what type of food
Chinese, Japanese, Indian, Italian, Danish.

You name it, and at all of these restaurants
there are people in the kitchen that look like my tios and tias
shouting en español
listening to mariachi music
and cooking.

These same people
who can't pronounce the names of the dishes they create
are the ones whose job it is

To suspend your disbelief.

These cooks use the knowledge passed down to them to
teleport you to another time and place—
The wood-fire warmed kitchen of an old grandmother living in the countryside
—and by some amazing feat
This time and place is completely foreign to them.

Once upon a time, my father was one of these cooks.
He worked at an American diner making comfort food favorites like
cheeseburgers, steaks, mashed potatoes.

Made people believe he was a little old American grandmother
named Delilah cooking from her family's handwritten recipes.

That was the only beautiful part of it though.

The hours were many and the pay was little.
But to put in his words
"Conseguir trabajo en la cocina es buen trabajo cuando no conoces a nadie"
"Getting work in the kitchen is good when you don't know anyone"

Hidden behind closed doors
He didn't have to know or speak with anyone to cook.

It was a job appropriate for anyone…
And no one.

And so he was rightfully upset when a Mexican like me
who grew up all in the same place,
knew many people,
and graduated from college
chose to follow in his footsteps and cook.

I tried to justify what I was doing
told him that I wasn't only cooking.
I was building a movement.
So that people like him
wouldn't have to stay in work appropriate for no one
for as long as he did.
So that people like him
could use it as a stepping stone.
So that people like him
wouldn't be judged unfairly based on their background.

He never really understood, though.
He cooked to survive.

But today
my father walked through the doors of my Middle Eastern inspired restaurant.
He remarked at the beautiful space
Made joyful comments about the pink-lit, glittery bathrooms.

He sat down to eat our
Shakshuka
Halloumi salad
and Greek yogurt with date molasses and turmeric granola.

And for a moment he believed

he had been transported to a continent he has never imagined he could visit
and that an old Tunisian grandmother had prepared his food.
Only, it was people like him in the kitchen.
People who face insane barriers in life.
People who are working towards something better.

He ate my food
And for the first time in what felt like forever
He began to glow with pride.
He finally understood.
And with his affirmation—

Today I became Mexican like my father.

Kevin Madrigal is a decolonizer of diets, art, and health in America. He is a
Chicano first-generation child of inmigrantes Mexicanos. In 2016, he founded
Farming Hope in San Francisco to provide employment opportunities in
culinary jobs for folks experiencing homelessness. He writes to honor his
ancestors, to connect with his community, and to work towards a better future.
He loves to listen to hip hop and dance in his free time.

Homeless Cubano with shopping cart. Photo by Shizue Seigel.

My Father's Journey of Resistance
Kenji G. Taguma

We find our heroes wherever we can, sometimes not by choice. They could be Super Bowl MVPs, or even more iconic figures like MLK, Malcom X or Cesar Chavez. But some heroes are not necessarily found in history books.

But what my dad taught me is that ordinary people can do extraordinary things in the face of adversity. Even a simple, unsophisticated farm boy like my father.

Growing up, I was ashamed of my heritage, as I was constantly teased for my slanted eyes, and called "Nip," "Jap" or "Chink" all too frequently. I used to run away from my own mother as she yelled my name in Japanese at the local supermarket. I just wanted to be a "regular" American. But now I realize that "America" is indeed in the heart, and that people of color, who have been marginalized in history textbooks, do have their rightful place in the great American mosaic.

My father's story saved me. It gave me a sense of purpose. It instilled an unbreakable sense of pride, an unshakeable sense of principle.

My personal relationship with my father, however, actually wasn't always so great, particularly in my teens, when I saw him as an easily irritable old man. It was probably partially my fault, however, that he appeared so mean. The fifth of five kids, I took it upon myself to rebel from the examples set before me by my other siblings, who were exceptional students, athletes, or both. One day, my English teacher took me outside of class, concerned about my academic performance when compared to my other siblings. I just laughed at him. I knew I wasn't dumb—I became the editor of our school yearbook, after all— but I felt more at ease goofing off in high school. Instead of the 4.0 GPAs of my siblings, sometimes I barely made a 2.0.

At home, I was a lazy, unfilial son. I wouldn't be quick to do any chores, and intentionally wouldn't try hard with homework. In addition, my father must have been disappointed with me, as I got into trouble with the law twice. He never even heard of my other run-ins with the law, including another time when police guns were drawn upon me.

Because of my lack of ambition, he kept yelling at me *"Prido ga nai! Prido ga nai!"*—or "You have no pride!" He also kept saying "They don't know about us guys. They don't know about us resisters" like a mantra.

It wasn't until my chance enrollment in an Asian American studies class at California State University, Sacramento that I started to understand what my father meant, and I began to discover the true heroism in his wartime actions. My semester-long project for Wayne Maeda's class was to interview my father, and research my father's history,

Noboru Taguma was born and raised in Broderick, California, directly across the Sacramento River from Sacramento. He was the eldest son—and second of seven children—born to Iwakichi and Iwa Taguma, two Issei immigrants from Yamaguchi Prefecture, Japan. In 1942, at the age of 19, he and his family were imprisoned first at the Merced Assembly Center, and then at the Grenada (Amache) concentration camp in Colorado. Like two-thirds of the 120,000 incarcerees, he was an American citizen, with the constitutional right not to be imprisoned without charge. In 1944, when the U.S. Army began drafting U.S. citizens directly out of the camps, my father became one of some 300 who resisted. As one of just 36 draft resisters at the Granada camp, he wrote a letter declaring that imprisonment without due process was unconstitutional, and he refused to serve in a segregated military unit. For his courage, he was sent to a Federal Labor Camp in the Catalina Mountains overseeing Tucson— the very same camp that Gordon Hirabayashi, himself a draft resister, would serve time at.

After my father was released for "good behavior," he relocated to the town of Granada, where he worked at a fish market. Banned from entering the camp where his family was still held, every night for a month he would either hitchhike or walk the 2- to 3-mile journey to the camp, sneak under the barbed wire fence, time the searchlights for his dash along the cesspool, and enter the mess hall to visit family, eat some musubi and maybe watch a movie. When told that the "MPs were coming," he would again sneak under the searchlights on his journey out of the camp. I call this a "reverse *Hogan's Heroes*"—instead of sneaking "out" of a detention camp, like in the popular TV show set in wartime, dad was actually sneaking "into" the camp. All at the obvious risk of getting shot on the spot. As the eldest son, he maintained a deep sense of obligation to his family.

Wanting to get his family closer to home at Tule Lake, dad renounced his citizenship. One day, staying with his friend Joe Norikane in Denver, he returned to the apartment to find Joe singing in Japanese: "You picked a bad time to come home, you picked a bad time to come home…" "Joe, what kind of song is that," dad would ask, as he peered behind the opening door to find two well-dressed FBI agents waiting to take him away. Instead of heading to Tule Lake with his family, he earned a one-way ticket to the Department of Justice camp at Santa Fe, New Mexico. After that camp closed, he was sent to the family reunification camp at Crystal City, Texas—ironically, without his family.

He was then paroled to Seabrook Farms, New Jersey, and was not free to return to California until September 20, 1947.

This research, which became part of Prof. Maeda's exhibit at the Sacramento History Museum, was an epiphany for me. I was about the age my father had been when he took his courageous stand. Learning his story transformed me from a relatively shy 20-something in danger of dropping out of college. It gave me my new calling as an activist. I changed my major from International Business to Ethnic Studies, and began organizing programs on the California State University, Sacramento campus—first on Nisei draft resistance during World War II and then forums on hate crimes, anti-immigrant legislation Proposition 187, anti-affirmative action Proposition 209, Asian Heritage Weeks and film festivals, while publishing three editions of my own Asian American newspaper. Within the course of eighteen months, this once painfully shy country boy was transformed to the most active student on campus, inspired by my father's own fight for social justice.

My father's story gave me a voice, and I committed to give his story the voice that he had been yearning for all these years. In spite of some community opposition, the story of the resisters began to be rediscovered on a local, national and even international level. Books, videos and forums would come out. The Florin JACL would honor the local resisters in 1994, and the recognition of this once-shunned group would culminate with the National JACL's Resisters Reconciliation Ceremony in 2002. Dad and I attended event after event together.

Now he could no longer say "They don't know about us guys."

Through it all, our family was by his side, even traveling to the former federal labor camp he was sentenced to near Tucson, Arizona. It is a testament to my father that his kids truly supported him every step of the way, as he finally received recognition for his gutsy stand some five decades earlier. The uncovering of his story, coupled with the arrival of his first granddaughter

Cheryl, helped to peel off layers upon layers of his tough exterior, and truly made him a happy Papa Bear.

His story continues to inspire me.

When the *Nichi Bei Times*, one of the last Japanese American newspapers in the country, was folding in September of 2009, it took a tremendous will for me as its editor to launch the first nonprofit ethnic newspaper of its kind in the country—especially in the worst of economic times in decades. It took courage and determination that I didn't even know I had. And while my family and others were supportive of this inspiring community movement, I believe that it was my father's resistance that gave me the courage to resist the demise of a treasured community institution, and the fight to move forward to give a voice to the voiceless.

My father's pride and principle, no doubt, will continue to inspire us as the years pass. He will forever be a guiding light as we face adversity. His love of family and his hard work ethic will forever be a part of our fabric, interwoven with the huge generosity and faith that is inherited from our mother.

On March 11, 2011, as Japan was losing so much in the devastating earthquake and tsunami, I lost my personal hero. But I'm sure that his spirit will live on in each of us who were touched by him.

His spirit certainly continues to drive me, each and every day.

A version was first posted on https://taguma.org/2015/03/11/3-11-2015.

Kenji G. Taguma is an innovative media professional and award-winning journalist. As the *Nichi Bei Times* was closing in 2009, he led the movement to create the Nichi Bei Foundation, an educational nonprofit organization that launched the first nonprofit ethnic community newspaper of its kind in the country, the *Nichi Bei Weekly*—which traces its legacy back to the *Nichi Bei Shimbun* in 1899. Committed to social justice and historical accuracy, his efforts to preserve and promote Japanese American history and culture include the Northern California Soy and Tofu Festival, the Films of Remembrance series and the Nikkei Angel Island Pilgrimage.

Paper Bullets
Colin Masashi Ehara
For Aya Haliya Ehara-Lopez & Nipsey Hussle

Hajimemashite.
It's nice to meet you
O genki desu ka?
I'm greeting you in Japanese 'cause
I am the Nihonjin blood inside Masashi
The Yonsei-hombre kamikaze
Little boy whose crippled joy they burned to death in Nagasaki
Stole my wealth when Roosevelt uprooted me
I told myself: "Just go with your community..."
A wounded crane whose bruised brain was locked up in a furnace
A choo-choo train and troopers came and put me in internment
The No-No Boy
A Sergeant in the 442nd
The poster boy for "Dirty Jap" back in the war
You remember?
The kid you thought was good at math
Who learned to drive in cooking class
The nerdy "herb" with crooked glasses inside the looking glass
I'm taking all your jobs
I'm why there's immigration laws
I serve your "stars" in sushi bars and build you cars for your *applause*
Uncle Sam, you can rock my war song
Because "Japanese American" is an oxymoron

.

I hate it when they say I shouldn't
Spray the world with paper bullets
Because paper cuts for hatred couldn't
Make up for this racial bullsh*t

.

Hey, how's it going?
This is Colin's Scottish blood:
Erased and labeled "white" with hatred
Fright
and
Lack of love
I never wanted privilege if it meant my skin would have the pleasure
To be setup as an infant to become a damned oppressor
When guilt consumes me

Sometimes I look away from the horror:
A filthy movie rated XXX we paid for and ordered
I don't want to be
A Cop
A Judge
or
A Politician
But
I benefit when any of them send a Black man to prison
Listen.
I'm beginning to understand
I'm given the upper-hand
And privilege from Uncle Sam
It cripples me inside the ways I've lost my culture
So I nip at ethnic pride like a demonic vulture
I'd better remember:
The ones who've got it better than ever
Made this hate to chase their blame away
Just like 11 - September
If only for a day
I'll know that I'm Scottish
And chop a lying tyrants head like William Wallace
I promise

.

I hate it when they say I shouldn't
Spray the world with paper bullets
Because paper cuts for hatred couldn't
Make up for this racial bullsh*t

.

Hi, I know it's hard to see me but I'm still alive and kicking
Surviving sickness and all that genocide's afflicted
I'm Colin's Native blood: Thin and hanging on for life
My skin's been lightened
Cries been silenced
Sick and strangling most my life.
Preparing ya…
I'm choosing to come clean
Because Amerika diluted my bloodstream
And it's embarrassing because Lucifer's one thing
But Amerikan hysteria is abusive and unclean
Shooting me for loot to seize my emeralds?
F*ck you.

Scrutiny for wounded knee and general Custer
My spirit flow is limitless:
No part retreating back
I'm Haudenosaunee
Turtle Clan
Mohawk to be exact.
Smallpox and firewater
Living in hell here
Locked in reservation
Just like Leonard Peltier
Colin has to represent me through his rhythm and rhymes
Because if he don't?
One
More
Indigenous
Dies

.

I hate it when they say I shouldn't
Spray the world with paper bullets
Because paper cuts for hatred couldn't
Make up for this racial bullsh*t

.

"The Last Samurai"
"The Last King of Scotland"
"The Last of the Mohicans"
Rolled into one.
My raps have to die
Like saplings in Autumn
Because everything is impermanent
It's over
I'm done

.

Colin Masashi Ehara is a Yonsei-Nikkei/Celtic/Haudenosaunee heritage Artist
and Educator, teaching in his hometown of Richmond, CA. He gravitates
towards those who cite Kendrick Lamar, E-40, Arundhati Roy, *Game of
Thrones*, and/or Paulo Freire, and is a core member of People's Education
Movement Bay Area—a collective of Educator-Organizers of Color who work
towards developing decolonial, humanizing, pro-people learning and teaching.
Colin and his wife/partner, Emalyn Lopez reside with their daughter, Aya in El
Cerrito.

This Is What Happens When You Corner a Poet in a 3 am Alley
Guy Biederman

Whoever said you can't draw with a typewriter never learned to write.
Whoever said you can't get news from poetry never went to an open mic.
A man face down in the street with bullet holes in his feet
is not fit for idle speculation over tea.
His home is on the front page of our minds in one thousand point font,
his life screaming in our mouths, sinking in our hearts.
The young woman killed while waiting
for a train
her skin a target. All the dreams she can't have won't be forgotten
if we are of a mind.
If we catch and carry, listen and hope. And act.
1200 children held in cages. Government issue. State sanctioned kidnapping.
Find that key.
I'm becoming a verb before my own eyes.
Even little actions lead to big.
Even drops of water crack open the rock of old belief.
Deaf ears can tune to deeper frequencies.

The act of expression is both a possibility and a tool.
Call it a weapon if you will. This is what happens when you corner a poet
in a 3 am alley and they pull out their pen.

Imagine poetry as currency. Imagine swapping a story for a bowl
of minestrone, a novel for a rack of ribs, haiku for tacos, a limerick
for a ripe yellow peach, prose poems for an open mind, flash fiction
for sudden truth.

Words peel back minds, jumpstart hearts, create the flow where poets &
listeners share in the fluid economy of understanding, dignity, and respect,
a free market exchange, if you will, built on the gold standard of love.

Confessions from the Resistance
Katie Simpson

I want to be informed but I can't read the news most weekdays. Not because I'm in denial, but because I can't cry in the office. There's only so much horror I can take. I don't need to listen to children crying to know we are in a dark, dark place. The anger and the horror sap me dry.

It gives me a kind of fatigue both personal and yet social. I was too tired to go to the Families Belong Together march. Days before, I sat on my therapist's couch, debating whether or not I should go. I had my excuses: I would be traveling in an unfamiliar city. If things went wrong, would I be prepared? The truth: I didn't have the energy.

The question I should've asked my therapist. Was I letting them win by taking it easy? I know I'm only one person but the boundary between self-care and privilege can feel as thin as fishing line. I could go back and forth, flailing for an answer in the empty air.

As a white woman, I know I have to carry more of the burden. I know people who voted for Trump. I've tried crossing that bridge, despite our different politics, despite familial etiquette that says it's improper. The scene is well rehearsed: We fight. I wait, like a melodramatic actor, until they leave to murmur my final line. Can you love me if you don't respect my basic humanity?

With only a pillow and bed, there's no applause—only the sheets sighing.

What part of the burden should I be carrying? I don't know how to win hearts and minds, only how to apply my own to the work. Is choosing that giving up or just moving to a different act? Let each critique have a different take.

So, I gave up my Facebook predictions, the Twitter hand wringing. It feels easier to write to Congress than a 3-day fight over the legacy of Martin Luther King, Jr. I can't make you believe victims of sexual assault, but I can donate to their legal fund. Is it enough? Most of my actions feel so small in this current darkness.

Yet, I feel guilty for only feeling the horror now. I knew before. I'd known about deportations under Obama. I know people in Berlin who have been harassed by racists for years. It's public knowledge that Flint hasn't had clean water for 3 years. It's one thing to know it and another to feel the threat of losing *Roe v. Wade*. It's one thing to know anti-Semitism is out there and another to hear "Blood and Soil" chanted 2 hours from my hometown. And now, I don't know how to forget that feeling.

The resistance is more than expiating my guilt. I still remember the day I discovered learned helplessness. Dogs were shocked no matter what they did. It trained them to be passive and depressed. As someone who has had multiple depressive episodes, I knew this administration could trigger another episode. Resistance, small and large, are my ways of fighting the darkness. It's true, my single donation or letter won't change the tide. But it's a little light I can shine into the dark. Each action helping me hold onto my sanity.

Despite all of this, I'm hopeful. It's not the naive idea that everything will be alright. As Rebecca Solnit beautifully put it:

> It is the belief that what we do matters even though how and when it may matter, who and what it may impact, are not things we can know beforehand. We may not, in fact, know them afterwards either, but they matter all the same, and history is full of people whose influence was most powerful after they were gone.

I wrap the unmet days like a rosary in my palm. There is the power to act, the ability to write the future. It's easy with optimism or despair to give that power up, trade it in for letting go and giving up.

In my head, I can hear the naysayers laughing at me. My family calls me naive at least once every Thanksgiving. You may too. Who am I up against the Koch brothers, the Super PACs, the political giants of the world? I don't claim the same power. I only know that I have power to do something. Nothing, well, that lets them win without a fight.

Ashley C. Ford said it best: "I'm all done with despair. Nothing left in me but love & fight."

Let's make them work for it.

Originally published on Medium July 8, 2018

Katie Simpson is a writer and photographer in San Francisco. Her work has been featured in *Eastern Iowa Review*, HitRecord's *Body Book,* and *Entropy Magazine,* among others. You can find her online at: https://twitter.com/honest_creative.

What is Poverty Scholarship?
Lisa "Tiny" Gray-Garcia

The notion of poverty scholarship was born in the calles, prisons, street corners, community centers, welfare offices, shelters, kitchen tables, assembly lines, tenements, favelas, projects, and ghettos—all the places people don't look for educators, experts, leaders, researchers, lecturers, linguists, artists, creative thinkers, writers, and media producers.

Poverty scholars are the people usually silenced: incarcerated, criminalized, displaced, homeless, disabled, marginalized, sorted, separated, and extinguished. Poverty scholarship is community newsrooms and indigenous news-making circles; impromptu writing workshops in welfare-office waiting rooms; reviews of a neighborhood's sources of free food; facilitated reporting about what's going on in the streets by people who live there; and poetic autobiographies of struggle.

Poverty scholars are told our knowledge is not valid or legitimate. Our speech is improper; our work and our choices, criminal; our words, inept. Our languages, writing, thinking, and art are deemed invalid through a process I call linguistic domination—a complex battery of tests and studies developed and promoted by formal institutions of learning that have gained power, authority, and legitimacy through their wealth and privilege, through white supremacy and power.

Formal institutions of learning were launched by wealthy people with access to land inherited or stolen from indigenous peoples. With their wealth and privilege, the formal institutions have been able to buy their legitimacy and position their forms of knowledge as the only knowledge that is valuable and important, therefore cornering the entire "market" of education. To keep their incredibly imbalanced market share, formal institutions of learning have a stake in the ongoing repression, destruction, and silencing of informal institutions of learning and of poverty scholars.

In relation to formal institutions of learning, we poverty skolaz are valued as subjects of research, surveys, curriculum, and study. Our situations and struggles are developed into complete degree programs, and graduates of these programs are fed into jobs in the ever-hungry nonprofit industrial complex, prison industrial complex, welfare system, and/or academia—all sites that use our struggles as a rationale for their existence. Our art is considered quaint or fetishized as "outsider" or folk art. If we don't ascribe to or have access to formal education, if we don't master its complex system of language, we are called "at-risk" and/or learning-disabled and/or speakers of an "invalid" tongue such as Ebonics or pidgin. Our writing is called mediocre and our research is deemed invalid. We are only important as the subject of other people's research.

For the last fifteen years I have been teaching, innovating, and developing complex curriculum based on my own poverty scholarship: the knowledge I've gained from my struggle to survive and care for my family in an underground economy, on welfare, or with nothing—all the while making media and art and doing research that has been continuously deemed invalid. I have worked tirelessly—in multi-racial, multi-lingual, multi-generational groups of poverty skolaz from all corners of Pachamama—to promote the expertise, creativity, literature, media, solutions, and research of silenced mamas, daughters, sons, fathers, grandfathers, tías, tíos, abuelitos, abuelitas.

Poverty skolaz' schools are everywhere. Our teachings are essential, haphazard and immediate, fluid and static. We are your mama, your cousin, your elders, your corner-store owner, and your recycler. Our research is based on our lives and our experience, our solutions, our vast knowledge of what works and what can work. Our visions are based on the dreams of our ancestors, our elders, and our youth. Our languages are many (albeit mostly of the colonizers' tongues, while we strive to move back to our indigenous, pre-colonized complex forms of communication).

With this book I hope to insert poverty scholarship into its proper place. Our crucial knowledge should be recognized and understood. My hope is not to destroy, dismantle, or disrespect formal institutions of learning. As indigenous peoples, we don't work to destroy and oppress, silence and contain; rather I hope that we, the poverty skolaz, can begin to engage in a dialogue with institutional scholars from a place of mutual understanding and respect between equal parties creating and promoting the knowledge, art, dreams, and thinking of all peoples. I hope that through this sharing we can be truly in relation with each other.

Excerpt of the "Introduction" to *Poverty Scholarship: Poor People-Led Theory, Art, Words and Tears Across Mama Earth,* Poor Press, 2019.

Tiny (aka Lisa Gray-Garcia) is a formerly unhoused, incarcerated poverty scholar, revolutionary journalist, lecturer, poet, visionary, and teacher. She is the single mama of Tiburcio, daughter of a houseless, disabled mama Dee, and the co-founder of POOR Magazine/Prensa POBRE/PoorNewsNetwork. She is the author of *Criminal of Poverty: Growing Up Homeless in America,* co-editor of *A Decolonizers Guide to A Humble Revolution* (2011), *Born 'n' Raised in Frisco* (2012), and *Poverty Scholarship: Poor People-Led Theory, Arts, Words and Tears Across Mama Earth.* In 2011 she co-launched The Homefulness Project—a landless peoples, self-determined land liberation movement in the Ohlone/Lisjan/Huchuin territory known as Deep East Oakland, and co-founded a liberation school for children, Deecolonize Academy.

Why We Love Jeff Adachi
San Francisco Bay View editorial, March 20, 2019
Dr. Willie and Mary Ratcliff

Tears flowed throughout San Francisco Saturday, Feb. 23, but especially in its darkest and poorest neighborhoods and encampments, at the painful news that Public Defender Jeff Adachi, our champion, is gone. Jeff was the only official in this city we could trust to fight for us, the Black and Brown and poor San Franciscans being bulldozed out by a city drunk on its wealth and power.

Jeff Adachi was so determined to win the best possible outcome for his clients, not a one of them able to pay him, that he spent countless hours with them, respecting their superior knowledge of their case and situation.

San Francisco's jails are 57 percent Black, yet Blacks are down to about 3 percent of the population. Those were his clients, and he visited them in their jail cells and wherever they lived—Mayor London Breed remembers him visiting her neighbors as she grew up in public housing. We believe Jeff had faith in London (pardon the first names, but in our part of town, we know them on a first-name basis) to carry on his legacy of compassion and inclusion.

Why do we love him? Primarily because he loved us. In a city where Blacks were never welcome and always pressured to leave, Jeff Adachi knew, he respected and he fought fiercely for Black people, a sense of kinship rooted in his family's tales of the atrocity of World War II Japanese internment. He poured out his love and all the funds he could find for our children—held annual backpack giveaways so they'd be eager to start the new school year, held book fairs and science fairs to tempt their curiosity, even held proms for youngsters who couldn't afford the one at school, outfitting them with formal clothes for free.

Yes, he even cared about Black teenagers, the ones with the mean mugs trying to scare you more than you scare them. He put smiles on their faces and hope in their hearts. Remember Tyrell Taylor, one of the four children, ages 12-14, corralled by cops on Martin Luther King Day 2002 on Kiska Road at the top of Hunters Point Hill? The kids were sitting in a parked car, a red car, listening to music at the end of a happy MLK Day barbeque for the whole neighborhood, when cops snatched them out, claiming they were suspects—someone having reported a suspicious red car.

Minutes later, after the four little children, two boys and two girls, were handcuffed, beaten and forced to sit on the curb by eight white cops with guns to their heads, everyone at the barbeque heard the bad news and ran up the hill—parents of the four kids who tried to retrieve them told, "If you move, I'll shoot you," as one mother watched a cop slam her little girl on the ground, grinding his knee into her back, then lifting her up by her handcuffs.

"Why are you doing this," the crowd shouted at the cops, and that's when we, the people of Bayview Hunters Point, learned for sure what we'd long suspected: San Francisco City Hall's real "Black policy" is "We want you out of here." The officer in charge could not have stated it more clearly when he said, "As long as you people are here, we will act like this." And they have. We ran that cop's picture on the front page.

In our editorial that week—the *Bay View* was a weekly paper for many years—Dr. Ratcliff described it as the "Third Hand," Nelson Mandela's term for a government's clandestine efforts to destabilize the people it oppresses, writing: "In San Francisco, the Third Hand is trying to drive African Americans out of the city." He called it "gentrification by terror."

Another child, Jerome Brown, 14, tall for his age, called out from the crowd, "Take the guns off my li'l cousin," and as soon as a cop called out, "Take him down," all eight cops jumped him. When his dad finally talked him out of the police station and took him to the hospital, "His mouth needed stitches inside and out, he'd suffered a concussion, couldn't stand alone and for a while didn't know who he was," the *Bay View* reported.

That's the "Black policy" Jeff Adachi fought morning, noon and night. Those children's families sued the city, infuriating the cops, who took it out on the kids.

Gwen Woods, the mother of Mario Woods, gunned down by an SFPD firing squad on Dec. 2, 2015, spoke of Adachi's unrelenting support following her son's murder and urged others to respect and continue his legacy.

As the only elected public defender in California and one of few nationwide, Jeff was independent enough to fight for a budget equal to the district attorney's to level the playing field for the poor. In the press release on his fifth swearing in, Public Information Officer Katy St. Clair wrote:

"Adachi has overseen the creation of the Clean Slate Program, which helps clear the records of approximately 2,000 clients per year. Mayor Breed also praised the office's MAGIC programs—Mobilization for Adolescent Growth In our Communities—as well as efforts the public defender made to eliminate costly fines and fees associated with clients' cases, a model that is being replicated nationally...

"Adachi also said that he was proud to preside over one of the most diverse public defender offices in the country, with a staff that is 40 percent people of color, 20 percent LGBTQ and 50 percent female."

Jeff's recent work was moving him closer to head-on conflict with the district attorney, which may be why the current DA chose not to run for reelection. Jeff believed that defending the poor was worth as much as prosecuting the guilty, and when police officers are clearly guilty, especially when they murder poor people, the DA should prosecute them.

Last May, in response to the district attorney's decision not to pursue charges against officers in the fatal shootings of Mario Woods and Luis Gongora Pat, an Indigenous man from Mexico, Jeff said:

"A hail of bullets is not an appropriate police response to people suffering mental health crises. In both the Woods and Gongora killings, officers were not in immediate danger when they fired their weapons. The San Francisco District Attorney's decision not to prosecute any officer on any charge is mindboggling and fails to hold police to the same laws we, as citizens, are expected to abide.

"To date, not a single officer in San Francisco has ever been criminally charged as the result of shooting a citizen, yet citizens are charged with crimes every day despite prosecutors being unable to prove their guilt beyond a reasonable doubt. It is clear prosecutors are using a different standard in judging police officers' conduct. The reforms proposed by the Department of Justice's review are empty promises without officer accountability."

Now you know why we love Jeff Adachi.

Excerpted from https://sfbayview.com/2019/03/why-we-love-jeff-adachi/

Dr. Willie Ratcliff, publisher of the *San Francisco Bay View* and lifelong contractor and organizer, has dedicated his life to winning equal opportunity and economic equity for Black and other oppressed people. He and his wife, Mary Ratcliff, an attorney who found her calling as editor of the *Bay View*, joined forces in 1976 and took on the *Bay View* in 1991. They can be reached at editor@sfbayview.com.

Days of Remembrance in the Era of Alternative Facts
by Anthony Brown, PhD

Music is a driving force in my life as a percussionist, composer, ethnomusicologist, and founder and director of San Francisco's Asian American Orchestra. But I am equally inspired by social justice and the rich musical and social legacies of my African American and Japanese roots. Music can invite audiences to think and feel deeply about human rights, mass incarceration, and war and peace.

My African/Native American father grew up in the American South before making a career in the military. He met and married my Japanese mother when he was stationed in Tokyo. Since she did not arrive in the US until 1952, none of my family was caught up in the WWII incarceration of Japanese Americans, although she did experience the horrific March 1945 fire bombing of Tokyo that killed over 100,000 people.

Since its inception in 1998 as the Asian American Jazz Orchestra, the group has been anchored by its original mission of creating musical experiences that address issues of social justice. Our first CD, *Big Bands Behind Barbed Wire*, included testimony from Japanese Americans—US-born citizens incarcerated during World War II. To emphasize their American perspectives, we underscored their narratives with the big band tunes that reminded homesick teenagers of life outside the camps. George Yoshida, a former incarceree who played jazz in a Poston, Arizona, camp band said, "We identified ourselves as Americans through our music."

I'm sometimes asked what this past has to do with me. I reply, "If Executive Order 9066 was passed today, my mother, children, brothers and I would be interned." This is an issue of social justice that should be of utmost importance to all Americans, especially given the current temper of the times.

The Asian American Orchestra celebrated its 20th anniversary in 2018 with *Go for Broke! A Salute to Nisei Veterans*, a CD and supporting performances marking the 75th anniversary of the signing of Executive Order 9066 by President Roosevelt on February 19, 1942. The presidential order unconstitutionally authorized the forced removal and incarceration of men, women and children of Japanese ancestry during World War II. More than 120,000 innocent people (over two-thirds US citizens) were imprisoned in ten desolate concentration camps with only what they could carry. Most lost their homes, businesses, and farms and were unable to recover them after their release.

Additionally, over 2,200 Japanese Latin Americans were forcibly brought to the US and held in camps to be used for hostage and POW exchange. The US policy of concentration camps began in the 1830s when Cherokee, Choctaw, Chickasaw, Creek and Seminole Indians were confined prior to their forced removal from the Southeastern US to Oklahoma on the Trail of Tears. Almost a hundred years later, in his book *Mein Kampf*, Adolf Hitler acknowledged that this US policy influenced his thinking about Jews and concentration camps.

Go for Broke! premiered in the Presidio of San Francisco where Gen. John L. DeWitt directed the mass incarceration in 1942. Some of the music was composed to accompany spoken word and original poetry by activist, former San Francisco poet laureate, and former incarceree Janice Mirikitani. As I researched the National Japanese American Historical Society archives, I was moved by stories of the Nisei (second generation Japanese in America) men and women who volunteered to fight and die in World War II while their families were imprisoned. As a vet myself and the son and brother of vets, I understood their sacrifice to prove their loyalty as Japanese Americans.

Some of the music also served as the score for Jon Osaki's new documentary, *Alternative Facts: The Lies of Executive Order 9066*. The film reveals that in the opening months of World War II, the US government distorted the threat that Japanese Americans posed to national security. (Not a single Japanese American was ever charged with espionage or sabotage.) *Alternative Facts* documents resistance to mass incarceration by the FBI, Navy Intelligence and the Attorney General of the US. They were overridden by pressure from politicians, the media and lobbyists who wanted to remove Japanese Americans from their lucrative California farms.

The Asian American Orchestra also premiered *Down by the Riverside: Requiem for a King* in 2018, marking the 50th anniversary of Martin Luther

King's assassination. The piece featured spoken word by Dr. Angela Davis and Voices Of A Dream Gospel ensemble. It premiered at the 2018 San Francisco International Arts Festival.

In 2013, the Voices Of A Dream vocal ensemble was founded to premiere *Our Eyes On the Prize: King's Dream 50 Years On*, to commemorate the 50th anniversary of the March on Washington and Dr. King's immortal "Dream" speech, and to celebrate female freedom fighters from Sojourner Truth to Ella Baker. In 2015, the Asian American Orchestra and Voices Of A Dream collaborated with activist/poet Genny Lim and the Ojala Bata ensemble to premier *1945: A Year of Infamy* at SF Japantown's Peace Plaza on the 70th anniversary of the nuclear holocaust of Hiroshima and Nagasaki. In 2016, the same collaborative group reimagined *We Insist! Freedom Now Suite*, the first overtly political jazz album, created in 1960 by band leader/percussionist Max Roach, with Oscar Brown, Jr., Abbey Lincoln, and Olatunji. The album featured poetry and songs advocating for international equality and justice. With *We Insist! Freedom Now Suite 2016*, the Asian American Orchestra celebrated the courage of our forbearers' convictions and commitment to human rights, and the work's continuing relevance to the #BlackLivesMatter Movement and the upsurge of anti-Muslim violence.

During my career, I've participated in thirty recordings and performed with musicians including my mentor Max Roach, Wadada Leo Smith and Pharoah Sanders, the poet Sonia Sanchez, and the San Francisco Symphony. The Asian American Orchestra has received international critical acclaim for our performances blending the sounds and styles of Asian and jazz traditions. We have performed at Jazz Festivals and have been in residence at the Smithsonian Institution, in Pittsburgh, Boston, Seattle, Chicago, Los Angeles and at universities and colleges nationally. In retrospect, my life's path has been one paved with progressive jazz and guided by social justice.

Adapted from "Day of Remembrance and the Music of Anthony Brown" by Ron Jacobs, posted on Counterpunch.org, February 19, 2019.

Anthony Brown is a Guggenheim and Ford Fellow, and a Smithsonian Associate Scholar with an MA and PhD in ethnomusicology from UC Berkeley, and a Master of Music from Rutgers. He's been Visiting Professor of Music at UC Berkeley, and Curator of American Musical Culture and Director of the Smithsonian's Jazz Oral History Program. He is the artistic director of Fifth Stream Music and the Asian American Orchestra. Its recordings include the Grammy-nominated *Far East Suite* (2000). http://www.fifthstreammusic.org.

Nikkei Resisters and community members at Families Belong Together protest, July 30, 2019. Photo by Roji Oyama.

A Love Letter to Nikkei Organizers:
Calling in Elders and Youth for #NeverAgainIsNow
Miya Sommers

"You know they call us elders now."

Deep, hearty laughs circle around the table.

It's June and far too cold in LA. I, born and raised in the Bay Area, didn't bother to check the weather before flying down to LA without a coat. Good thing laughter warms you up.

I was in LA as Nikkei Resister's "young person"—even though I was a month away from leaving the actual young person age bracket of 18-25—as we attended Nikkei for Civil Rights and Redress' book launch party. The next day, we met with other community-based Japanese American (JA) organizers from Nikkei Progressives for brunch so we could better organize together against the current administration's racist policies.

Naturally, we also began to dwell on the challenges that our communities are facing—from the fight against displacement in J-Towns, to historical amnesia around incarceration, to the ever prevalent fears about future community leadership. Throughout my time in Nikkei Resisters, this question about who will continue JA community work remains a constant source of worry. Various community members have lamented about the "lack of young people" in their organizations. Folks have come up to me asking "How do we find more young people? We need more young people to take over." This same concern came up again, in between bites of chashu and pancakes at JiST Cafe, and that's when it was clarified that millennials—like me—now call these older organizers "our elders." The laughter was there to cover up the shock since the over 40 crowd couldn't imagine being elders up there with the Nisei and Issei they once organized with.

Since then, the elders have jokingly started calling me and my peers #TheYouth as we try to navigate what it means to build an intergenerational organization. This is an exciting moment as the JA community is more activated due to the current political climate, but that new engagement doesn't come without strings attached.

Of those strings is the pervasiveness of "not wanting to be too political" within the JA community. The idea that the nail that sticks out gets hammered— a method for survival in a white supremacist world after the horrors of camp —made me feel guilty for wanting to honor the anger within me, born from the intergenerational trauma of war, through action. This meant that at many times growing up, I had felt at odds with my social justice beliefs and being what I believed was "JA." Despite being a part of a variety of Nikkei specific spaces, there was always an internal tension about experiencing the social and cultural aspects devoid of any political context.

Just when I had completely given up on the community, I met my elder organizers in Nikkei Resisters. These were activists who mobilized folks to demand reparations, fought against evictions in J-Town, protested police brutality, and made art and music for revolution. These are folks who, in the past and present, politicized their JA identities to act against state violence. Being able to find myself reflected in both past and current organizing spaces enabled me to know that I am encompassed in the hxstory and the future of the JA experience. This is where we can start finding answers for what can come next for Japanese America.

I want my elders to know that there are young folks here and ready. We may be in smaller number than the coalitions you all had during times like Redress, but we need you not to give up on us. We look to you to teach us our hxstory, the parts that are left out of our classrooms. We need your experience to help us strategize. And we need your energy to inspire us that activism can be a lifestyle we sustain, not just showing up when it's convenient.

But we need you also to learn from and with us. #TheYouth aren't here as just labor for your events. We need to be in positions to act as your collaborators, with our opinions and visions holding weight. In strategizing, welcome the new organizing tactics and new language that serve to deepen our conscientização.

Become comfortable with pronouns, ditch blood quantum expectations, honor self-care, and learn more about intersectionality.

This message is for all the young folks too. Our communities are being engulfed in tech booms, our hxstory is being distorted to detain and surveil immigrants, and our traditions are being commodified for diversity brochures. You can leave the safety of white visions of assimilation to advocate for a just world. You will not be alone. Our elders are here to catch you.

Despite all the hxstory I still have to learn, all the books I need to read, the many people to meet—all while having to explain what is a retweet, a meme, a hashtag—we are foraging this path ahead. On August 9th, with the support of a national JA network that was created by participants at the Tule Lake Pilgrimage wanting to stop family separations at the border, Nikkei Resisters and Nikkei Progressives released our #NeverAgainIsNow campaign. This 6 point campaign is a call for the Nikkei community to fight against racist policies from the Muslim Ban to indefinite detention at ICE facilities. Our slogan came from past JA organizers fighting to ensure what happened to our communities would never happen again.

And yet, in 2018, the current parallels are the stuff of Nisei's nightmares.

Nonetheless, this JA network continues to grow. I'm excited that I'm now one of many "young" voices and getting to know more "old" voices as we struggle together for liberation.

So, I end this love letter to my community—to those I've met, those I will meet, and those who I will only know through a diasporic connection from an archipelago in the Pacific—by inviting you to be a part of this new chapter. I love you for your nuance, your complexity, and your resilience. I love you for being willing to fight again. #NeverAgainIsNow and we will only win if we are in this together.

Yours truly,

miya

First published online at *Eastwind: Politics and Culture of Asian Pacific America*, September 13, 2018.

Miya Sommers (she/they) is a Gosei from the Bay Area. An organizer with Nikkei Resisters, Miya's family's hxstory as survivors of the WWII incarceration camps and Hiroshima atomic bombing informs her commitment to resist against state violence through an anti-imperialist, anti-capitalist, and anti-racist lens.

Welcome to the Queer Rebellion
KB Boyce, Celeste Chan, and Queer Rebels

Welcome to the queer rebellion.

A seven-year-old girl flees war in Iran, escaping into a night of ancestral fairytales with the spirit of her deceased Grandmother.

A multiracial women of color collective traverses the New Mexico desert, enacting new rituals as children of Sun Ra.

A Latina drag queen, 6'6" in heels, screams "Stop being poor" to a San Francisco museum audience.

A Black femme re-imagines her life and that of Gladys Bentley—both of them gender warriors. She questions, "Dear Gladys, women like us are supposed to feel ashamed.... You fat, you Black, you only one of a kind, how did you ever get your fingers to fly?"

A Chinese femme documents her ancestors' Malaysian Memories through layers of cellophane and experimental video.

A Mexicana artist dons gold lame cockroach attire, her performance a "fuck you" to the colonial gaze.

A Black Two-spirit sings and strums on their guitar, "some say it's the end of the world, but it's a brand new day to be...and I howl cuz I feel free."

These works can be seen on the stage, the screen, on the streets and in the halls of museums through Queer Rebels.

There are invisible threads weaving our lives together. We recognize the language of racism as violence—through police brutality and state violence, through war, through poverty. Our art goes beyond binaries that say some of us do not exist. We show performances and films that revere queer Black brilliance...while grieving and fighting anti-Black racism. We deepen and carve space for Asian, Arab, Latin@ and Indigenous stories.

Queer Rebels is a production company and a space of liberation. We are artists who met and fell in love in 2008. We are a Black/Native Two-Spirit trans/butch and a Chinese/Jewish femme. We created Queer Rebels to make a home for queer and trans artists of color, forging voices and visions in QTPOC movement building. Though we divorced in 2019, the production company lives on.

For so long, queer people of color have been whitewashed or erased from history. There's a deliberate absence. We are queer as in outsider, as in exile. From young Iranian refugees to Latina drag queens fighting for their homes; from Afropunk teens living out and proud in Bed-Stuy; to Korean adoptees addressing war; from South Asian radicals in Berkeley to Blasian teens raised in Brooklyn—we believe in our voices and visions, telling our whole stories.

So we create. We crack open artistic freedom in black box theaters and cultural centers, block-long warehouses and small arts spaces, libraries and museums, in parking lots and public parks. The time is now. We are creating an archive for the future. We are all in it together—audience and artists alike.

We are showcasing queer and trans artists of color outside the mainstream gaze. Experimentation gives us new ways of seeing and believing. Nobody will make this space for us. We are choosing to work together across difference.

We honor the culture makers who came before us, and we create anew. We are inspired by outsider artists...from Vaginal Crème Davis to Gloria Anzaldúa, Yayoi Kusuma to Guillermo Gómez-Peña and Coco Fusco, Yoko Ono and Sun Ra.... We could go on and on!

We want to give space to our differences, to our lived experiences of racial hierarchies. We want to create a queer third world liberation zone. WE ARE OUTSIDERS—AND WE ARE STRONGER WHEN WE CREATE TOGETHER.

First published in *Ada: A Journal of Gender, New Media, and Technology*, No. 6.

KB aka Kali Boyce is a Two-Spirit musician whose adventures have brought hir from teenage punk band appearances at CBGB in NY, to B-grade horror movies in LA, and on to solo Drag King blues performance as TuffNStuff in San Francisco. TuffNStuff composes and performs music that pays homage to African American and Indigenous legacies of resistance through art. S/he conjures the spirit of cross-dressing Blues performers—reflecting the history, creativity, and aesthetics of the ancestors.

Celeste Chan is a writer schooled by DIY and immigrant parents from Malaysia and the Bronx. She's toured her work with Sister Spit, launched Queer Rebels festival, and joined *Foglifter Journal* as board member. Her writing can be found in *AWAY, cream city review, Gertrude, The Rumpus*, and elsewhere.

They are co-founders of Queer Rebels, a Queer People of Color arts company.

xi. Together We Are More

Leon Sun, "Sanctuary," from *Faces of NOpression; Faces of Truth, Love and Resistance* series, photograph, 2018.

Soulmemory 2
Dee Allen.

My soul remembers

Discrimination, barred from entering
Society's doors, initially open,
Hastily shut once they saw
Black faces coming.

My soul also remembers

How my ancestors
Fought to throw
Those doors wide
Open to them—
The *separate*
And *but*
In *separate but equal*
Was sought to be dropped
So everybody's *equal*—

So they
Sang, marched, picketed,
Protested, sat in,
Risked arrest, filled
Jail cells to capacity,
Endured spit, slaps, sharpened
Slurs, high-powered
Water hoses, dog bites,
Middle finger salutes,
Confederate flags on sticks,
Noxious tear gas, thrown bricks

Walked on their way
To Freedom
From living as
Second Class
Taking non-violent steps, letting
Nobody and nothing
Turn around
The mass exodus.

Nowhere to go but ahead—

Yassuh, boss
Were words
They wanted
Extracted from
Their vocabulary.

Beneath dusty
Boots of bigots
Were the places
They wanted
To leave.

Someone among my ancestors yelled
For POWER
BLACK POWER
And the walking mass took
Bolder, more militant strides.
     Toward setting cities to flames.

They've won fights
And their gains
And my people's
Civil rights

Remain
Under
Constant
Siege—

Thousands of us
Make it to
The morgue and
The boneyard quicker
Than to the university.

If not
Those sites,

The prison, end-line
To a pipe-line
From grade school trouble.

I refuse all of this. I want respect,
    not elimination.

As we always have
Since Jim Crow and before,
Resistance is
The thing
To turn to

In an era
When open
Hate for different
Skin shade is declared
The New Normal.

For defending our
Right to exist
On the streets,
We get the name
Terrorists.

These misinformed
Assholes just
Missed the memo:
Protesting isn't terrorism.
White Supremacy is.

I resist

A hate escaping
From under rocks,
A hate emboldened
From the top
The nationalist
And proud

White House
These past
Few years

With head
And hand
And pen
And paper
And laptop
And mic.

I move toward

Unity between
Different colours
And nationalities
Through the Written
And Spoken Words

Sending hate running
Until there's no shelter
Left to hide itself in.

My social justice
Street warrior dues
Are paid in full. Now I choose the
stage for my
    resistance exclusively.

My soul remembers

Past fights for equality and respect.
The path to department stores,
    lunch counters
And fair housing didn't clear
    themselves.

My ancestors' struggle
Also belongs to me—

There Has Always Been Drumming in Oakland*
Norma Smith

There has always been drumming in Oakland. There has always been
church-song. Since the early days when you could stand on the shore,
back to the bay, before there was a bay, feel the surf
pulling and thrumming at your heart, before dawn,
when the bay was a delta, falling sharply
into the sea, before they connected St. Francis
to Marin with gold. Before the mission, before the presidio.

Since people stood before dawn
among the poplars—that long stretch of alameda—watching
the eastern hillside, to sing the sun up over the oaks,
there has been drumming in Oakland. There has been church-song.
The people believed back then, as we do now, that the bright orbs—
sun and moon—were listening, because
why wouldn't they

Listen to their relations. There has been barbeque
in Oakland, since mussels and wild onion, rabbit
and tender deer bits lay on the fire, ready
to be dropped into the acorn stew held
in dry-grass receptacles, ready
to be stirred into this rock-boiling water
to add flavor, simmering.
Mmmmmmm.
There has been song in Oakland.

And Oakland has been multilingual and multicultural
for tens of thousands of years, since people first began
to gather here to trade, a crossroads where the creeks ran down to the bay,
where steelhead and coho climbed up to spawn while grizzly watched
their chance, hungry and irritable, mumbling to each other.
There have always been

Complaints about the neighbors.   We live next door.
Marry in.   Bird and bear, turtle and wasp.   The locals let us know
what's what if we can hear them: There has always been song.

We have always moved to it, each of us,
as we—the two-leggeds, no fins, no leaves—have moved here:

ex-soldiers, land grabbers, opportunist ranchers
and our yanqui lawyers, a new police force, murderous.
Alongside refugees from land-grabs, from impoverishment
and massacre elsewhere. Workers crossing oceans or borders
to flee viciousness elsewhere
do the dirtiest work.

While some come as tailors, to cover us in denim—that warp-faced fabric
sewn in goldfields—some arrive later, to build steel warships, wanting
an honest day's work for a day's pay. And safety
for their families. Respect.

Fishers and sailors move here
to the canneries, processors, foundries,
factories. Adding mussels and wild onions
to cioppino, to mae un-tang. Gardeners arrive—
Lao, Mien, Hmong, Kanjobal, Mam, Ibo, Ahmara, Punjabi, Sicilian—
cooks and politicians,

Mexican and Palestino panaderos, bring their own
recipes, their own steps. Their own ways.
The children become office workers, teachers, librarians,
historians. Police. Physicists and medicine seekers.
Artists and other sex workers.

Now we gather against the drought, the fire, the storm,
assess the damage, organize
a promise: a living wage, a house, some vision.
There has been drumming.
There has been song. We find

A place that's home. Where there has always been
song. Song has been here. Song has welcomed us.

Song draws a line
we can dance across, if we can hear
the drum.

If we can weave
this basket into something
that will hold.

---

*In the past few years, during a time of gentrification/push-out of long-time residents, newcomer gentrifiers have called on local police force to confront and harass community members engaged in communal activities such as drumming circles, family barbecues in public parks, or singing in churches on Sunday mornings.

Norma Smith was born in Detroit, grew up in Fresno, California, and has lived in Oakland since the late 1960s. She has worked as a journalist, a translator/interpreter, an educator, and as an editor and writing coach. Norma's writing has been published in academic, political, and literary journals. She has been part of white anti-racist organizing networks since the 1970s. Her book of poems, *Home Remedy,* was published in 2017 by Nomadic Press.

We Are More Than Even We Know
Lorraine Bonner

In the future, history teachers will also be grief counsellors
for children bewildered and sorrowful over us.
Every part of our lives will grieve them:
gasoline, coca cola, body cams.
Only a few will study incarceration,
and only in small groups
with the most compassionate mentors.

Our calendar passes by the holidays
they will celebrate
days when grace filled our trembling souls
and we became their ancestors.

We don't know yet how it will happen
the flowering:
Heart and mind
Compassion and brilliance
Courage and genius

The children beg to hear
the thrilling stories
again and again

Lorraine Bonner, "We Are More Than Even We Know,"
Multi-Hued Humanity series, 21 x 12 x 9 in.

…The Everpresent Rhythm Of Dreams
Avotcja

In an inappropriately humble attempt
To take
Some of the overwhelming (purifying) pressure
Off the hard working folks of Arizona & Alabama
I rented an upscale storefront
And opened a ritzy Employment Office
To help Anglicize the workforce in the fields
It was just my small way to silence the fury
To put an end
To the rage of the unemployed American citizenry
And fill all the seats
Behind every Sewing Machine in the Garment Industry
With card carrying children of
The Daughters of the American Revolution
It was my hope
To replace the ungrateful, rabble rousing College kids,
Wild Afro hair, Dashiki wearing & minimum wage earning
Paperless Farm-workers, as well as all those alien looking
Service Workers & Janitors in the Office Buildings,
And Hotels & Hospitals with
A patriotic army of "all American good old Boys"

On the day we finally opened
We stood feeling good, we had done our homework well
And had left no stone unturned
We were ready for the job hungry crowds
We opened those doors @ five thirty Monday morning
Complete with smiling faces
And a Cappuccino with every Application
Nobody came…
Tuesday, Wednesday, it was the same old story
Thursday, Friday, Saturday & even Sunday
Nobody came…
And the following Monday
To add insult to injury
We only had one applicant who could barely stand up
And he thought we were a Blood Bank

Oh well, I tried
Many have tried to turn this stupidity around
Many, much wiser than me, have died
Trying to make this world, a world worth living in
Truth is,
We are everywhere, we just don't sell newspapers
I can only hope
The powerful beauty of the un-newsworthy majority
Will succeed
In drowning the ugliness of the disciples of hate
But life goes on
And I continue to dance & write & cry & laugh
And scream in the face of madness
And I'll go to my grave singing about castles in the sky
Still hanging on to rainbows
Still standing
Standing strong
And still living in the rhythm of my dreams!!!

Joan Osato, untitled photograph, *Honoring Our Ancestors* series at the *Dia de los Muertos* exhibition, SOMArts Cultural Center, 2018.

In My 3 Michelin Star Restaurant
Kevin Madrigal

There are no servers.
you hang out in the lobby
which feels more like a living room
waiting until at an arbitrary time
you hear a Mexican mother yell from the kitchen:
"YA ESTAAAAAAAA!"

In my 3 michelin star restaurant
the chefs are all black and brown women
and the dishwashers are all white men.

In my 3 michelin star restaurant
we don't have any menus in English.
Sorry, you'll have to read in Español.

In my 3 michelin star restaurant
we don't have a kitchen
just one big ass comal for the tortillas
and one wood fired stove for the huge pot where everything is cooked.

In my 3 michelin star restaurant
we don't buy ingredients.
the farmers give them to us
and in exchange
they bring their family to come to eat every day for free.

In my 3 michelin star restaurant
we obtain any other ingredients needed with SNAP.

In my 3 michelin star restaurant
You don't need to ask for more tortillas
there are always more tortillas
Already on the way.

In my 3 michelin star restaurant
My loud ass, had 1 too many shots of tequila
uncle visits each day looking for free food
and I feed him
Cause even if he's annoying and cutting into the bottom line—he's still family.

In my 3 michelin star restaurant
we serve beans, corn, squash, and nopales
prepared the same way
they've been prepared
for centuries.

In my 3 michelin star restaurant
Apprentices are treated with love and care
that we hope one day
they will pass on to those they teach.

In my 3 michelin star restaurant
We serve
Ube ice cream
And Ritz crackers
For dessert.
Cause my mom loves Filipino dessert.
And even though I'm the "professional" cook
She has always been and forever will be ahead of me in combining flavors.
(Mixing sweet and salty, smooth and crispy, earthy and buttery.)

In my 3 michelin star restaurant
It takes 30 minutes to leave
Cause you hug and thank each staff member on your way out.

In my 3 michelin star restaurant
We ban all michelin restaurant inspectors.
Not a single one has ever stepped foot inside.

And regardless, my 3 michelin star restaurant is still reviewed.
And will always have 3 stars to the outside world

but on the inside—

we have reached for the system that upholds three stars
and destroyed it.
We've repopulated the dark night sky with galaxy
an endless number of microscopic suns
Illuminating all darkness in the world.
Impossible to count
Exactly like the stars
at my michelin starred restaurant.

Latinos
Tony Aldarondo

Latinossss!!!!
Latinos are the colors of the rainbow…
I said the rainbow yo…
Latinos are blancito, negrito, triguenito
and afaro…
Afrolistic! Realistic! Simplistic!
Always mystic!
Always real…really real…
Sometimes too real!
Always told…we love to steal…

So some latinos… become angered!
So angry and angered…
Some become…
Endangered!
Or mis-informed…
Un-informed…
Then uniformed….
Into the penitentiary…
Right into the next century…
Some mis-informed
Un-informed…
Then uniformed
Into the war…
turned into uncle sam's whore…
Latinos….
I can't take it no more…
I said the u.s. military!
Where we're first
On the front lines…
First to die…
Then…
We…have to bury…
Have you seen how many latino soldiers
are in your national cemetery?
We are used in the u.s.!
Abused in the u.s.!
Confused in the u.s.!
And told "we are less!"

In the u.s.…
Come on system…confesss…
We have been infected!
Rejected!
Corrected!
And almost never…
Almost never…
Elected…
Yet always selected to
Clean, clean, clean, clean, clean
Those pissed on urinals…
And shitty stalls…
We are the latina nannies
That wipe the mielda
Out of el presidentes
Grandchildren's draws…
Then kiss his ass…
To cut his grass…
For a visa pass…

Latinosss!!!
Latinos are runaway slaves
Runaway slaves
With eyes open wide
And
No place to hide…
Latinos risk their lives…
Risk their lives to reach the u.s.!
And
Can't come…inside…

Latinos are young men
And women
Who serve this country
With pride…
We're here, there—
And everywhere…
Tall, short, bald—
And even indio looking

With long hair…
Latinosss!!!
Latinos…
Can become what we dream
Can become what we dream…
If given a chance…

Latinos are stars…
Sports stars, movie stars—
And superstars like Celia Cruz!

Latinos—
Influence people—
Around el mundo
Like "orquesta de la luz!"

Latinos are—
United farm workers!
Teachers!…preachers!…
Activists!…poets!…
Your sisters and brothers!
From now until infinity—
We are you!
And you are we!
We'll forever be—
In this country…
We're all many branches
But one tree…
Straight, queer and l,g,b,t…
We spell latinos—
L.o.v.e…… latinosssssss!!!!

Joan Osato, untitled photograph, *Honoring Our Ancestors* series, *Dia de los Muertos,* SOMArts Cultural Center, 2018.

Ang Ngiping Leon (The Dandelion)
Darzelle Oliveros

Wild Flower growing in the open
an arena among green and gold
Although, as not everything
that glitters is golden,
not everything that's gold
is pure. Not everything green
is a pasture of heaven;
not everything clean
means innocence nor
can Ignorance itself know
what it truly means. For
Nature inhabits the in between

Wild Flower dances in the midst
of rain and heat. The blowing
of the winds will want it
to submit in defeat; yet the Lion
stays as king of the jungle
not because it's as tall as the trees
—no, it isn't—nor does it even have
the fastest feet, but its power
comes from within
inside the heart and mind
Because it does not bow down
to its enemies, it does not run
or hide from what it eats.
The Lion is proud and shows
its teeth, wearing its crown
as it feasts

Ang Ngiping Leon ay umiindak
Ang Ngiping Leon ay umiindak
Ang Ngiping Leon ay umiindak

The Dandelion dances,
with grace
    and strength

and belief
is where it gets its courage.
It bends and
grooves and
                sways
back and   forth

The Dandelion blooms,
with Time,
into a beautiful flower
into a beautiful gold
whose truth is given by the Sun
whose love is given by the Moon
Light reflected by the heavens,
day and night
so it could still
see its own
roots

The Dandelion was birthed by the
Earth, sprouted as the touch
of Heaven had told it so.
The Dandelion dances
even when it doesn't know
exactly why it goes with the
seasons; but its faith will
reap the reasons just as soon
as it has grown.

They say a dandelion is a weed,
going in and out of places
Cut for its growth
Uprooted for its resilience,
but still picked up for its beauty
Admired for its abundance,
for the sense of Hope it gives,
for its seeds of eternity.

Legends do live and leave
a legacy

Ang Ngiping Leon ay umiindak

Right when you thought that
it had
died,
dried,
and
    had
      gone
      cold
—It resurrects and rises like a tide
but now moving even softer
than before
like ebb
       and flow
and so
         it goes

even once it loses its
beautiful gold, Ngiping Leon will then

be a part of the sky. Blown into the
vastness of space; traces of
stardust once they've scattered
endlessly, Children of the Heavens

The Dandelion dances,
and dances,
and dances

No matter what form or where
From Earth to Sky
It Will Dance with Time.
And come back down to
Home [Him]
with the roots of where
it came from

The Lion will dance,
and dance,
and dance again

Wild Flower will not be tamed.

Darzelle Oliveros was born and raised in Las Piñas. In the Philippines, her childhood consisted of sweet mango smoothies and sun-drenched streets. Growing up in San Francisco made her adolescence in America an interesting journey of finding herself and her home. As a young adult, she is discovering that her adventure is far from over. She is currently pursuing her interest in philosophy and is constantly developing a passion for giving back to her community. "Ang Ngiping Leon" was first published in {m}aganda magazine, issue 32: Indak, April 2019.

Aquí por vida
Rafael Jesús González

Aquí estoy—
llevo el jade de los ancianos—
es la vida, decían, y preciosa;
turquesa que he buscado
para darles filo a mis visiones;
y coral para cultivar el corazón;
madreperla para la pureza.

Me he puesto el poder que pude
para decirles que hay montañas
donde duermen las piedras —
            los halcones anidan allí
y liquen más viejo
de lo que el hielo es frío.

El mar es vasto y profundo
guardando secretos
más oscuros
de lo que las rocas son duras.

Aquí estoy para decirles
que la Tierra es hecha de cosas
tan suyas mismas
que hacen a los ángeles arrodillarse.
Caminamos entre ellas
y son ciertas como la lluvia es húmeda
y son frágiles como el pino es alto.

Nosotros también les pertenecemos;
cuentan con nuestro cantar,
los pasos de nuestro bailar,
los gritos de nuestros hijos, su risa.

Aquí estoy por la canción no acabada,
el baile incompleto,
el sanar,
las terribles adujas del amor.
            Aquí estoy por vida
                    y no me iré.

Here for Life
Rafael Jesús González

I am here—
I wear the old-ones' jade—
it's life, they said & precious;
turquoise I've sought to hone my visions;
& coral to cultivate the heart;
mother of pearl for purity.

I have put on what power I could
to tell you there are mountains
where the stones sleep—
       hawks nest there
& lichens older than the ice is cold.

The sea is vast & deep
keeping secrets
darker than the rocks are hard.

I am here to tell you
the Earth is made of things
so much themselves
they make the angels kneel.
We walk among them
& they are certain as the rain is wet
& they are fragile as the pine is tall.

     We, too, belong to them;
they count upon our singing,
the footfalls of our dance,
our children's shouts, their laughter.

I am here for the unfinished song,
the uncompleted dance,
the healing,
the dreadful fakes of love.
     I am here for life
        & I will not go away.

Written in prison for blocking the testing of a nuclear weapon. First published
in *Voices for Peace Anthology*, Barbara Nestor Davis, Ed.; Rochester, N.Y. 1983.

No easy answers
Shizue Seigel

The joy lies in the search
strength arises from struggle
Know your own history notice
how it shapes the daily ripple of events
understand sources and motivations behind
lies and manipulations—including your own
Do not be confused
by the breakup of hardened assumption
Do not succumb to oblivion
however tempting

Beware of borrowed experience
cinematic fury and inflated expectations
Forgive—and forgive yourself
We all know it can't last:
Comfort borne on the backs of lessers
Safety shielded by expendable bodies
Bottom lines built atop glass ceilings
inevitably fall of their own weight

Let go of panic, drop our human hubris
and settle into the knowledge
that life has never been easy.
Yet grace is always present.

Civilization as we know it may indeed be dying.
What is wrong with turning away
from a roboticized future and seeking our answers?
—relearning how to use our hands
like our ancestors to haul water, dig a well,
plant seed and thank the living for feeding us.
Look truth in the eye, join hands in love,
commingle our energies to cradle our young
weave wisdom into our baskets,
shape the clay of a reborn society
where the heart spirit wisdoms
of animate and inanimate worlds entwine—
bubbling up through our feet and
and receiving a bareheaded message from the sky.

Index

About the Editor

Shizue Seigel is a third-generation Japanese American writer, visual artist, and community activist who explores complex intersections of history, culture, and spirituality through prose, poetry, and visual art. Her work is informed by seven decades of experiential explorations across age, class, continents, and cultures. Her work is informed by her family's release WWII incarceration, her experiences in segregated Baltimore, Occupied Japan, California farm labor camps, and skid-row Stockton, the Haight-Ashbury, Indian ashrams, corporate cubicles and public housing. www. shizueseigel.com.

Civil Liberties United is her sixth book. She also edited *Endangered Species, Enduring Value* (2018), *Standing Strong! Fillmore & Japantown* (2016) and *Distillations: Meditations on the Japanese American Experience* (2010), all from Pease Press. She authored *In Good Conscience: Supporting Japanese Americans During the Internment* (AACP, Inc., 2006) and co-authored *A Century of Change* (2002)

Her prose and poetry have appeared in *All the Women in My Family Sing, Your Golden Sun Still Shines, InvAsian, Cheers to Muses, Empty Shoes, My Words Are Gonna Linger, Away Journal, sPARKLE + bLINK, Eleven Eleven, Persimmon Tree, Whirlwind Magazine,* and elsewhere. She is a three-time VONA/Voices fellow aad has been awarded grants and residencies from the San Francisco Arts Commission, the Asian Pacific, Cultural Center, Center for Cultural Innovation, Zellerbach Family Foundation, Jental, Newnan Art Rez, and Hypatia-in-the-Woods. Her papers are archived at UC Santa Barbara's California Ethnic and Multicultural Archives.

She facilitates Write Now! SF Bay's free monthly writing workshops at the San Francisco Main Library. For details, see www.WriteNowSF.com and www. facebook.com/EndangeredSpeciesSF/.